Microsoft Works on the Macintosh

Phyllis Yasuda and **Vivian Frederick**
with
Judy Yamada and **Ann Koda** and **Barbara Buckley**

 *Mitchell Publishing, Inc.*
INNOVATORS IN COMPUTER EDUCATION
55 PENNY LANE, SUITE 103   WATSONVILLE, CA 95076
(800) 435-2665   IN CALIFORNIA (408) 724-0195

Cover Design: Juan Vargas
Printer: Malloy Lithographing, Inc.
Product Development: Raleigh S. Wilson
Product Management: BMR, of Mill Valley, California
Sponsoring Editor: Roger L. Howell

Copyright (c) 1989 by BMR, Inc.
Innovators in Computer Education

All rights reserved under International and Pan-American Copyright Conventions. No part of this book may be reproduced in any form or by any means, electronic or mechanical, including photocopying, without permission in writing from the publisher. All inquiries should be addressed to Mitchell Publishing, Inc., 55 Penny Lane, Suite 103, Watsonville, CA 95076, (408) 724-0195 or (800) 435-2665. Published in the United States by Mitchell Publishing, Inc., a McGraw-Hill Book Company.

Printed in the United States of America
10 9 8 7 6 5 4 3 2 1

Library of Congress Catalog No.: 88-062419
ISBN: P/N: 557912-X (text only)
0-07-909408-2 (text and data disk)

Macintosh is a registered trademark of Apple Computer, Inc.
Microsoft, MS, Excel, and Word are registered trademarks owned by
 Microsoft Corp.
How to Use This Book   vii

Preface and Acknowledgements

Microsoft Works on the Macintosh is designed to introduce *Microsoft Works* to students of varying backgrounds, but it is particularly geared toward the computer novice. Throughout this text, our assumption is that the student has little experience with the Macintosh and has never used *Microsoft Works* before. Therefore, our approach is comprehensive and gently encouraging. This book consists of a series of worksheet exercises that build gradually on themselves. It is essential that the student read the section, "How to Use This Book," before beginning to work with the individual chapters.

Note that a data disk is packaged with this book. (See the inside back cover.) This disk contains practice files that are needed to complete the exercises.

Throughout the exercises in the text, reproductions of screen images guide the student every step of the way. These reproductions match the students' own screen as they work through the program.

This book covers Version 1.1 of *Microsoft Works*, with changes for Version 2.0 noted in the Appendix F.

An instructor's guide is available to accompany this book. The guide provides an annotated copy of the text and contains suggestions for using the book, as well as numerous tips for teaching the material.

A glossary appears at the end of the text. It contains words that are introduced in the book, along with common computer-related terms that the student may be curious about.

We want to thank the classroom instuctors at De Anza College, who have used our exercises for the past four years to teach computing concepts to more than 2,000 students. Suggestions from all of them—particularly Rod Riggenbach, Eric Nagler, and Peggy Miller—have been incorporated into the final version of this book. And we give special thanks to Doris Tengan for sharing her experiences in operating an ice cream shop.

We dedicate this book to our long-suffering husbands and companions, Stan Yasuda, Bob Frederick, J.J. Yamada, Ben Koda, and Michael Buckley, all of whom patiently endured our erratic schedules and marathon writing sessions. Thanks, fellows.

— P.Y., V.F., J.Y., A.K., & B.B.

Contents

For a hands-on introduction to the Macintosh, see **Appendix A**, page 197.

How to Use This Book   vii

1. INTRODUCING MICROSOFT WORKS   1
    Objectives   1
    Setting the Scene   1
    Getting Started   2
    Dialog Boxes   4
    Some Things to Remember   6
    More Scene Setting   6
    Opening a File   6
    Inserting Text   8
    Centering Text   8
    Deleting Lines   9
    Changing Text Size and Style   10
    Saving a File Under a Different Name   11
    Printing a File   13
    Quitting *Works*   14

2. WORD PROCESSING: WORKSHEET 1   17
    Word Processing Background   17
    Objectives   18
    Some Things to Remember   18
    Setting the Scene   18
    Getting Started   18
    Opening a File   18
    Typing a Centered Bold Heading   21
    Underlining Text   23
    Inserting Text   23
    Replacing Letters   24
    Replacing Words   24
    Searching and Replacing Text   25
    Saving a File Under a Different Name   26
    Viewing Two Open Files   28
    Printing a File   29
    Think About It   30
    Quitting *Works*   30

3. WORD PROCESSING: WORKSHEET 2   33
    Objectives   34
    Getting Started   34
    Opening a File   34
    Creating a Larger Top Margin   34
    Capitalizing a Title   35

    Typing a Byline   35
    Inserting Paragraphs   36
    Setting First-Line Indents   36
    Double Spacing Paragraphs   40
    Changing a Tab Stop   42
    Inserting Blank Lines   43
    Moving a Paragraph   44
    Saving a File   46
    Printing a File   46
    Review   46
    Think About It   46
    Quitting *Works*   47

4. WORD PROCESSING: WORKSHEET 3   49
    Objectives   49
    Setting the Scene   49
    Getting Started   49
    Typing the Letter   50
    Making Changes in the Page Setup   50
    Saving a File   52
    Printing a File   53
    Review   53
    Quitting *Works*   53

5. SHORTCUTS AND OTHER TECHNIQUES: WORKSHEET 4   55
    Objectives   55
    Setting the Scene   55
    Shortcuts   55
    Opening Programs and Files   57
    Selecting Text   57
    Changing Margins and Tabs   57
    Formatting Hints   59
    Page Breaks   60

6. SPREADSHEETS: WORKSHEET 1   63
    Spreadsheet Background   63
    Objectives   64
    Setting the Scene   64
    Getting Started   65
    Opening a File   66
    Identifying Rows, Columns, and Cells   66
    Cell Contents   67

    Labels   *68*
    Scrolling Through the Spreadsheet   *68*
    Selecting Parts of a Spreadsheet   *70*
    Using the Go To Method   *72*
    Entering Data   *72*
    Correcting Errors   *74*
    Values and Alignments   *75*
    Deleting a Column   *75*
    Changing Cell Contents   *76*
    Viewing a Formula   *77*
    Using a Function   *78*
    "What If?"   *80*
    Printing a File   *81*
    Saving a File Under a Different Name   *82*
    Review   *83*
    Summary   *83*
    Quitting *Works*   *83*

7. SPREADSHEETS: WORKSHEET 2   *85*
    Objectives   *85*
    Setting the Scene   *85*
    Getting Started   *85*
    Opening a File   *86*
    Inserting a Column   *86*
    Changing a Column Width   *88*
    Using the Fill Down Command   *88*
    Relative and Absolute Values   *90*
    Changing a Formula   *91*
    Copying a Formula   *92*
    Formatting Numeric Values   *92*
    Formatting Labels   *94*
    Identifying Your Work   *94*
    Printing a File   *95*
    Saving a File Under a Different Name   *95*
    Review   *95*
    Summary   *96*
    Quitting *Works*   *96*

8. SPREADSHEETS: WORKSHEET 3   *97*
    Objectives   *97*
    Setting the Scene   *97*
    Getting Started   *97*
    Opening a File   *97*
    Repositioning a Title   *98*
    Inserting a Blank Row   *99*
    Inserting a Row at the End of a Range   *99*
    Creating a Formula   *101*
    Copying a Formula   *101*
    Aligning Columns and Their Headings   *101*
    Identifying Your Work   *103*

    Protecting Cells   *103*
    Saving a File Under a Different Name   *104*
    Printing a File   *104*
    Review   *104*
    Summary   *104*
    Quitting *Works*   *104*

9. SHORTCUTS, CHARTING, OTHER TECHNIQUES: WORKSHEET 4   *105*
    Objectives   *105*
    Setting the Scene   *105*
    Shortcuts   *105*
    Entering Functions   *106*
    Charting   *107*
    Getting Started   *107*
    Opening a File   *107*
    Creating a Pie Chart   *107*
    Sizing Windows   *109*
    Printing a Pie Chart   *112*
    Creating a Bar Chart   *113*
    Printing a Chart   *116*
    Saving a Chart   *117*
    Showing Formula(s)   *118*
    Printing Options   *118*
    If Statement   *119*
    Summary   *120*
    Quitting *Works*   *120*

10. DATABASE: WORKSHEET 1   *121*
    Database Background   *121*
    Objectives   *122*
    Setting the Scene   *122*
    Getting Started   *122*
    Opening a File   *122*
    Viewing a Database File As a List   *123*
    Viewing a Database File As a Form   *125*
    Selecting Records   *125*
    Entering New Data   *127*
    Sorting a Database   *129*
    Modifying a Form   *129*
    Searching a Database   *131*
    Saving a File   *132*
    Review   *133*
    Think About It   *133*
    Quitting *Works*   *133*

11. DATABASE: WORKSHEET 2   *135*
    Objectives   *135*
    Setting the Scene   *135*

Getting Started   *135*
Creating a New Database File   *135*
Creating a Form   *136*
Changing the Size and Location of Fields   *137*
Entering New Data   *138*
Changing the Size of a Column   *141*
Sorting a File   *141*
Saving a File   *143*
Review   *144*
Summary   *144*
Quitting *Works*   *144*

12. DATABASE: WORKSHEET 3   *145*
Objectives   *145*
Setting the Scene   *145*
Getting Started   *145*
Opening a File   *145*
Sorting Fields in a Report   *146*
Creating a New Report   *147*
Selecting Fields for a Report   *148*
Widening Margins   *150*
Widening Columns   *151*
Using a Report Header (Title)   *153*
Printing Without Lines   *154*
Printing a Report   *154*
Renaming the Report   *155*
Saving a Report   *155*
Review   *156*
Summary   *156*
Quitting *Works*   *156*

13. DATABASE SHORTCUTS & OTHER TECHNIQUES: WORKSHEET 4   *157*
Objectives   *157*
Setting the Scene   *157*
Database Shortcuts   *157*
Copying Information   *158*
Using Calculated Fields   *161*
Dividing a List Window Into Panes   *162*
Summary   *164*
Quitting *Works*   *164*

14. INTEGRATION WORKSHEET   *165*
Objectives   *165*
Setting the Scene   *165*
Opening Two Files   *167*
Viewing the Open Documents   *169*
Changing Text (the Salutation)   *172*
Selecting Data (January Birthdays)   *173*

Adding a Picture   *173*
Printing a Merged Document (The Letter)   *176*
More Scene Setting   *176*
Opening a New Word Processor Document   *176*
Typing the Memo   *176*
Opening the Spreadsheet Document   *177*
Drawing a Frame   *178*
Saving the File Under Under a Different Name   *180*
Printing a File   *181*
Review   *182*
Summary   *182*
Quitting *Works*   *182*

15. USING THE SPELLING CHECKER   *185*
Objectives   *185*
Setting the Scene   *185*
Using Spellswell   *185*
Homonyms   *187*
Spelling Errors   *189*
Viewing the Dictionary   *191*
Adding Words to the Dictionary   *191*
Redundant Words   *192*
Quitting Spellswell   *192*
More Scene Setting   *193*
Formatting   *193*
Page breaks   *193*
Numbering Pages   *194*
Saving and Printing Your File   *194*
Quitting *Works*   *194*

Appendix A: Meeting the Macintosh   *197*

Appendix B: Laboratory Procedures   *211*

Appendix C: Printing With a LaserWriter   *214*

Appendix D: Installing Works on a Hard Disk   *217*

Appendix E: Communications   *219*

Appendix F: Version 2.0 Changes   *228*

Appendix G: Glossary of Terms   *242*

INDEX   *251*

How to Use This Book

Microsoft Works is a powerful, integrated productivity tool that includes word processing, database, spreadsheet, communications and drawing functions. As a user, you can work with any one or all of these functions as you need them. *Microsoft Works on the Macintosh* has been written for the beginning user of the *Microsoft Works* (Version 1.1) program. If you are a novice computer user—as well as a new user of Microsoft Works—this book will gently guide you through your first encounter with a computer.

Although you may be an expert user of many other software packages, learning a new application presents new challenges and requires a considerable investment of your time. For the experienced user, this book is intended to reduce the amount of time you need to achieve meaningful results with *Microsoft Works* and your Macintosh. You will probably skip many of the step-by-step tutorials, but the detailed information in these exercises will be there when you need them.

Microsoft Works on the Macintosh consists of a worksheet that leads you through the creation or alteration of one or more documents using *Microsoft Works*. The worksheets are presented in the form of keystroke tutorials, in which we list all keyboard entries needed to achieve the stated purpose and then describe the results. Each chapter includes many screen illustrations to supplement the instructions in the text.

Chapter 1 is an introduction to the program, *Microsoft Works*. Chapters 2 through 5 cover word processing features. Chapters 6 through 9 focus on spreadsheet capabilities of the program. Chapters 10 through 13 concentrate on database applications, including report generation. In Chapter 14, you will integrate the major applications. Chapter 15 covers the use of the spelling checker and a few other advanced features.

The seven appendices address some specific needs of individual users. Appendix A is a short introduction to the Macintosh computer and keyboard and is especially important for those who have never used one.

We have then developed the worksheets in an easy-to-follow format, as shown below:

- Names of files are in italics: *Filename*.

- The first time a term is used, it appears in ***italicized boldface***.

- Section headings are designed to help you quickly locate the information you need.

- When you are to take action, the instructions are typed **in bold** and preceded by an arrow.

We have also used many screen illustrations throughout the text to show you *approximately* what your screen should look like as you work through the material. However, due to minor differences in hardware and software, your screen may not look *exactly* like the one in the book. As long as the basic information is there, you are doing fine, but do ask questions when you are uncertain.

Read Ahead! Read the section before you actually begin to follow its instructions. Experience has shown that students who read only as they go along miss the action taking place on the screen—and with any computer, that's half the fun! Reading computer screens is also the best way to learn to use any computer program.

Take your time as you work through the exercises, and review the material often. The original document will usually appear on your data disk so that you can start over again whenever you wish.

Feel free to experiment. This book was designed to help you explore some of the operations of *Microsoft Works*. And before you even begin the chapter worksheets, make a backup copy of the data disk that accompanies this book. Then, if you should damage the data disk, you can easily make a new copy and start over again. After you have completed a chapter, see if you can, on your own, get *Works* to do what *you* want it to do. Remember, you don't need to worry about making mistakes. In fact, we've found that people learn more from making mistakes, trying to figure out what went wrong, and then making the necessary corrections. So don't hesitate to jump right in!

If you get stuck, try one of these methods:

- Browse through the available options. Experienced users often learn a new application program this way.
- Use the Help facility.
- Ask questions of your classroom neighbor, instructor, or lab assistant.
- Read the manufacturer's manual *Microsoft Works Reference*, which accompanied the program. We recommend it as a source for all kinds of useful facts. (*Note*: The goal of this book is to teach you enough to get started with *Works*. It is *not* designed to replace the *Works* manual.)

Of the hundreds of students who have used this material during its development, one stands out for her ability to express our goals for this book in poetic fashion. When Sylvia Riveness began using this material, she suffered from an advanced case of "computer phobia." Her following original poem describes her progression through the course.

MY GOD! That's a computer that is staring
    back at me
I really think it's sneering in superiority.
My hands are feeling clammy and my head
    begins to throb.
Oh surely I could find a nice new <u>un</u>computer
    job?!

The teacher says it's time to start;
    I summon up my nerve;
I meet the mighty Macintosh
    My courage doesn't swerve.

I double check the manual;
    Stare at the sketch that's drawn;
I take a breath and push a switch—
    OH LORD—I've turned it on!

I'm in the lab for 2 straight hours;
    The struggle is intense.
Please let me do just *one* thing right.
    My pride would be immense.

And FINALLY I'm on Page 10,
    Rewriting what I've done.
It did just what it said it would—
    You know—this *might* be fun!

Copyright 1988 S. Riveness

1 Introducing Microsoft Works

Microsoft Works is an integrated software package for professionals and small businesses. The program combines a word processor, a database manager, a spreadsheet, a telecommunications module, and a spelling checker. The program includes capabilities for mail merging, report generation, simple drawing, and chart generation. Separately, each function (application) is less comprehensive than an individual program; but together, the functions become powerful. They simplify and speed up tasks such as

- Creating and maintaining small databases
- Preparing and managing spreadsheets
- Writing letters and reports
- Dialing up information services
- Inserting graphics into documents

Currently two versions of *Works* are in general use. This text addresses Version 1.1, with changes for Version 2.0 given in Appendix F.

Objectives

In this worksheet, you will learn how to

- Start up *Works* on a two-disk-drive system
- Open and close *Works* documents
- Use *Works* dialog boxes and menus
- Insert and delete text
- Center text
- Change text size and style
- Save your document on your disk
- Print a document

Setting the Scene

Suppose you are the manager of a small ice cream shop called The Ice Cream Factory. Your boss, Chris Hughes, owns The Factory and seven other ice cream shops. For each shop, Chris has purchased a Macintosh SE computer equipped with two disk drives, a modem, and an Imagewriter printer. In addition to the hardware, she has purchased eight copies of *Microsoft Works*. She wants you and the seven other managers to use *Works* to maintain and create all the records and reports needed to manage the shops effectively.

Your first assignment is to learn more about the software. This worksheet will help you to do that. In order to complete the assignment, you will need the data disk (practice files) that comes with this text.

Getting Started

In this introductory worksheet, you will get detailed instructions on starting your Macintosh and loading *Works* into its memory. In later worksheets, you will simply be told to insert the *Works* disk and load the program.

Reminder: Appendix A contains a short introduction to the Macintosh if you need a review.

How you start up *Works* depends on the state of the computer. From Steps 1-3 below, select the step that corresponds to the condition of your computer. Then follow the lettered instructions.

1. **If the computer is off**

    a. **Turn the computer on.** You will see a flashing **?** disk similar to Figure 1-1. It reminds you that the computer needs a system disk.

Figure 1-1. The flashing question mark disk

   b. **Insert the *Works* program disk into the upper disk drive.** At this point, you should see the *Works* program-disk icon in the upper right corner of the screen. Your screen should look like either Figure 1-2a (page 3) or Figure 1-2b (page 4).

   c. **If your screen looks like Figure 1-2a, continue with Step d.** If your screen looks like Figure 1-2b, skip down to Step f.

   d. **Click on the *Works* disk icon to select (highlight) it (if it is not already selected).**

2   *Microsoft Works on the Macintosh*

Figure 1-2a. Desktop with *Works* Program-disk icon in the upper right corner

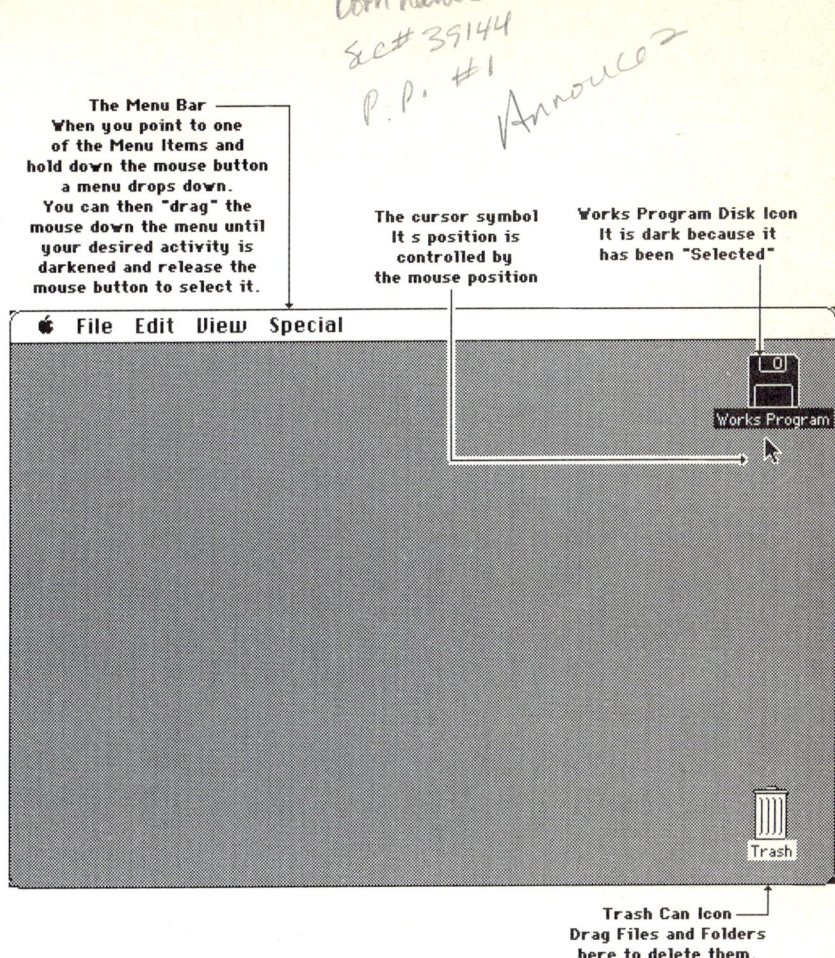

e. **Pull down the File Menu and select Open to open the disk on the desktop.** You see a desktop like Figure 1-2b.

f. **Click on the *Works* program-disk icon.**

g. **Move the pointer to File. Hold down the mouse button while you drag the pointer to Open and then release the mouse button.** You see the *Works* Open dialog box. It looks like Figure 1-3 on page 5.

h. **Now read the next text section.** It's headed Dialog Boxes.

2. **If the computer is on and you see the flashing ? disk from Figure 1-1, follow Steps 1b through 1h from page 2.**

1 Introducing Microsoft Works   **3**

Figure 1-2b. Desktop with *Works* program disk open and showing files as icons

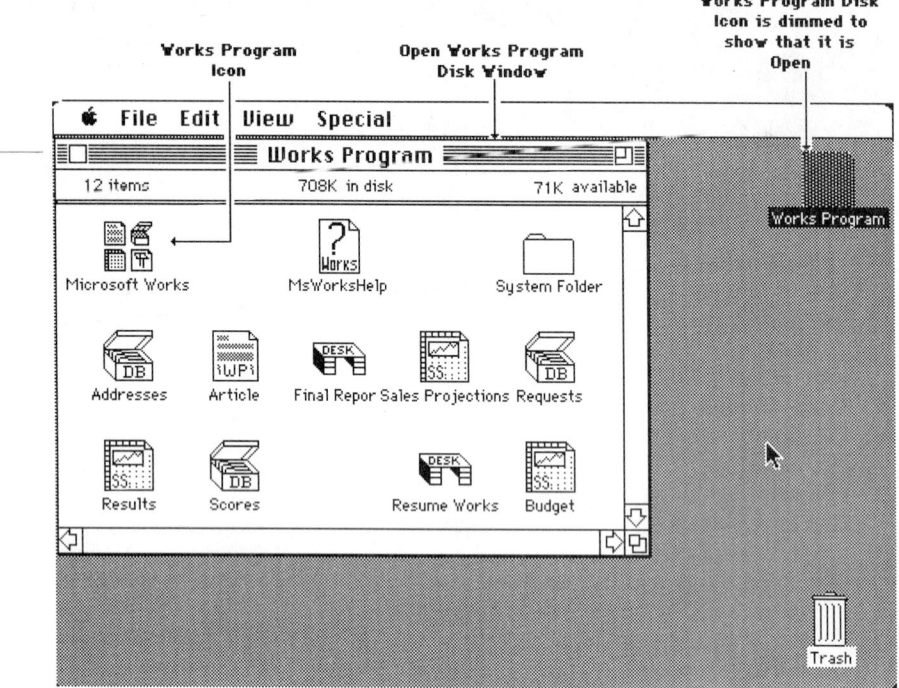

3. **If the computer is on and and you see anything other than the flashing ? disk, it means that the previous user did not properly shut down the computer.** Because it is best to close down before beginning your session, you must

   a. **Pull down the Special Menu and select Shut Down.** The Macintosh will eject any disks in the disk drives and display the flashing ? disk as shown in Figure 1-1.

   b. **Return the ejected disks to their proper storage places.**

   c. **Follow Steps 1b through 1h from page 2.**

Dialog Boxes

Now you should see the *Works* Open ***dialog box*** on your screen. It looks like Figure 1-3. This dialog box is the first of many that you will encounter as you use Microsoft *Works*. Dialog boxes ask you to select one or more actions before you can complete a task.

The dialog box on your screen may be slightly different from the one in Figure 1-3 (page 5). For example, if you are working on a system that contains a hard disk, the disk name may be different. The filename list may also be different (It may show the files

4 *Microsoft Works on the Macintosh*

Figure 1-3. *Works* Open dialog box. Note that because you have not yet inserted the data disk, the list box shows files from the *Works* program disk.

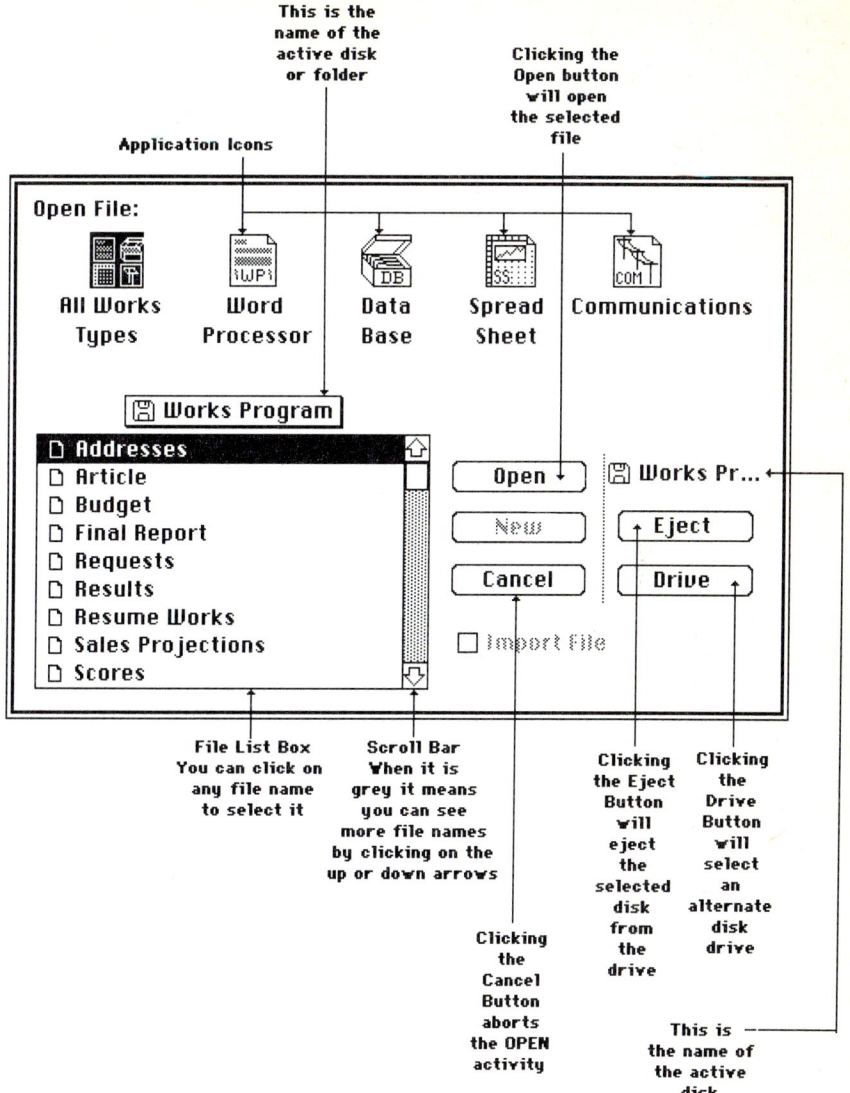

that are stored on the active disk.) Look at Figure 1-3 again. Try to identify the parts of the dialog box and account for any differences you find.

By clicking on one of the buttons on the lower right side of the box, you can use the Open dialog box to open a file, create a new file, cancel the open command, eject the active disk, or change the active drive. Across the top of the box, you see symbols (icons) that represent the applications that *Works* makes available: Word Processor, Database, Spreadsheet, or Communications.

1 Introducing Microsoft Works **5**

You can use the icons to request lists of types of documents stored on the active disk. As you can see, the All Works Types icon is presently selected (highlighted). Therefore, the list box on the lower left includes the names of files created by *all* applications. If you click on one of the other icons, the filenames in the list box will change to display only the names of files created by using the selected application.

Some Things to Remember

- A **file** is simply another name for a document that is currently stored in memory or that is electronically stored on a disk where the computer can easily retrieve it for processing. Each document (or file) must have a unique name.

- **To open an existing file** means to make the file ready for use by bringing it from the disk into the computer's main memory. Opening a file is the same as going to a file cabinet and removing the desired document.

- **To save a file** means to copy the content of the file that is currently in memory into a storage place on the disk. Saving a file is the same as putting a copy of the file into the file cabinet. The file remains open (in memory) and you can continue to work with it.

- **To close a file** means to clear the computer's memory in order to make room for another task or to quit the program. Closing a file is the same as dropping the document currently in memory into the waste basket. You will lose any changes you made in the file unless you save it before closing. Luckily, *Works* always prompts you to save changes whenever you try to close a file to which changes have been made.

More Scene Setting

The Ice Cream Factory is almost ready for business, and you want to create a flyer to announce the grand opening to the neighborhood. Chris has created a rough draft of the flyer, but you need to make changes in it. The draft is stored on your data disk under the filename *Announce*.

Opening a File

To open the *Announce* file on the *Works Data Disk*, follow these steps:

1. **Insert the data disk into the second disk drive.** You probably remember that in the dialog box the name of the disk

6   *Microsoft Works on the Macintosh*

in the active drive appears to the right of the disk icon (as in Figure 1-3). When you insert the data disk, the active drive should change to "Works Data." If it does not, move the pointer to the Drive button and click once. The files you see in the list box are now those stored on the data disk.

2. **Move the pointer to the Word Processor icon at the top of the dialog box and click once to select it.** Because *only* word processing files are now listed in the list box, it is much easier to find *Announce*.

3. The filename *Announce* should already be highlighted in the list box. **If it is not, move the pointer to the filename *Announce* and click once to select (highlight) it.**

4. **Move the pointer to the Open button and click once.** Your screen should now look like Figure 1-4.

Figure 1-4. The *Announce* File. Your screen should look like this.

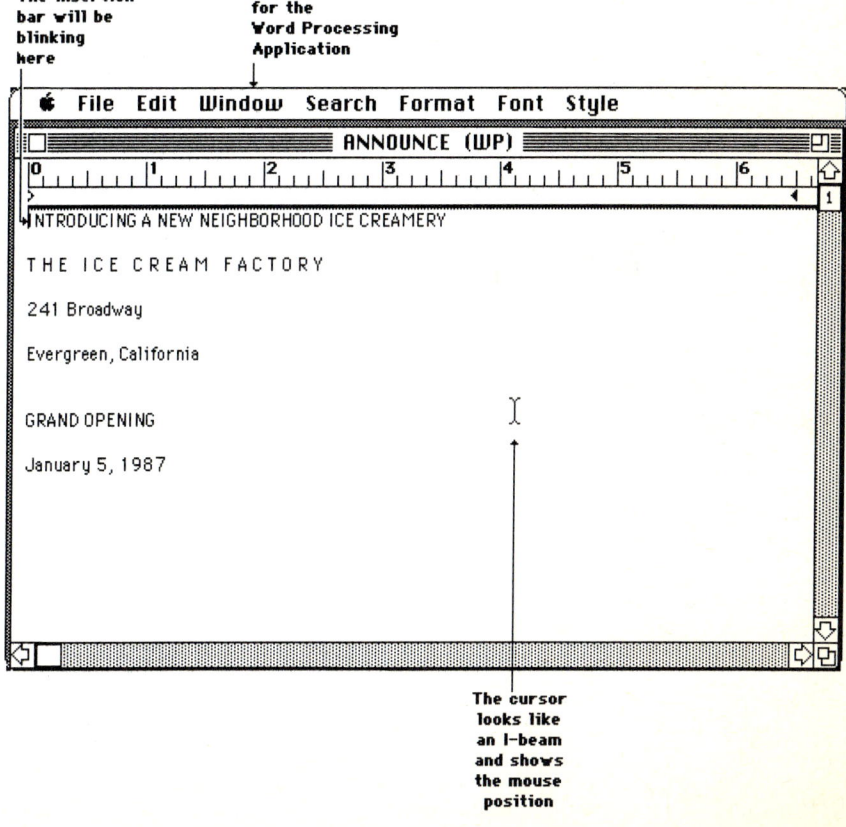

1 *Introducing Microsoft Works*   **7**

Inserting Text

As you can see from Figure 1-4, Chris has forgotten to include hours for the Grand Opening.

Follow the instructions below to add the open hours 1:00 p.m. to 4:00 p.m. below the date.

1. **Move the *I-beam*** (it marks the present position of the mouse and is shown in Figure 1-4) **to the end of the file** (the space immediately after the date) **and click once.** The ***insertion bar*** cursor (the blinking vertical line that marks the position for your next action) appears at that point. To add another line to the file,

2. **Press:**   [RETURN] **once.** The insertion bar moves to the next line.

3. **Type:**   1:00 p.m. to 4:00 p.m.

Centering Text

The announcement would look much better if all the lines were centered. The ***menu bar*** across the top of the screen contains options that enable you to do just that. Follow the directions below to select (highlight) and center all the lines. You can select text for editing purposes in several ways. Since you want to select the entire document,

1. **Move the I-beam to the menu bar.** As you move the I-beam, it becomes an arrow (pointer) as shown in Figure 1-5. You use the pointer to pull down a menu.

Figure 1-5. The menu bar with the pointer on the Edit Menu option

```
  File  Edit  Window  Search  Format  Font  Style
```

Note that the I-beam and the arrow perform the same function— to indicate the location of the mouse at all times. When the I-beam is in the working area where you type, it is an I-beam. Anywhere else, it is usually an arrow.

2. **Move the pointer to Edit. Hold down the mouse button, drag the pointer down to Select All, and then release the mouse button.** The entire announcement is now selected.

3. **Move the pointer to Format. Hold down the mouse button, drag the pointer down to Centered, and then re-**

8   *Microsoft Works on the Macintosh*

lease the mouse button. Each line of the document will now be centered. Click anywhere on the screen to deselect text.

From this point on, instructions for making selections from the menus will be abbreviated. For example, Step 3 above will read: **"Pull down the Format Menu and select Centered."**

Deleting Lines

One more change! Delete the blank line between the address and the city/state lines.

1. **Move the I-beam into the line between the street address and the city/state.** See Figure 1-6.

2. **Click to place the insertion bar.** Note that the insertion bar jumps to the center of the line. That is because you just formatted these lines to be centered.

3. **Press [BACKSPACE] or [DELETE].** The line disappears.

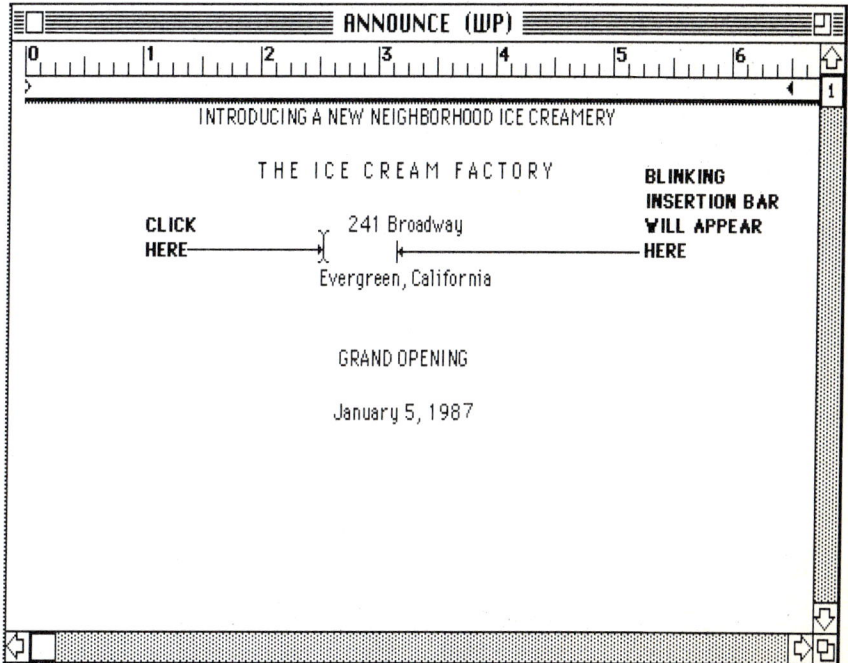

Figure 1-6. The *Announce* file with every line centered and the insertion bar cursor in the line between the street and city address

1 *Introducing Microsoft Works*   **9**

Changing Text Size and Style

The styles and sizes of **typefaces** (called **fonts**) depend upon your printer's capabilities. The term *font* in the Macintosh world refers to the design used to print characters (for example, Courier, Helvetica, Times). Type *style* refers to the appearance of the characters (bold, italic, underline, outline, shadow). When choosing the size, the larger the number you choose, the larger the print.

To add a little variety to the announcement, you will now increase the size of the text and change the type style of the first line. When you pull down the Font Menu, you will see a checkmark next to the current font setting. If you select a different option, the checkmark will appear next to that setting, but only for selected text. You do not have to use the same font for an entire document. If you have a dot matrix or laser printer, you can change typeface, typestyle, and size anywhere within a document.

1. **Position the I-beam to the left of the word "Introducing." Hold down the mouse button, drag to the right to select the entire line, and then release the mouse button.**

2. **Pull down the Font Menu and select any font other than Geneva.** (We used Boston in Figure 1-7.) Do you see the change in the type style? If you don't like the face, you can try another font. Keep changing the font style until you find one that pleases you. With the line still highlighted,

3. **Pull down the Style Menu and select 18.** The line now appears in extra large letters.

4. **Pull down the Style Menu and select Outline.**

5. **Pull down the Style Menu and select Shadow.** The line now appears as shown in Figure 1-7.

Figure 1-7. This heading appears in Boston, outline, shadow, 18 points

```
┌─────────────────────────────────────────┐
│      INTRODUCING A NEW                  │
│   NEIGHBORHOOD ICE CREAMERY             │
└─────────────────────────────────────────┘
```

Warning: Be sure to deselect text after you reformat it. Here's an exercise to illustrate a problem that may occur if you don't. First,

10   *Microsoft Works on the Macintosh*

the heading should still be selected (highlighted). If it is not,

1. **Repeat Step 1 on page 10.**

2. **Press the [BACKSPACE] or [DELETE].**

The entire heading has disappeared! But don't panic. As you can see, if you accidentally press a key while text is selected, that keystroke will *replace* all the highlighted text. (In this case, [BACKSPACE] or [DELETE] erases text.) Undoing the damage, fortunately, is easy:

3. **Pull down the Edit Menu and select Undo.** (See Figure 1-8.) The line reappears.

Figure 1-8. Edit Menu with Undo option selected

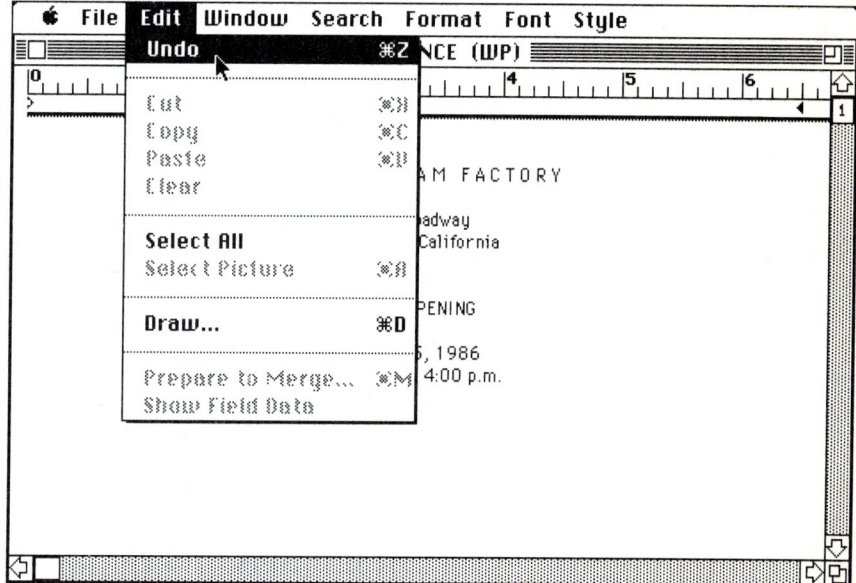

4. **Click the mouse button once to deselect the heading.**
   Now you can't accidentally change the heading.

Saving a File Under a Different Name

At the present time, your revision exists only on the screen and in the memory of your computer. If the power goes off, you would have to start over with the original version of *Announce* because the computer does not automatically save a file as you create it.

1 Introducing Microsoft Works **11**

By completing the following steps, your revision of *Announce* will be saved with a different filename so that the original file will remain unchanged on your disk in case you want to repeat this worksheet at another time. We will now rename the new file *Announce2*.

 1. **Pull down the File Menu and choose Save As.** The Save As dialog box shown in Figure 1-9 appears. Since the filename box is already selected,

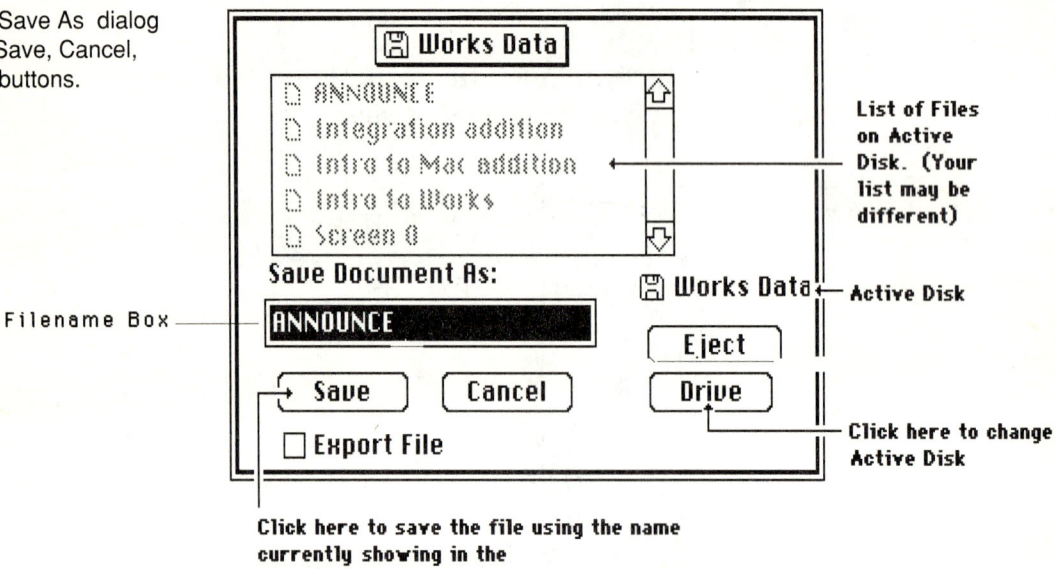

Figure 1-9. The Save As dialog box. Shows the Save, Cancel, Eject, and Drive buttons.

2. **Type:**   Announce2

Your data disk should be in the active drive and its name displayed next to the active disk icon on the middle right of the dialog box. **If the *Works* program disk is displayed instead of your *Works Data Disk*,**

3. **Click once on the Drive button.** "Works Data" should now display as the active disk.

4. **Click once on the Save button.** Your revised announcement now exists on your data disk as well as in the computer's memory.

12 *Microsoft Works on the Macintosh*

Printing a File

To print your announcement,

1. **Turn on your printer and be sure that it is ready to print.**

2. **Pull down the File Menu and select Print.**

   You see a Print dialog box similar to Figure 1-10. It offers many options. The options that are currently selected have highlighted buttons.

Figure 1-10. The Print dialog box for the Imagewriter printer

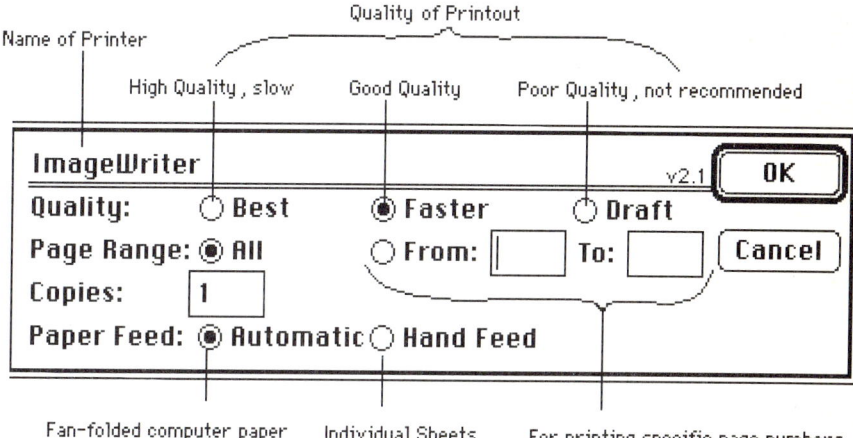

3. **If the dialog box on your screen does not show the same options selected as in Figure 1-10, click the appropriate buttons on your screen to make the boxes agree.** Don't worry, nothing happens until you click the OK Button in the next step.

Note: For general use, use Faster quality printing. Best takes longer to print and quickly wears out ribbons.

4. **When your dialog box matches Figure 1-10, move the pointer to the OK button and click once.** The disk drive whirs as the Macintosh prepares the file for printing. Be patient — printing should begin in about 30 seconds. You will see the printing message before printing begins. If for any reason you want to cancel printing, hold down [COMMAND] or [⌘] and type a period. If the paper jams, use the printer on/

1 Introducing Microsoft Works **13**

off button to turn the printer off, readjust the paper, and begin again with Step 1.

Quitting Works

Now that you have printed and saved your revised announcement on disk, you can safely put your announcement file away in preparation for quitting.

- **Pull down the File Menu and select Close.**

If you have made any changes to *Announce2* since saving it, you will see a dialog box similar to Figure 1-11.

Figure 1-11. The Save Changes dialog box. Note how the program identifies the file as a word processing file: WP.

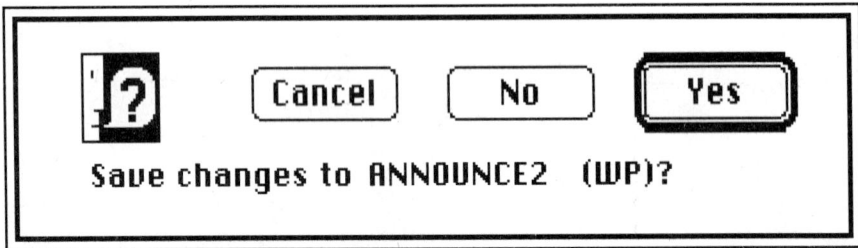

- **If you want to save any changes you have made, move the pointer to the Yes button and click once.**

- **If you do not want to save changes, simply move the pointer to the No Button and click once.**

After closing *Announce2*, you see the *Works* Open dialog box on the screen. If you want to continue to the next worksheet, you can do so now and skip the rest of this worksheet. If, however, you are finished for this session, follow the steps for quitting.

Remember that when you quit *Works*, the file in the computer's memory disappears, but the files stored on the disk (either floppy or hard) are not lost. It is always best to formally quit the program before turning off the Macintosh. If you do not, you may lose information because the Macintosh updates the directories on the disks during the quitting process. The following steps will guide you through quitting *Works*.

1. **Pull down the File Menu and select Quit.** When the Macintosh has returned you to the desktop, tidy it up for the next person by closing all the windows.

14 *Microsoft Works on the Macintosh*

2. **Move the pointer to the upper-left corner close box of each open window and click once.** See Figure 1-12.

Figure 1-12. The Macintosh desktop showing in Icon View the contents of the *Works* program disk

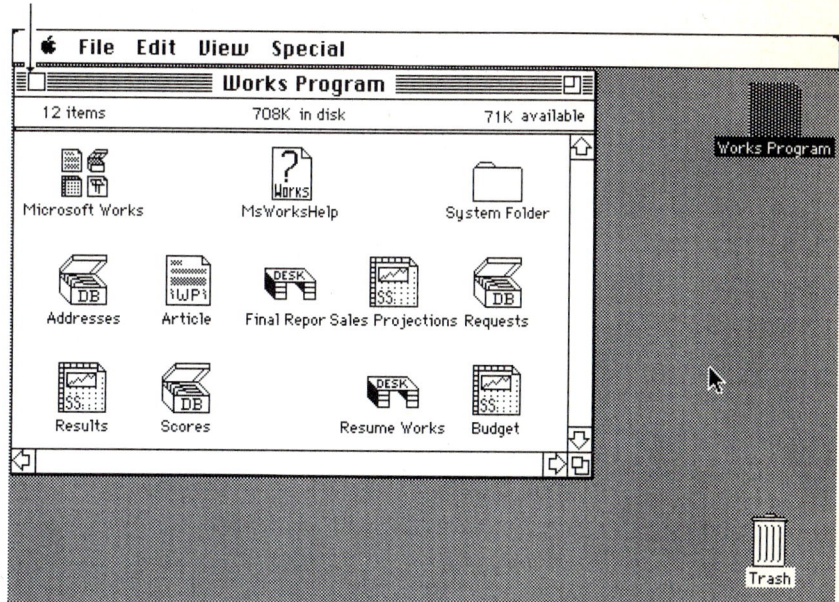

3. **Pull down the Special Menu and select Shut Down.**

4. **Remove the disks from the drives and return them to their appropriate places.**

Congratulations! You should now be able to open and close word processing files, use *Works'* menus and dialog boxes, insert and delete text, center text, change type size and style, save files, and print documents.

1 Introducing Microsoft Works   **15**

2 Word Processing Worksheet 1

Word Processing Background

Word processing is perhaps the easiest application to understand—as well as the most useful to learn. A word processing program enables us to use the computer's ability to save keystrokes in memory, thus allowing us to make changes before printing a final copy.

When relieved of the burden of correcting typographical mistakes, we are able to concentrate on the purpose of writing—to communicate ideas. Revisions are no longer chores but opportunities to improve. *MacWrite*™ was the original word processing program for the Macintosh computer. Now *WordPerfect*™, *Word*™, and *FullWrite*™ are other popular Macintosh word processing programs.

For some time, the combination of computer hardware and word processing software has allowed us to print documents using varied typefaces, styles, and sizes, including headers (text that automatically appears at the top of each page), footers (text that automatically appears at the bottom of each page), and personalized form letters. Recently, some word processors have acquired additional features that, for example, allow them to print in columns, incorporate graphics into text, check spelling, and create indexes.

An extremely useful feature of word processing programs is that they facilitate collaborative writing. For example, this book was written by several authors, each using the same word processing program. Disks were exchanged and files edited and revised until no one had any sense of ownership of any individual part of the manuscript. The ability to collaborate in this manner means that each writer brings his or her major strengths to bear on the entire project.

So it is natural then that the first application in the *Works* program that you will use is word processing. You were, of course, introduced to word processing in the previous worksheet.

Objectives

In this worksheet, you will learn how to

- Start the computer with the *Works* program
- Open a file
- Insert, delete, and replace text
- Center, underline, and bold text
- Search and replace text
- Save changes using a new name
- Print a file and quit *Works*

Some Things to Remember

As you probably recall, the position at which the action takes place on the screen is marked by the insertion bar, or **cursor**. In *Works* the cursor is a blinking, vertical line.

Remember also that when typing you don't need to press [RETURN] at the end of a line. The program will **wordwrap** and automatically begin a new line. However, don't forget to press [RETURN] or [ENTER] whenever a new line is required (for example, to begin a new paragraph or a new item in a list).

Setting the Scene

As the manager of The Ice Cream Factory, you have been given a Macintosh and *Works* to help you manage the store. You have decided to finish that article on ice cream trivia that the local newspaper has been asking you to submit for some time. You drafted the article earlier, but it needs revision.

Getting Started

- **Turn on the computer and load *Works* into the computer as described in Getting Started, Chapter 1.** You should see the Open dialog box shown in Figure 2-1 (page 19).

Opening a File

A word processing file containing the draft of your article is stored on your *Works Data Disk* under the filename *Trivia*. (The name "*Trivia*" will help you remember the content of the file.)

1. **Insert your *Works Data Disk* into the second disk drive.** The name next to the active disk icon changes from "Works Program" to "Works Data." As shown in Figure 2-2 (page 19), the files in the list box are now those stored on the data disk.

2. **Move the pointer to the Word Processor icon at the top of the dialog box and click once to select it.** You now see *only* word processing files in the list box, making it is easier to find *Trivia*.

18   *Microsoft Works on the Macintosh*

Figure 2-1. The Open dialog box showing the files from the *Works* program disk (the active disk)

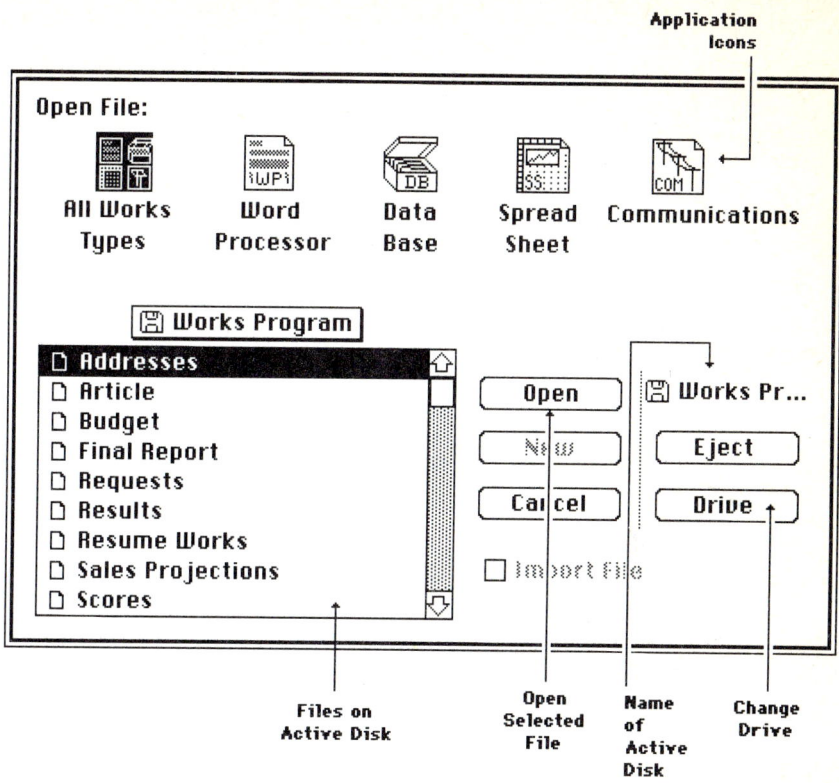

Figure 2-2. The Open dialog box showing files from the *Works* Data Disk

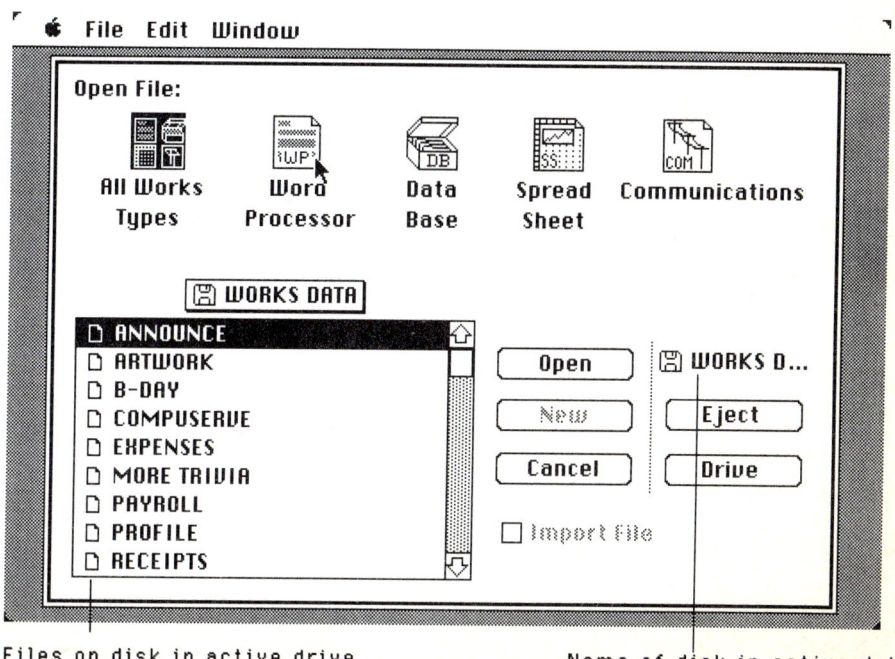

2 Word Processing: Worksheet 1   **19**

3. **Move the pointer to *Trivia* in the list box and click once to select (highlight) it.**

4. **Move the pointer to the Open button and click once.** Your screen will now show the beginning of the *Trivia* file. See Figure 2-3.

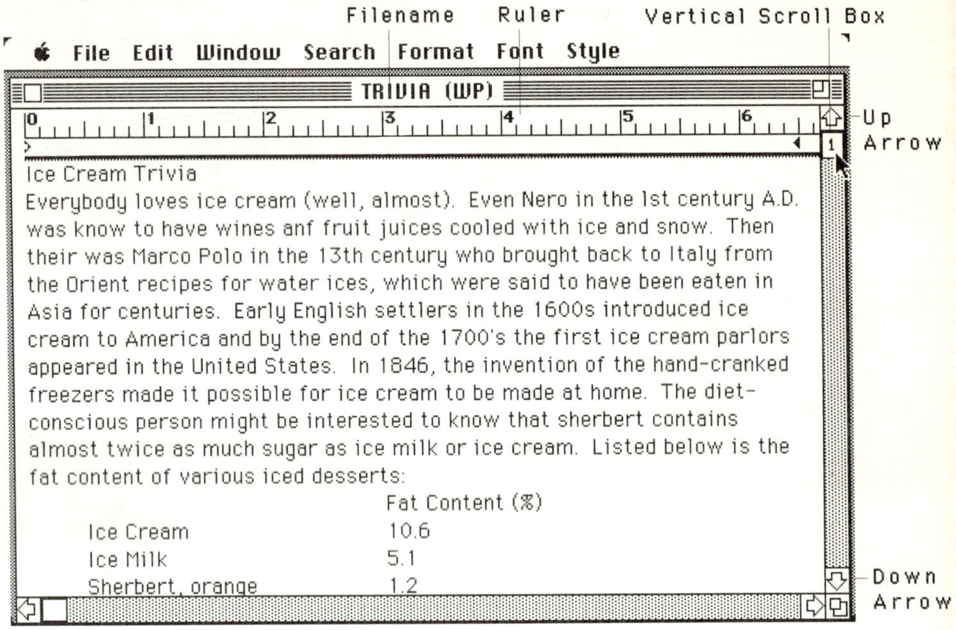

Figure 2-3. The *Trivia* file. You see the ruler, the filename, the vertical scroll bar, and the vertical scroll arrows

To display the remainder of the document, you will use the vertical scroll bar at the right of the screen.

1. **Move the pointer below the scroll box in the vertical scroll bar.**

2. **Click once.** The screen displays the remainder of the document.

To scroll up and down the document one row at a time,

3. **Move the pointer to the up arrow at the top of the vertical scroll bar.**

4. **Click once.**

20 *Microsoft Works on the Macintosh*

To move back to the top of the text,

5. **Move the pointer to the vertical scroll box.**

6. **Drag the box to the top of the vertical scroll bar.** Now you see the beginning of the file.

In this worksheet, you will revise *Trivia*. The revisions are shown by number in Figure 2-4 (page 22).

Typing a Centered Bold Heading (Revision 1)

To make the main heading stand out, you will center it and make it bold

Figure 2-5   1. Center and in bold

```
Ice Cream Trivia
Everybody loves ice cream (well, almost).  Even Nero in the 1st
century A.D. was know to have wines anf fruit juices cooled with
```

1. **Move the I-beam to anywhere within the headline and click once.**

2. **Pull down the FORMAT Menu (notice that Left Justified is presently selected) and select Centered.** The heading should now be centered. To change the typestyle of the entire heading to bold,

3. **Select the line "Ice Cream Trivia" by moving the I-beam to the left of the first letter, holding down the mouse button, and dragging the I-beam across it.** If you highlight the wrong line, simply click on the mouse to deselect the text and begin again.

In the future, when you are asked to select (highlight) text, follow the procedure used in Step 3 above.

4. **Pull down the Style Menu and select Bold.** To deselect the text and eliminate the highlighting,

5. **Click the mouse once.**

Important Reminder: If, as you work, you find that a previous action is not what you intended, you can pull down the Edit Menu

2 Word Processing: Worksheet 1   **21**

1 ——— Ice Cream Trivia
2 ——— Everybody loves ice cream (well, almost). Even Nero in the 1st century A.D.
3 & 4 ——— was know to have wines anf fruit juices cooled with ice and snow. Then
5 ——— their was Marco Polo in the 13th century who brought back to Italy from
the Orient recipes for water ices, which were said to have been eaten in
6 ——— Asia for centuries. Early English settlers in the 1600s introduced ice
cream to America and by the end of the 1700's the first ice cream parlors
appeared in the United States. In 1846, the invention of the hand-cranked
freezers made it possible for ice cream to be made at home. The diet-
7 ——— conscious person might be interested to know that sherbert contains
almost twice as much sugar as ice milk or ice cream. Listed below is the
fat content of various iced desserts:

	Fat Content (%)
Ice Cream	10.6
Ice Milk	5.1
Sherbert, orange	1.2

For you trivia buffs, here are more facts about ice cream:

8 ——— 1. Most popular flavor in the United States is vanila, followed by chocolate and strawberry.
9 ——— 2. Average serving (1/6 of a quart) of vanila ice cream is about 200 calories.

Figure 2-4. The revisions are shown by the numbers 1 through 9.

and select Undo to reverse the action. To undo more than one action, you must select the portion of the text you want to correct (as in Step 3) and make the corrections by using the menu bar options or, if necessary, by retyping the text.

Underlining Text (Revision 2)

To emphasize the first word of the article, "Everybody," you will underline it. By now you probably know that you can make changes in the appearance of groups of characters by using the Style Menu. You will select the material you want to underline by highlighting it, and then you will underline it.

Figure 2-6

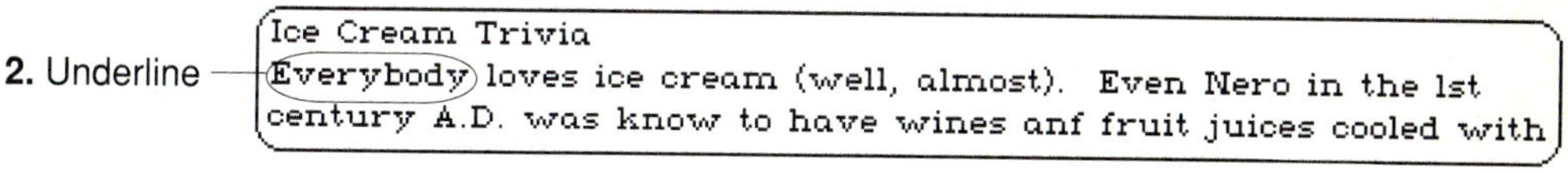

2. Underline

```
Ice Cream Trivia
Everybody loves ice cream (well, almost).  Even Nero in the 1st
century A.D. was know to have wines anf fruit juices cooled with
```

1. **Select the word "Everybody" by dragging the I-beam across it.** See Step 3 under Revision 1 if you have forgotten how to select text.

2. **Pull down the Style Menu and select Underline.**

That's it! To deselect and eliminate the highlight, click once on the mouse.

Inserting Text (Revisions 3 and 6)

Works always inserts letters at the blinking insertion bar and at the same time moves the remaining letters to the right. Therefore, you must always place the I-beam at the position where you want the correction to appear and click once to position the insertion bar.

Figure 2-7

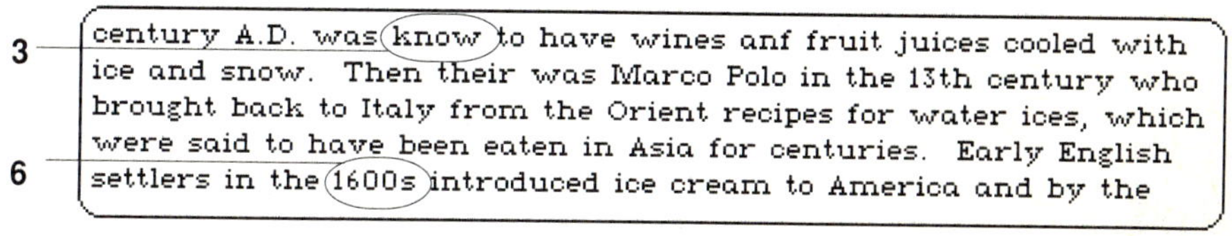

3

6

```
century A.D. was know to have wines anf fruit juices cooled with
ice and snow.  Then their was Marco Polo in the 13th century who
brought back to Italy from the Orient recipes for water ices, which
were said to have been eaten in Asia for centuries.  Early English
settlers in the 1600s introduced ice cream to America and by the
```

1. **For Revision 3, move the I-beam immediately after "know" and click once.** The blinking insertion bar appears.

2. **Type the letter n:**   n

2 Word Processing: Worksheet 1   **23**

3. **Move the I-beam between "1600" and "s" in Revision 6 and click once.** The blinking insertion bar appears.

4. **Type an apostrophe:** '

In the future, when you are asked to "place the insertion bar," move the I-beam to the desired location and click once on the mouse button (as you did in Step 1 above).

Replacing Letters (Revisions 4 and 5)

There are many ways to replace letters when using *Works*. Usually, the easiest way is to use [BACKSPACE] or [DELETE] to erase the character immediately preceding the insertion bar and then type the correct text. For example, for Revisions 4 and 5, you will correct two misspellings.

Figure 2-8

4 ─
5 ─

century A.D. was know to have wines (anf) fruit juices cooled with ice and snow. Then (their) was Marco Polo in the 13th century who brought back to Italy from the Orient recipes for water ices, which were said to have been eaten in Asia for centuries. Early English settlers in the 1600s introduced ice cream to America and by the

1. **Place the insertion bar immediately after the "f" in "anf"** Remember, to place the insertion bar, you must first place the I-beam and then click the mouse.

2. **Press:**   [BACKSPACE] **or** [DELETE] **to delete the incorrect letter.**

3. **Type:**   d

4. **Place the insertion bar immediately after the "r" in "their."**

5. **Press:**   [BACKSPACE] **or** [DELETE] **twice to delete the unwanted letters "ir."**

6. **Type:**   re

Replacing Words (Revision 7)

We want to replace "person" with "eater." You can replace words in the same way as you replace characters. However, the following method is usually faster.

24   *Microsoft Works on the Macintosh*

Figure 2-9

7 — person might be interested to know that sherbert contains almost twice as much sugar as ice milk or ice cream. Listed below is the

1. Select the word "person" by dragging the I-beam across it.

As you may remember from the warning in Deleting Lines (page 10), if you type characters when text is highlighted, you will replace the selected text with the characters you type. Therefore,

2. Type: eater

The highlighted text "person" was replaced by "eater."

Searching and Replacing Text (Revisions 8 and 9)

Suppose that you are worried that you have misspelled "vanilla" throughout the article. This is a good opportunity to use the search and replace feature. With it, you can search for a misspelled word throughout a file and replace it with a correct spelling.

Figure 2-10

8 —
9 —
1. Most popular flavor in the United States is vanila followed by chocolate and strawberry.
2. Average serving (1.6 of a quart) of vanila ice cream is about 200 calories.

1. Pull down the Search Menu and select Replace.

At the bottom of the screen, you see a Replace dialog box similar to Figure 2-11, page 26. Study the dialog box carefully, and then follow the steps. For the Replace command, you need to give the text you want to find (Find What), the replacement text (Replace With), and the conditions under which you want the text replaced. With the insertion bar in the Find What box,

2. Type: vanila If you make a mistake, simply backspace and retype.

2 Word Processing: Worksheet 1   **25**

Figure 2-11. The Find What box, the Replace With box, and the search options

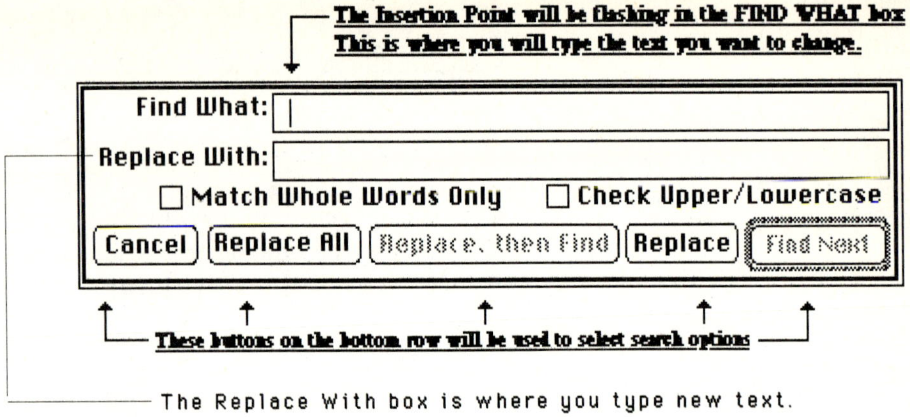

The Insertion Point will be flashing in the FIND WHAT box. This is where you will type the text you want to change.

Find What:
Replace With:
☐ Match Whole Words Only   ☐ Check Upper/Lowercase
[Cancel] [Replace All] [Replace, then Find] [Replace] [Find Next]

These buttons on the bottom row will be used to select search options

The Replace With box is where you type new text.

3. **Press:**   [TAB] to move the insertion bar to the Replace With box.

4. **Type the correct spelling:**   vanilla

5. **Move the pointer to the Replace All button and click once.** In a few seconds, you see a message telling you that all occurrences have been found and the replacements made.

6. **Move the pointer to the OK button and click once.**

The corrected file appears in Figure 2-12 (page 27).

If you wanted *Works* to stop at every occurrence of "vanila" and display it for your confirmation, you could click on the Find Next button (instead of the Replace All). Then, when *Works* displayed an occurrence, you could have clicked the Replace button to make the change or the Cancel button to abort the search.

Saving a File Under a Different Name

At the present time, your revisions exist only on the screen and in the memory of the Macintosh. If the power goes off, you will have to start over with the original version of *Trivia*. Remember that the computer does not automatically save a file as you create it.

There are times such as this when you will change a document but want to keep the unchanged as well as the changed version. For that reason, you will save the changed version as a new document under a different name. The original file will remain on your disk:

26 *Microsoft Works on the Macintosh*

Ice Cream Trivia

<u>Everybody</u> loves ice cream (well, almost). Even Nero in the 1st century A.D. was known to have wines and fruit juices cooled with ice and snow. Then there was Marco Polo in the 13th century who brought back to Italy from the Orient recipes for water ices, which were said to have been eaten in Asia for centuries. Early English settlers in the 1600's introduced ice cream to America and by the end of the 1700's the first ice cream parlors appeared in the United States. In 1846, the invention of the hand-cranked freezers made it possible for ice cream to be made at home. The diet-conscious eater might be interested to know that sherbert contains almost twice as much sugar as ice milk or ice cream. Listed below is the fat content of various iced desserts:

	Fat Content (%)
Ice Cream	10.6
Ice Milk	5.1
Sherbert, orange	1.2

For you trivia buffs, here are more facts about ice cream:
1. Most popular flavor in the United States is vanilla, followed by chocolate and strawberry.
2. Average serving (1/6 of a quart) of vanilla ice cream is about 200 calories.

Figure 2-12. Shows document after revisions 1-9 have been completed

1. **Pull down the File Menu and select Save As.** The Save As dialog box appears.

2. **Check to see that your data disk is the active disk.** Its name should appear to the right of the active disk icon in the dialog box. If it is not, click on the Drive button until the active disk name is "Works Data."

3. **For the new filename, type: Trivia2** When you type, the old name disappears. The rest of the options don't need to be changed.

4. **Move the pointer to the Save button and click once.** You now have two versions of this article on your disk. Note that the document name at the top of the screen has changed to *Trivia2*.

Viewing Two Open Files

To assure yourself that you did not destroy the original *Trivia* file, open it again.

1. **Pull down the File Menu and select Open.**

2. **When the Open dialog box appears (page 29), check to determine if your *Works Data Disk* is the active disk. Then, search the list box for your two *Trivia* files.** The list box can show only a limited number of files at a time; and since the files are listed alphabetically, you may have to scroll down to find them.

As you can see, the file you just created, **Trivia2**, appears in the list box along with the original file **Trivia**. To load the original *Trivia* file,

3. **Click on the filename *Trivia* to select it.**

4. **Click on the Open button.** The original file is now open and resident in memory. (See the document name at the top of the screen.) To check that you have two files open,

5. **Pull down the Window Menu and note that both files are now listed.**

28 *Microsoft Works on the Macintosh*

Figure 2-13. The Open dialog box with scroll bar, active disk icon, and options buttons

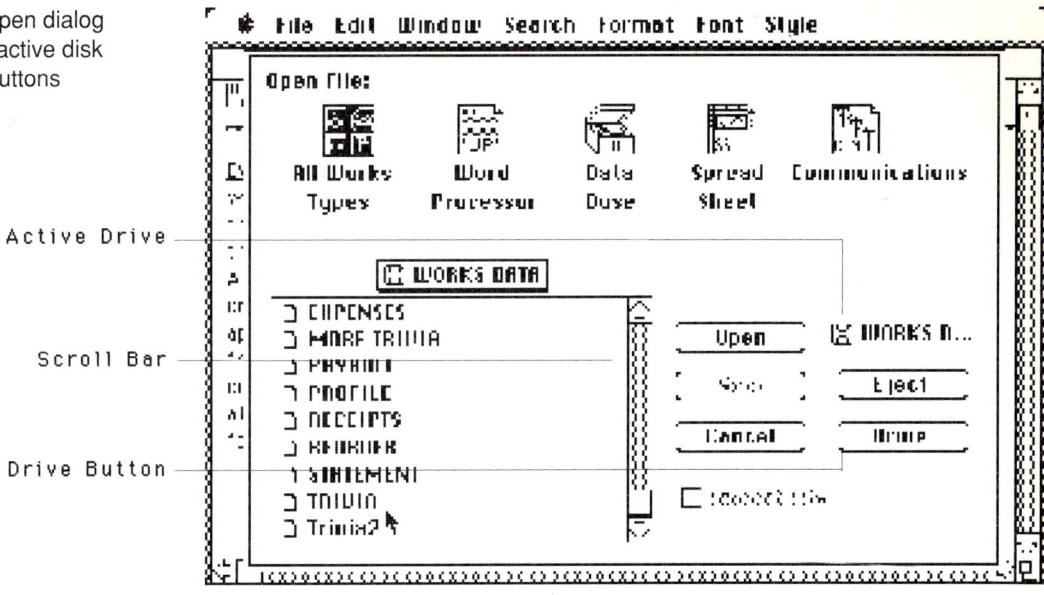

Active Drive

Scroll Bar

Drive Button

6. To return to your revised file, pull down the WINDOW Menu and select *Trivia2*.

Printing a File

Now you will print the *Trivia2* file.

1. Turn on your printer and be certain that it is ready to print.
2. Pull down the File Menu and select Print.

You see the Print Dialog Box. The options currently selected have highlighted buttons. Look at Figure 2-14. If the dialog box on your screen does not have the same options selected, click the buttons on your screen to make it conform with Figure 2-14.

Figure 2-14. The Print dialog box. Selected options have highlighted buttons.

2 Word Processing: Worksheet 1 **29**

Note: For general purposes, use FASTER printing. BEST takes longer to print and quickly wears out ribbons. When your dialog box matches Figure 2-14, move the pointer to the OK Button and click once.

The disk drive whirs as the Macintosh reads the printer file from the system folder and writes a print file to the disk before it actually starts printing. You will see the printing message and then printing will begin. If you want to cancel printing, hold down [COMMAND] or [⌘] and type a period. If the paper jams, use the on/off button to turn the printer off, readjust the paper, and begin again with Step 1.

Think About It

Before quitting *Works*, let's review what you have accomplished in this worksheet. You have opened a file, moved the cursor all around the file, inserted and deleted text, centered and made bold the heading, underlined text, searched and replaced text, and saved a file using a new name. Do you remember which menu was used for each? For example, under which menu will you find the Undo feature? Which menu would you use to change the type size? Take the time to review the menus on the screen before you leave this worksheet.

Quitting Works

Now that you have saved and printed *Trivia2*, you can safely quit the program. Remember that when you quit *Works*, the file currently in the computer's memory disappears, but a file stored on a disk is not lost.

When you have finished using a program, always try to formally quit. If you do not, you may lose information because the Macintosh updates disk directories during the quitting process.

➡ **1. Pull down the File Menu and select Quit.**

If you have made any changes to *Trivia2* since saving it, you may see a dialog box similar to Figure 2-15.

    a. If you want to save changes, move the pointer to the Yes button and click once.

    b. If you do not want to save changes, move the pointer to the No button and click once.

Figure 2-15. The Save Changes dialog box with the Cancel, No, Yes buttons

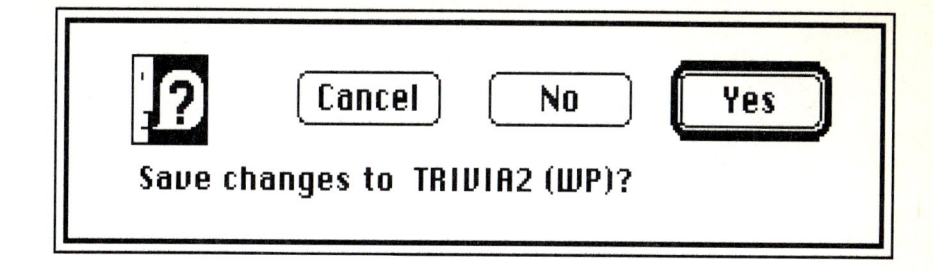

When the Macintosh has returned you to the desktop, tidy it up for the next person.

2. Move the pointer to the upper left corner close box of each open window and click once.

3. Pull down the Special Menu and select Shut Down.

4. Remove the disks from the Macintosh and return them to their appropriate places.

5. Turn off the Macintosh.

2 Word Processing: Worksheet 1 **31**

3 Word Processing Worksheet 2

Setting the Scene   Your article on ice cream trivia now looks like Figure 3-1. Areas that you still want to revise are marked.

1

2 ─────────────── Ice Cream Trivia

6 ── <u>Everybody</u> loves ice cream (well, almost). Even Nero in the 1st century A.D. ── **3**
was known to have wines and fruit juices cooled with ice and snow. Then there was Marco Polo in the 13th century who brought back to Italy from the Orient recipes for water ices, which were said to have been eaten in
4 ── Asia for centuries. Early English settlers in the 1600's introduced ice
7 ── cream to America and by the end of the 1700's the first ice cream parlors appeared in the United States. In 1846, the invention of the hand-cranked freezers made it possible for ice cream to be made at home. The diet- ── **5**
conscious eater might be interested to know that sherbert contains almost twice as much sugar as ice milk or ice cream. Listed below is the fat content of various iced desserts:

	Fat Content (%)
Ice Cream	10.6
Ice Milk	5.1	── **8**
Sherbert, orange	1.2

For you trivia buffs, here are more facts about ice cream:
  1. Most popular flavor in the United States is vanilla, followed by chocolate and strawberry.
9 ──
  2. Average serving (1/6 of a quart) of vanilla ice cream is about ── **10**
     200 calories.

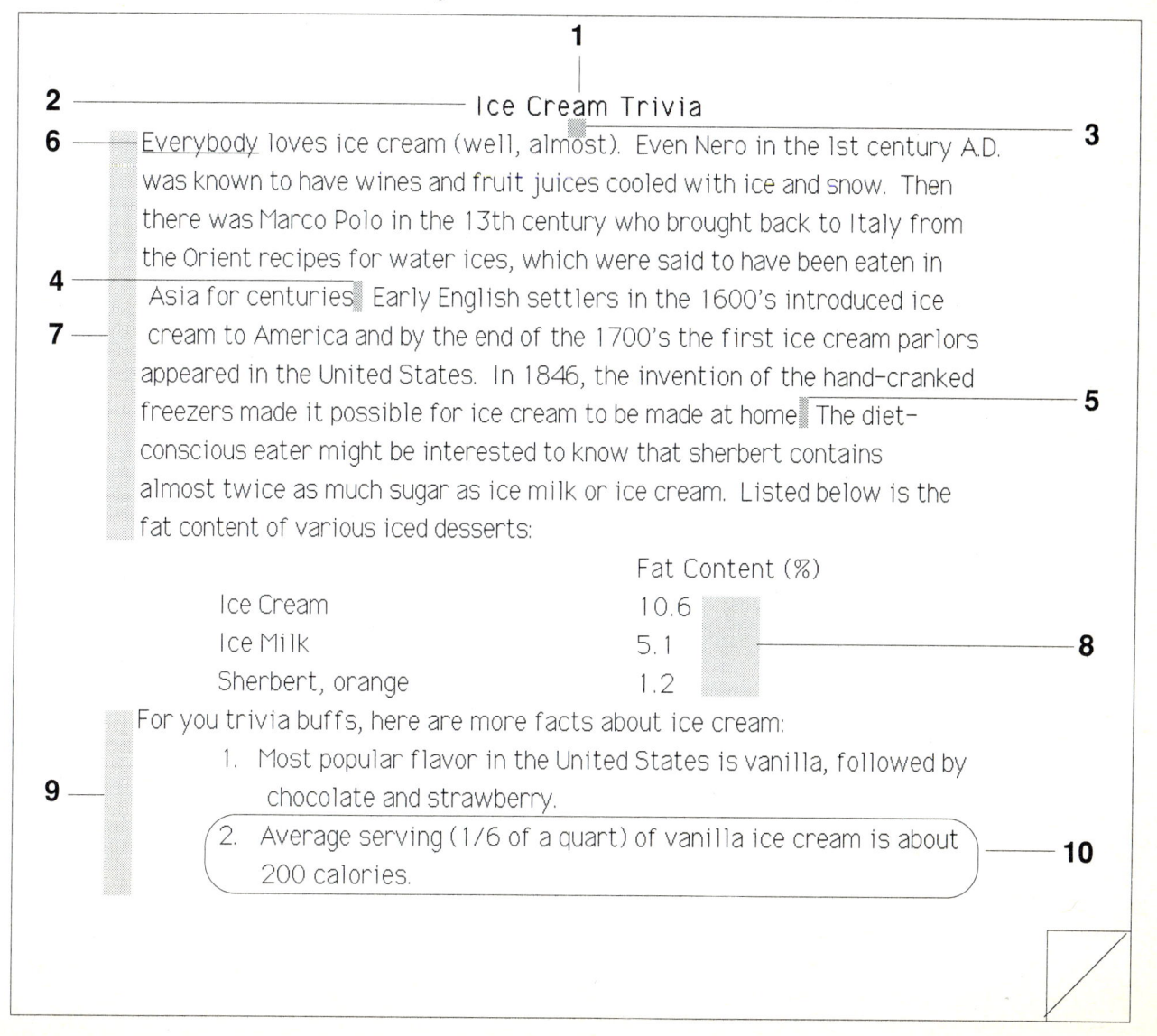

Figure 3-1

Objectives

In this worksheet, you will learn how to

- Create a top margin by inserting blank lines
- Type and delete at the same time
- Insert a new paragraph
- Use tabs to indent lines
- Double space paragraphs
- Change a tab stop
- Insert blank lines between lines
- Move a paragraph

Getting Started

You will need to use the file you prepared in the last worksheet. If you followed the directions there, the file is stored on your data disk under the name *Trivia2*.

➡ • **Turn on the Macintosh and load *Works* into the computer as described in Getting Started, Chapter 1.** You should see the Open dialog box on your screen.

Opening a File

If you have forgotten how to open an existing file, refer to Opening a File, Chapter 1.

➡ • **Open *Trivia 2* from your data disk.**

Figure 3-1 on page 33 shows the entire document.

Creating a Larger Top Margin (Revision 1)

Works automatically assigns 1-inch top and bottom margins to word processor documents. Since the standard top margin for the first page of a report is usually larger, add a few lines before the beginning of the first page.

Figure 3-2

```
┌─────────────────────────────────────────────────┐
│                          ←────── #1 Insert 3 blank lines here
│    Ice Cream Trivia                             │
│  eam (well almost.)   Eve                       │
└─────────────────────────────────────────────────┘
```

34   *Microsoft Works for the Macintosh*

➡ 1. **Move the insertion bar before the first letter of the first line of the document** (the "I" in "Ice"). **Reminder**: To move the insertion bar, move the I-beam to the location you want and then click on the mouse.

2. **Press:** **[RETURN] three times.** You have now added three lines above the title.

Capitalizing a Title (Revision 2)

Titles are normally typed in capitals (upper-case letters). To make this revision, you will first select the title and then type it in capitals.

Figure 3-3

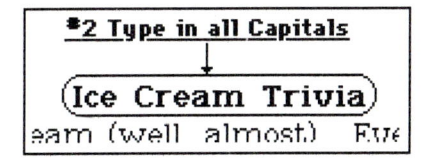

```
*2 Type in all Capitals
        ↓
 (Ice Cream Trivia)
 eam (well almost.)  Eve
```

➡ 1. **Select the title.** If you have forgotten how to select text, see Typing a Centered Head on page 21.

You do not need to delete the title. When you start retyping it, the program deletes the selected text and displays the letters of the new title as you type.

2. **Press:** **[CAPS LOCK].** This is a toggle key. It is used to alternate between upper and lower case. Until you press it again, all typing will appear in upper case.

3. **Type:** **ICE CREAM TRIVIA** To return to lower-case typing,

4. **Press:** **[CAPS LOCK].**

Typing a Byline (Revision 3)

You will want to identify yourself as the author of your article. First insert one blank line after the title.

Figure 3-4

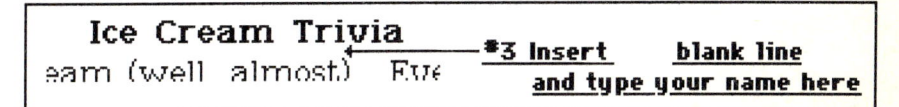

```
  Ice Cream Trivia       *3 Insert    blank line
  eam (well almost.)  Eve          and type your name here
```

➡️ 1. **Move the insertion bar immediately after the last letter of the title if it is not already there.** Any text you type at this point will retain the format of this line.

2. **Press: [RETURN] two times.** Since the heading was centered, note that the insertion bar for this inserted line is also centered.

3. **Pull down the Style Menu and select Normal Text.**

4. **Type your name.**

Inserting Paragraphs (Revisions 4 and 5)

The first paragraph is very long. Revisions 4 and 5 divide it into shorter, more logical paragraphs. To start a new paragraph, you press [RETURN] or [ENTER].

Figure 3-5

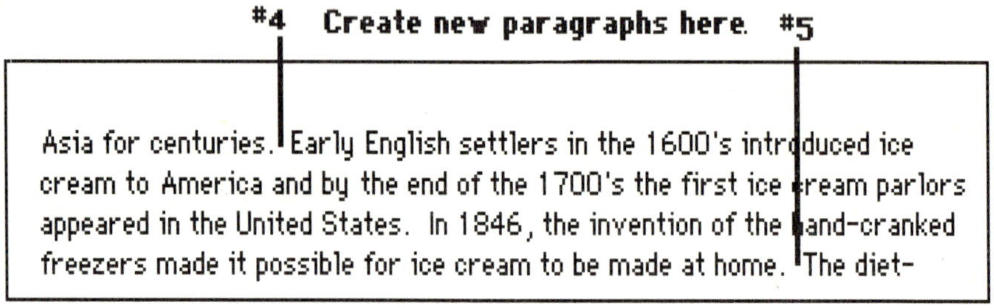

#4   Create new paragraphs here.   #5

```
Asia for centuries. Early English settlers in the 1600's introduced ice
cream to America and by the end of the 1700's the first ice cream parlors
appeared in the United States.  In 1846, the invention of the hand-cranked
freezers made it possible for ice cream to be made at home. The diet-
```

➡️ 1. **Place the insertion bar just before the "E" in "Early."**

2. **Press: [RETURN].**

3. **Follow the same procedure to insert the new paragraph in Revision 5.**

Setting First-Line Indents (Revision 6)

You are going to add the same paragraph indentations to the first three paragraphs. Look at Figure 3-6, page 37.

Works allows you to indent or outdent (*hang*) a paragraph. The terms *indent* and *outdent* derive from the position of the first line in the paragraph. For example, look at Figure 3-7, page 37. The first line of the first paragraph is indented. The first line of the second paragraph is outdented so that the rest of the paragraph "hangs" from it. Study Figure 3-7 carefully.

Figure 3-6

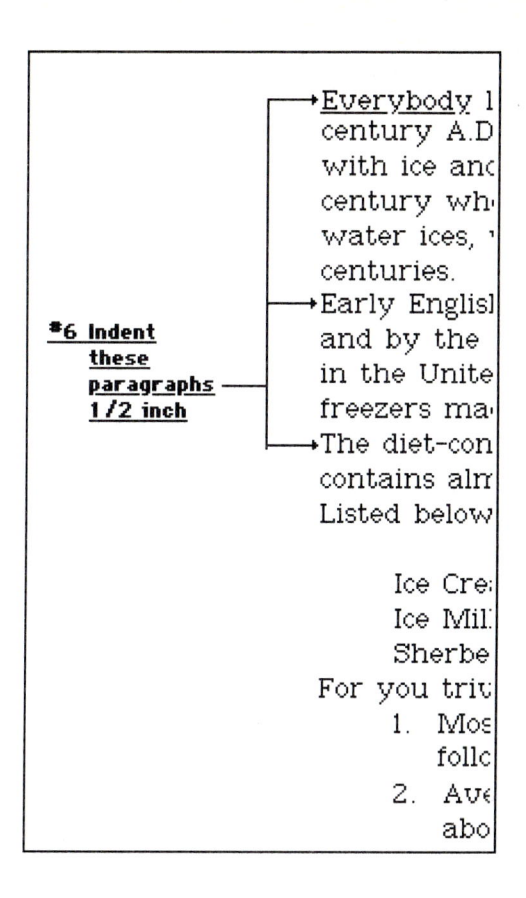

```
                    →Everybody l
                     century A.D
                     with ice anc
                     century wh
                     water ices,
                     centuries.
  #6 Indent         →Early Englisl
    these            and by the
    paragraphs ─┐   in the Unite
    1/2 inch     └  freezers ma
                 └→The diet-con
                    contains alm
                    Listed below

                        Ice Cre
                        Ice Mil
                        Sherbe
                    For you triv
                       1. Mos
                          follc
                       2. Ave
                          abo
```

Figure 3-7. Indented paragraph and hanging paragraph

>   This is an example of an indented paragraph. Notice that the first line of the paragraph begins further to the right of the left margin than do the rest of the lines.
>
> This is an example of an outdented, or
>   hanging paragraph. Notice that the
>   first line of the paragraph begins at
>   the left margin and the rest of the
>   lines begin further to the right.

➡️ **1. Move the I-beam to the beginning of the first paragraph, just before the "E" in "Everybody." Hold down the mouse button, drag down and across the text, and stop when the I-beam immediately follows the colon at the end of the third paragraph. Release the mouse button to select the first three paragraphs.**

In the future, whenever you want to select more than one line, follow Step 1 above.

Now look at the ruler at the top of your screen. Then study the illustration in Figure 3-8. The ruler shows the present format of the selected text. You use the ruler for setting tab stops, left margin, right margin, and paragraph indentations. You can hide the ruler if you want to.

Figure 3-8. Use the ruler to set tabs, margins, and indentations.

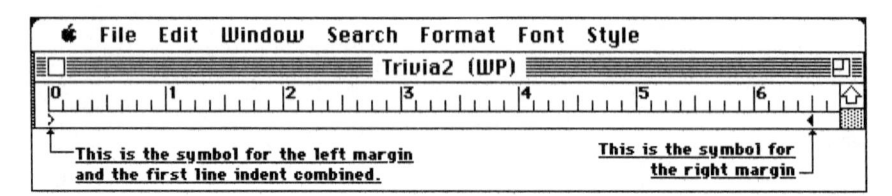

2. **Pull down the Format Menu and select Hide Ruler.** The ruler disappears and there is room to see a couple of more lines of text on the screen.

3. **Pull down the Format Menu and select Show Ruler.** The ruler reappears.

The ruler is marked in inches relative to the left margin of the page. The left margin is set to start at 1 inch from the edge of the printed page. You will learn how to change that setting in a later worksheet. In this exercise, any text that appears at the 0-inch mark of the ruler will actually print 1 inch from the left edge of your paper.

You use the ruler to control the left indent (where the body of a paragraph will begin) and the first-line indent (where the first line of a paragraph will begin). The first line of a paragraph is the first line you type after you press [RETURN] or [ENTER]. (You also use the ruler to control tab stops and the right margin. But you'll learn about these later in this worksheet.)

As shown in Figure 3-9, the symbol at the left edge of the ruler is actually made up of two separate symbols.

38 *Microsoft Works for the Macintosh*

Figure 3-9. The ruler shows the first-line indent symbol, the left-indent symbol, and the right-margin symbo.l

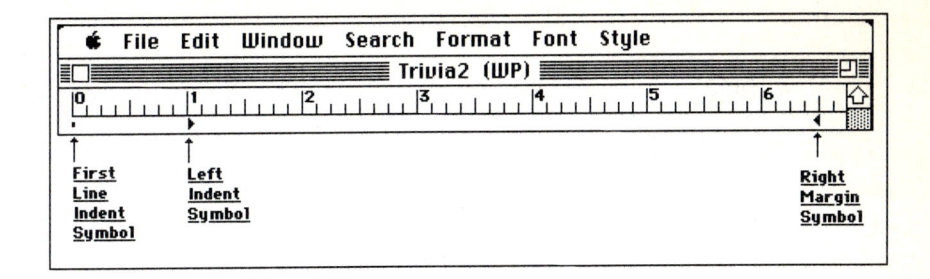

The left-indent symbol is the solid triangle with the straight edge on the left side. The first-line indent symbol is a solid, square dot. When the two symbols are together, they form the combined symbol shown in Figure 3-8.

You can move the left-indent symbol (and thus change the indentation of the paragraph body) by clicking the combination symbol near its top and dragging the left-indent symbol to a different position, as follow:

4. **Move the pointer to the top part of the combined symbol. Hold down the mouse button, drag the symbol to the 1/2-inch mark, and release the mouse button.** See how the symbols have separated and how your text has changed. Well, that was fun, but that's not the way you want your article to look.

5. **Drag the left-indent symbol back to the left edge of the ruler.** Now you again see the combined symbol.

6. **Move the pointer to the bottom edge of the combined symbol and drag the square dot to the 1/2-inch mark.** Now look at Figure 3-10. It shows you how the ruler should look.

Figure 3-10. The ruler shows the left indent and the first-line indent.

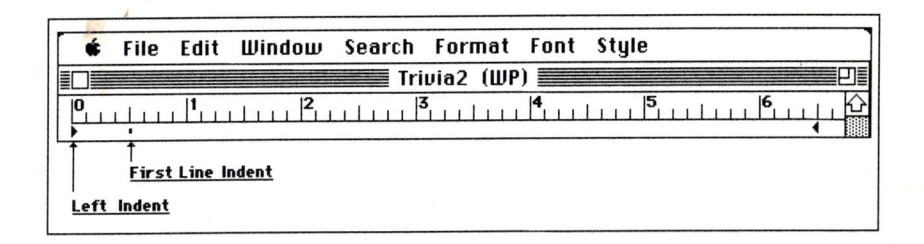

7. **Click anywhere on the screen to deselect the text.**

3 Word Processing: Worksheet 2

Figure 3-11

8. **Look at your text.** The first line of each paragraph is indented. The left side of your text should resemble Figure 3-11.

```
     Every
1st century
with ice an
century wh
water ices,
centuries.
     Early
America ar
appeared ir
cranked fre
home.
     The di
sherbert co
cream.  Lis
```

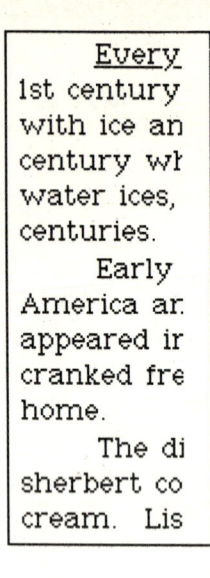

Double Spacing Paragraphs (Revision 7)

Reports are normally double spaced (one blank line between each line of typing). Now follow the steps to double space three paragraphs. See Figure 3-12.

Figure 3-12

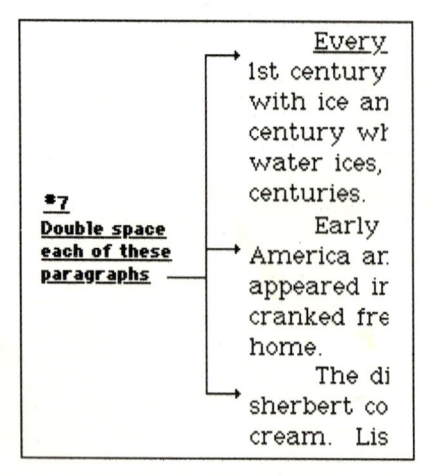

```
                 Every
              1st century
              with ice an
              century wh
              water ices,
   #7         centuries.
Double space      Early
each of these America ar
paragraphs    appeared ir
              cranked fre
              home.
                  The di
              sherbert co
              cream.  Lis
```

➡ 1. **Move the I-beam to the left of the first line in the first paragraph.** See its position on Figure 3-13 on page 41. (Note: You may have to use the vertical scroll bar to get the first paragraph on the screen.)

40   *Microsoft Works for the Macintosh*

2. **Select the first three paragraphs. Reminder**: Drag down and across.

3. **Pull down the Format Menu and select Spacing...** (The three dots following the word mean that you will be shown a dialog box from which you will select the spacing.

4. **Click on Double to select it.**

5. **Click the OK button to activate your selection.**

6. **Click anywhere on the screen to deselect the paragraph.** It looks like part of your report has disappeared!

Figure 3-13

```
 The I-Beam should be                              This is the
 here                                              vertical scroll bar
┌─────────────────────────────────────────────────┐
│              Trivia2 (WP)                       │
│ 0    1    2    3    4    5    6                 │
│                                                 │
│                                                 │
│              ICE CREAM TRIVIA                   │
│              Vivian Frederick                   │
│  I   Everybody loves ice cream (well, almost).  │
│  Even Nero in the                               │
│  1st century A.D. was known to have wines       │
│  and fruit juices cooled                        │
│  with ice and snow.  Then there was Marco       │
│  Polo in the 13th                               │
│  century who brought back to Italy from the     │
│  Orient recipes for                             │
│  water ices, which were said to have been       │
│  eaten in Asia for                              │
│  centuries.                                     │
│     Early English settlers in the 1600s         │
│  introduced ice cream to                        │
│  America and by the 1700's by the first ice     │
│  cream parlors                                  │
│  appeared in the United States.  In 1846,       │
│  the invention of the hand-                     │
└─────────────────────────────────────────────────┘
```

It hasn't. What really happened was that the extra lines introduced by double spacing made the article longer and it now takes up more than one screen. Note that double spacing has not occurred after the last line of paragraph 3. To double space between the last line of the third paragraph and the first line of the table,

7. **Position the insertion bar after the colon following "desserts:" and press [RETURN].**

3 Word Processing: Worksheet 2 **41**

Changing a Tab Stop (Revision 8)

Figure 3-14

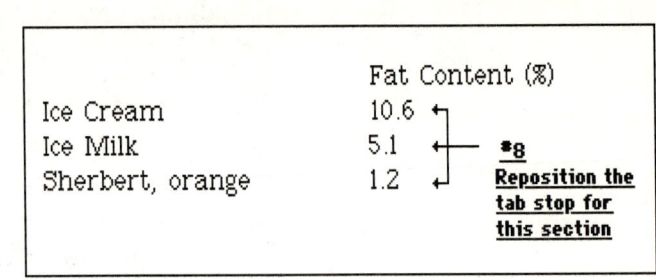

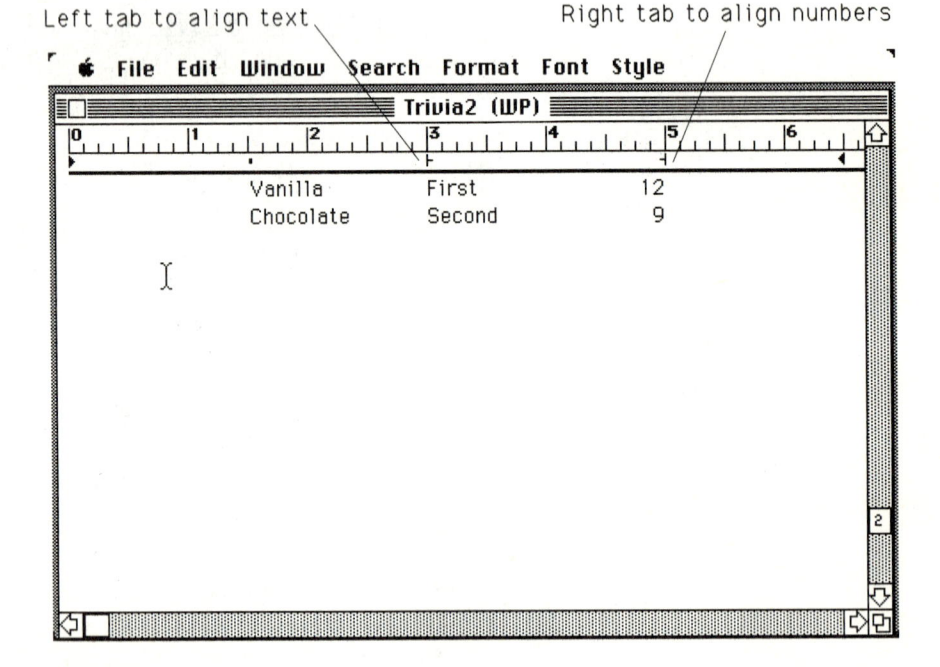

Figure 3-15. The ruler shows left and right tab stops.

When Works first opens a word processing document, tab stops are automatically set every .05 inch. You can change these default tab stops by setting manual tab stops. When you set a tab stop, you see a tab symbol like the one in Figure 3-15. It appears in the ruler and deletes all preset (*default*) tabs to the left of it. The preset tabs to the right of the new tab remain the same. As shown in Figure 3-14, you will change tab stops for the table.

```
                    Fat Content (%)
Ice Cream           10.6      ┐
Ice Milk            5.1       ├─ #8
Sherbert, orange    1.2       ┘   Reposition the
                                  tab stop for
                                  this section
```

Left tab to align text   Right tab to align numbers

[Screenshot of Trivia2 (WP) window showing ruler with tab stops and the text:]
```
Vanilla      First       12
Chocolate    Second      9
```

You can have different tab stops for each new line or paragraph. You set the tab stops on the ruler after you position the insertion bar anywhere in the line or paragraph you want to change.

To set a tab, you must position the tip of the pointer on the bottom of the ruler at each place where you want the tab stop. Click once to create a left-tab stop. (Text will *begin* at the left tab.)

42   *Microsoft Works for the Macintosh*

Click twice to create a right tab stop (and text will *end* at the right tab). Right tab stops are useful for aligning numbers.

To improve the appearance of the Fat Content table, you can align the figures at the right by setting a right tab and then center the column under the heading "Fat Content (%)." You can accomplish both of these tasks by moving the current tab stop for the percent column to the right and changing it to a right tab so that the column will print about 1/2-inch farther to the right.

➡ 1. **Position the I-beam to the extreme left margin of the line beginning "Ice Cream." Drag down and to the right to select the three lines of the table.** (See Figure 3-16.)

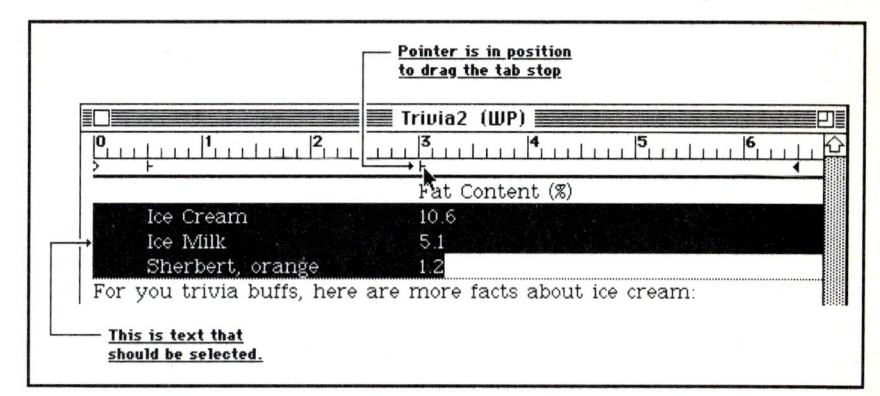

Figure 3-16

2. **Move the pointer to the tab stop for the second column (at the 3-inch mark) and drag the tab symbol to the 4-inch mark.** Now, to align the numbers at the right instead of at the left,

3. **Click once on the tab stop at the 4-inch mark. This changes the left tab to a right-tab stop.** The numbers should now align at the right. If the column of numbers does not look exactly centered, click the tab stop and drag it to the left or right until you are satisfied with its location. When you have the column positioned to your liking,

4. **Deselect the table by clicking anywhere on the screen.**

Inserting Blank Lines (Revision 9)

Double spacing is desirable above and below the paragraph under the table and between the enumerated paragraphs. Since the lines involved are so few, we will *not* use the Format Menu. Instead, we will simply use [RETURN] to insert these blank lines.

Figure 3-17

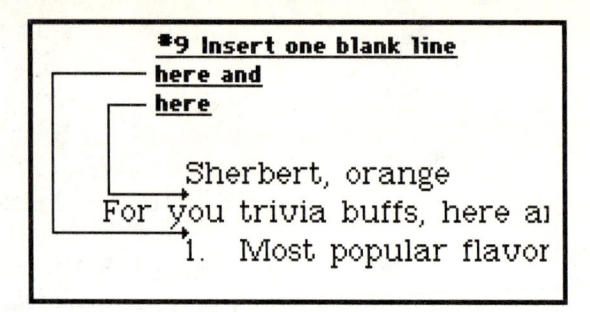

```
┌─ #9 Insert one blank line
│  ┌─ here and
│  │  here
│  │
│  │   Sherbert, orange
│  └→ For you trivia buffs, here a1
└──→ 1.  Most popular flavor
```

▶ 1. **Position the insertion bar at the left margin before the word "For" in the paragraph below the table.**

2. **Press: [RETURN].** Now you have a blank line between the table and the paragraph. If you see a dotted line, it indicates that the program has started a new page.

3. **Position the insertion bar at the left margin of the enumerated paragraph ("1. Most . . .").**

4. **Press: [RETURN].** Now you have a blank line between this paragraph and the enumerated paragraph.

5. **Position the insertion bar at the left margin of the second enumerated paragraph.**

6. **Press: [RETURN].**

This completes the inserting of blank lines.

Moving a Paragraph (Revision 10)

Very often, you will type a paragraph and then decide that it belongs in a different part of your document. When this happens, you can move the paragraph. (This action is sometimes called "cut and paste.") In this exercise, you will reverse the order of enumerated paragraphs. Look at Figure 3-18.

▶ 1. **Position the I-beam at the beginning of the blank line between the first and second enumerated paragraphs.**

44   *Microsoft Works for the Macintosh*

Figure 3-18

```
            #10 Exchange these two paragraphs

    1.  Most popular flavor in the United States is vanilla,
        followed by chocolate and strawberry.

    2.  Average serving (1/6 of a quart of vanilla ice cream is
        about 200 calories.
```

   2. Drag down to select the second enumerated paragraph.

Figure 3-19

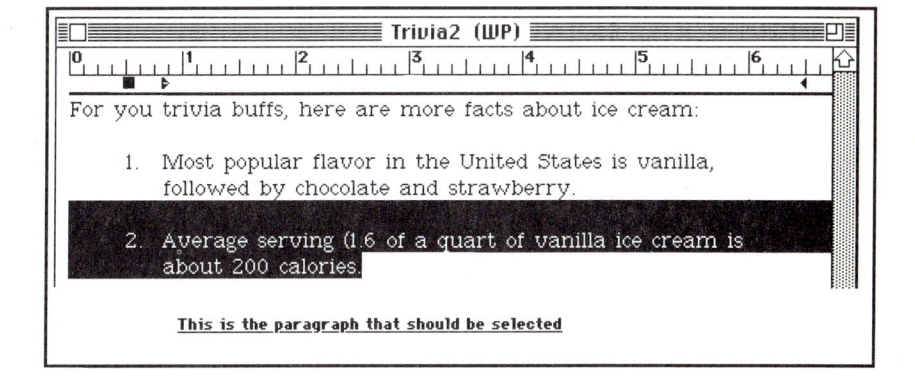

```
                         Trivia2 (WP)
    |0        |1        |2        |3        |4        |5        |6

    For you trivia buffs, here are more facts about ice cream:

        1.  Most popular flavor in the United States is vanilla,
            followed by chocolate and strawberry.

        2.  Average serving (1.6 of a quart of vanilla ice cream is
            about 200 calories.

    This is the paragraph that should be selected
```

   3. Pull down the Edit Menu and select Cut. You have deleted the second paragraph. It's now stored on the Macintosh clipboard.

   4. Position the insertion bar on the line above the first enumerated paragraph.

   5. Pull down the Edit Menu and select Paste.

   Although the paragraphs are now in the reversed order, they need to be renumbered.

   To renumber each paragraph,

   6. Highlight the paragraph number and type the correct number.

3 Word Processing: Worksheet 2   **45**

Saving a File

Because you have made numerous changes in this file, you should save it under a different name so that if you decide that the original is better than your current revision, you will still have the original to go back to. Use the skills you developed in Worksheet 1 to save your revisions under the filename *Trivia3*.

➡ 1. **Pull down the File Menu and select Save As.** The Save As dialog box appears.

2. **Check to see that your data disk is the active disk.** (Its name should appear to the right of the active disk icon in the dialog box.) To enter the new filename,

3. **Type:** *Trivia3* As you type, the old name disappears. The rest of the options don't need to be changed. So,

4. **Move the pointer to the Save button and click once.** You now have two versions of this article on your disk. Note that the document name at the top of the screen has changed to T*rivia3*.

Printing a File

➡ 1. **Turn on your printer to be certain that it is ready to print.**

2. **Pull down the File Menu and select Print.**

3. **Click on OK if all the defaults are correct as shown in Figure 1-10 (page 13).**

Review

If time permits, load *Trivia2* again and try to make the revisions without looking at the directions. To achieve this, you will have to

- Correct spelling
- Change margins
- Set tabs
- Change line spacings

Think About It

Congratulations! Your article is now ready to submit to the local newspaper. By now, you should be able to type text, insert and

46   *Microsoft Works for the Macintosh*

delete text, change line spacing, set tabs and indents, and move text. If Chris asks you to make more changes, you can easily recall this file, make changes, and print a new version with minimum effort.

Quitting Works

The following instructions will guide you through the steps for quitting *Works*.

1. **Pull down the File Menu and select Quit.** If you get a dialog box that asks if you would like to save changes, click on Yes or No.

When Macintosh has returned you to the desktop, tidy it up for the next person.

2. **Move the pointer to the upper left corner close box of each open window and click once.**

3. **Pull down the Special Menu and select Shut Down.**

4. **Remove the disks from the Macintosh and return them to their appropriate places.**

5. **Turn off the Macintosh.**

4 Word Processing Worksheet 3

Objectives

In this worksheet, you will learn how to

- Create a file (a letter)
- Edit the file (using techniques from previous worksheets)
- Change the layout (appearance) of the file
- Change margins for printing a file

Setting the Scene

As part of your sales promotion for The Ice Cream Factory, you have sponsored a Birthday Club. Each Birthday Club member receives a free ice cream cone during the month of his or her birthday and is invited to bring a guest. You are now going to create a form letter to mail to eligible Birthday Club members with each month's gift certificates.

Getting Started

You are going to create your document from scratch. Therefore, there is no file stored on your data disk for you. You must open a blank word processor document. Think of this activity as reaching into your desk drawer and pulling out a fresh sheet of paper.

➡ 1. **Follow the directions from Getting Started, Chapter 1 to boot the Macintosh and load *Works*.** You should see the Open dialog box.

2. **Click on the Word Processor application icon.**

3. **Click on the New button.** An empty screen is now available for creating a new document.

When you open a new file, you will see two symbols on the ruler. Each resembles a triangle. On the extreme left, you see an open triangle and at the 6.5-inch mark, you see a closed triangle. These symbols represent the left and right margins. (You worked with the left-margin symbol in Chapter 3.) The insertion bar will be blinking on the first line at the extreme left of the screen.

The filename located in the middle of the Title Bar is the *default* filename automatically assigned by *Works*. When you save your Birthday Club letter, you will give it a more descriptive filename.

Figure 4-1

```
Filename ─────────────────────────┐                      Title Bar
                                  │
First line and                    │
left indent symbols ──────────┐   │
                              │   │
Insertion bar ────────────┐   │   │
```

[Screen showing menu bar with File, Edit, Window, Search, Format, Font, Style; window titled "Untitled (WP)" with ruler marked 0-6 and Right margin symbol]

You are now ready to type the text of the letter. Don't worry about any typing errors. You can easily correct these later. However, if you feel compelled to correct errors as you make them, simply press [BACKSPACE] or [DELETE] and type the correct character(s).

Typing the Letter

In your short letter, you want to encourage birthday celebrants to come in for their treat. If you have no time to think of a letter, copy the example on page 51. Try to personalize the letter as you type. Remember to use [RETURN] *only* when you want to leave blank lines or start a paragraph. Proofread and correct any errors by using the techniques you have learned. Use the vertical scroll box to view all parts of your letter.

Making Changes in the Page Setup

The Page Setup option in the File Menu controls the placement of a document on the printed page as well as the appearance of a header or a footer on each printed page. When you save a document, *Works* stores your settings with the document.

➡ 1. **Pull down the File Menu and select Page Setup.** You see the Page Setup dialog box. See Figure 4-3, page 52.

50   *Microsoft Works on the Macintosh*

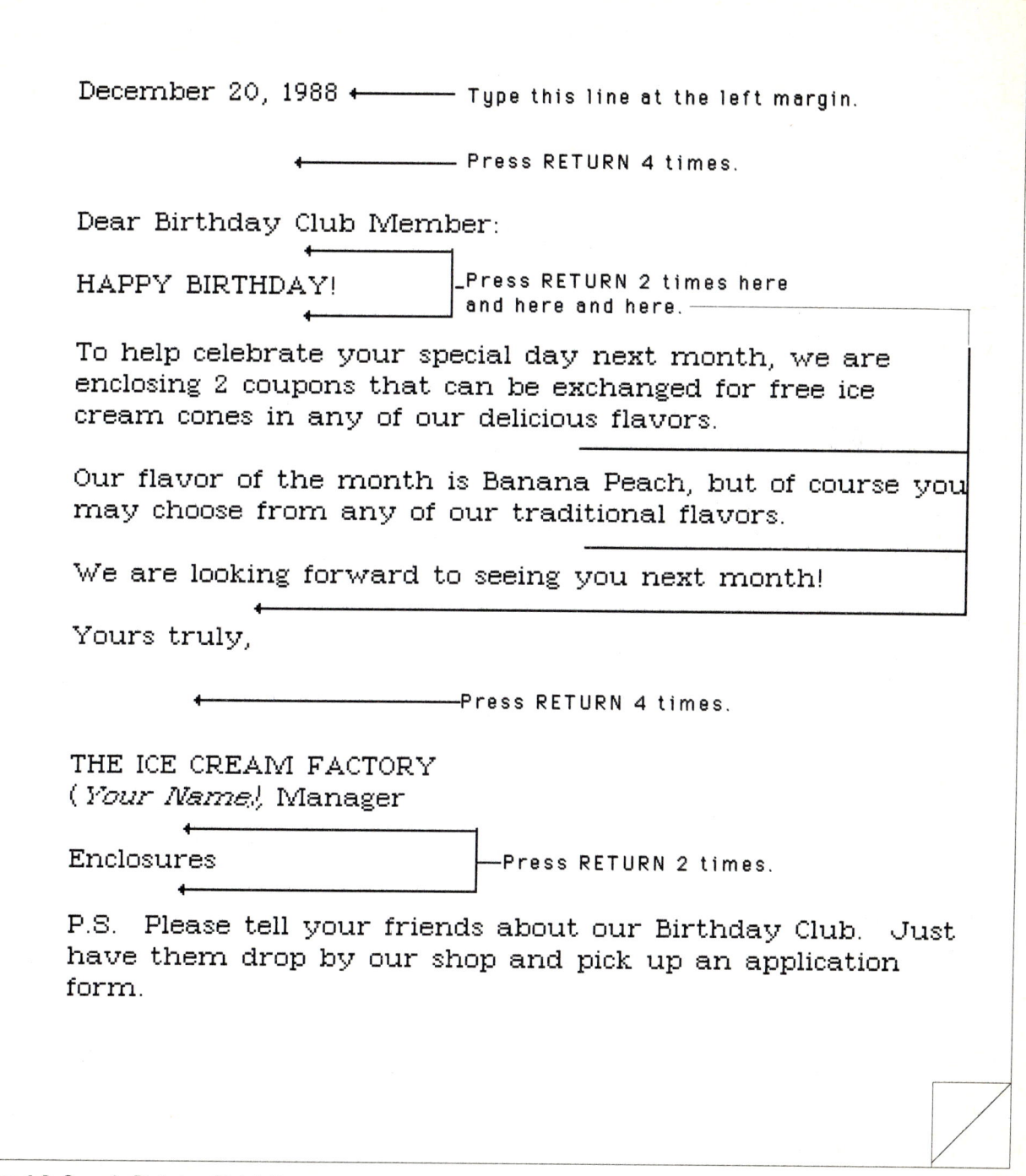

December 20, 1988 ←———— Type this line at the left margin.

←———— Press RETURN 4 times.

Dear Birthday Club Member:

HAPPY BIRTHDAY! ─Press RETURN 2 times here and here and here.

To help celebrate your special day next month, we are enclosing 2 coupons that can be exchanged for free ice cream cones in any of our delicious flavors.

Our flavor of the month is Banana Peach, but of course you may choose from any of our traditional flavors.

We are looking forward to seeing you next month!

Yours truly,

←———————Press RETURN 4 times.

THE ICE CREAM FACTORY
(*Your Name*), Manager

Enclosures ─Press RETURN 2 times.

P.S. Please tell your friends about our Birthday Club. Just have them drop by our shop and pick up an application form.

Figure 4-2. Sample Birthday Club letter

Figure 4-3. The Page Setup dialog box

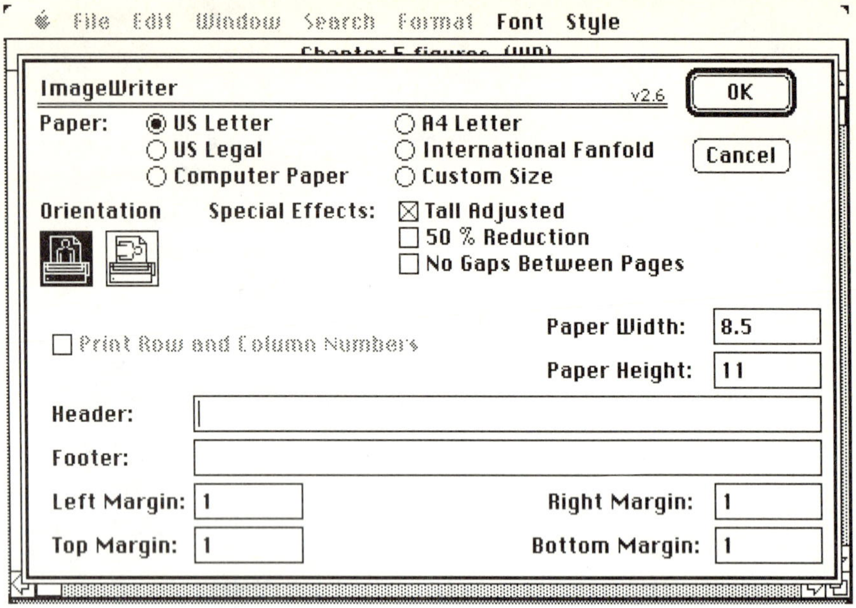

Note that the margins are set at 1 inch. You want to increase the size of the top margin to 2 inches so that this short letter will appear better centered on the printed page.

2. **Click after the number 1 in the Top Margin option box.**

3. **Press: [DELETE] or [BACKSPACE].**

4. **Type: 2**

5. **Click on the OK button to save the setting and return to the file.**

Saving a File

Now that you have your document typed correctly and formatted properly, it's time to save it so that you can use it over and over again. You will use the filename *Birthday*.

1. **Pull down the File Menu and select Save As.**

2. **Check that your data disk is the active disk.** The disk name appears next to the active disk icon. If you don't see

52   *Microsoft Works on the Macintosh*

"Works Data," click on the Drive button. Since the Save Document As: box is already selected,

3. **Type: Birthday** to replace the default "Untitled."

4. **Click on the Save button.**

Printing a File

1. **Turn on your printer and be certain that it is ready to print.**

2. **Pull down the File Menu and select Print.**

3. **Click on the OK button.** Printing should start shortly.

Review

If time permits, create another letter with different margins and tabs. How about a letter to the authors suggesting improvements for this book? Try using the bold, underline, and center options for emphasizing ideas. In case you have forgotten how to get started with a new file, pull down the File Menu and select New.

Quitting Works

The following steps will guide you through quitting Works.

1. **Pull down the File Menu and select Quit.**

2. **Close all windows.**

3. **Pull down the Special Menu and select Shut Down.**

4. **Remove the disks from the Macintosh and return them to their appropriate places.**

5. **Turn off the Macintosh.**

4 Word Processing: Worksheet 3

5 Shortcuts and Other Techniques Worksheet 4

Objectives

In this worksheet, you will learn how to

- Use keyboard shortcuts to edit and format text
- Change the style and size of typefaces
- Change margins and tabs
- Change layouts
- Insert page breaks

Setting the Scene

Now that you can produce simple documents, you are ready for some keyboard shortcuts and techniques. This worksheet gives you the opportunity to explore the *Works* word processing application on your own. You will notice that the instructions in this worksheet are less detailed and leave more to your imagination.

In order to try out these shortcuts and techniques, create a new document or recall your latest version of *Trivia*. You should feel a real sense of accomplishment when you complete this worksheet!

Shortcuts

You can invoke many of the menu options from the keyboard instead of using the mouse to pull down a menu and select an option. The keyboard commands available in each menu are shown at the right of the options. For example, pull down the File Menu to view the File options that have keyboard commands. To invoke an option from the keyboard, hold down [COMMAND] (⌘)* and press the letter for the particular option.

As you can see from Figure 5-1, to print a file, for example, you can avoid using the menu and simply hold down [⌘] and type P. Since you will be printing frequently, you will probably find it easier to press [⌘] and type P than to pull down the File Menu and select Print.

---

*On some keyboards, there is no [COMMAND] key and on some there is no [⌘] key. Nevertheless, whenever you see the symbol [⌘], it means to use either the [COMMAND] or [⌘] key, whichever is appropriate for your keyboard.

Figure 5-1. The File Menu and the File Menu options

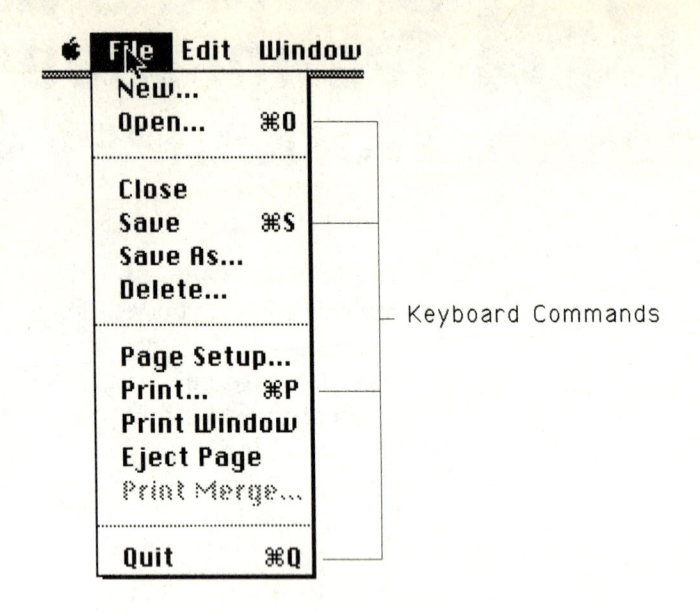

```
 File   Edit  Window
 New...
 Open...      ⌘O

 Close
 Save         ⌘S
 Save As...
 Delete...

 Page Setup...
 Print...     ⌘P
 Print Window
 Eject Page
 Print Merge...

 Quit         ⌘Q
```

— Keyboard Commands

The following table lists some of the more commonly used keyboard commands. The list is not complete. Consult your *Microsoft Works* manual for more information.

Menu	Option	Key to type while you press [⌘]
File	Open	**O**
	Save	**S**
	Print	**P**
	Quit	**Q**
Edit	Undo	**Z**
	Copy	**C**
	Cut	**X**
	Paste	**V**
Search	Find	**F**
	Replace	**R**
Style	Normal text	**N**
	Bold	**B**
	Italic	**I**
	Underline	**U**

Opening Programs and Files

As with all Macintosh programs, you can quickly open a program or file from the desktop or from the Open dialog box by double clicking. (See Figures 5-2a and 5-2b on page 58.) To use double clicking to open the file or program, simply

1. **Move the tip of the pointer over the filename or program icon.**

2. **Click twice in rapid succession.** The Macintosh will immediately begin loading the file or program into memory.

Selecting Text

You can use three methods of selecting text (other than dragging the mouse). To select:

- A **word**, double click anywhere on the word.

- A **line** or **paragraph**, move the I-beam to left of desired line until the I-beam changes into an arrow. Then click once. Double click to select an entire paragraph.

- Entire **document**, pull down the Edit Menu and select Select All.

Changing Margins and Tabs

Changing Margins

Margin size and paper size are controlled in the Page Setup dialog box shown in Figure 5-3, page 59. Margins are preset to 1 inch on the top, bottom, and sides. Paper width and length are preset to 8.5 by 11 inches. Click on the appropriate button to change the Paper size, Orientation, and Special Effects settings. You can use TAB to cycle through selection boxes, or you can simply click in the desired box.

Changing Tabs

Figure 5-4, page 59, illustrates left and right tab stops. If you want to change either tab, simply point to the tab marker and drag it to the left or right. To delete the tab, drag the marker down and off the ruler into the text field. When you release the mouse button, the tab marker disappears.

Figure 5-2a. Desktop with arrow on *Works* program icon. Double click to open.

Double click here to open Works.

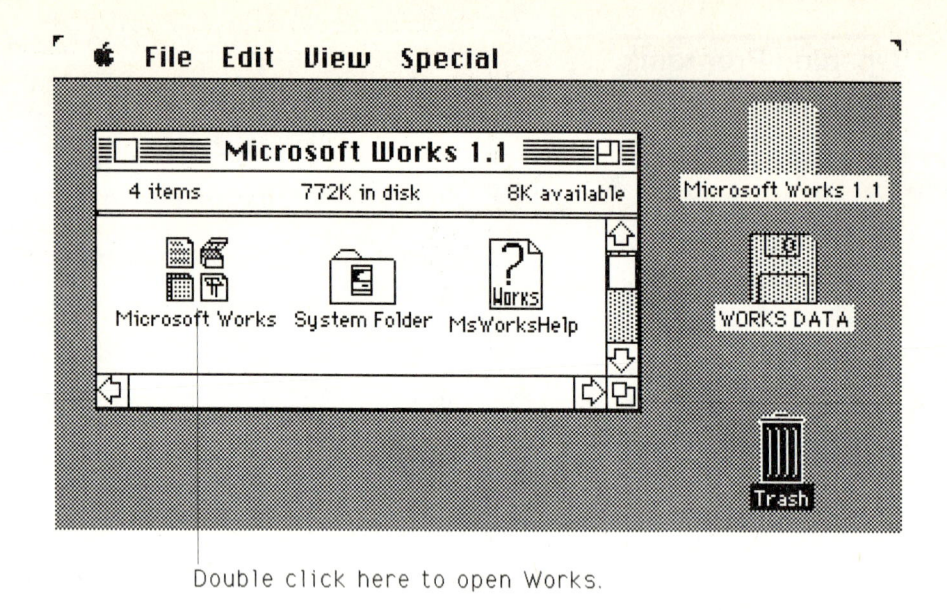

Figure 5-2b. The Open dialog box with arrow on filename. Double click to open.

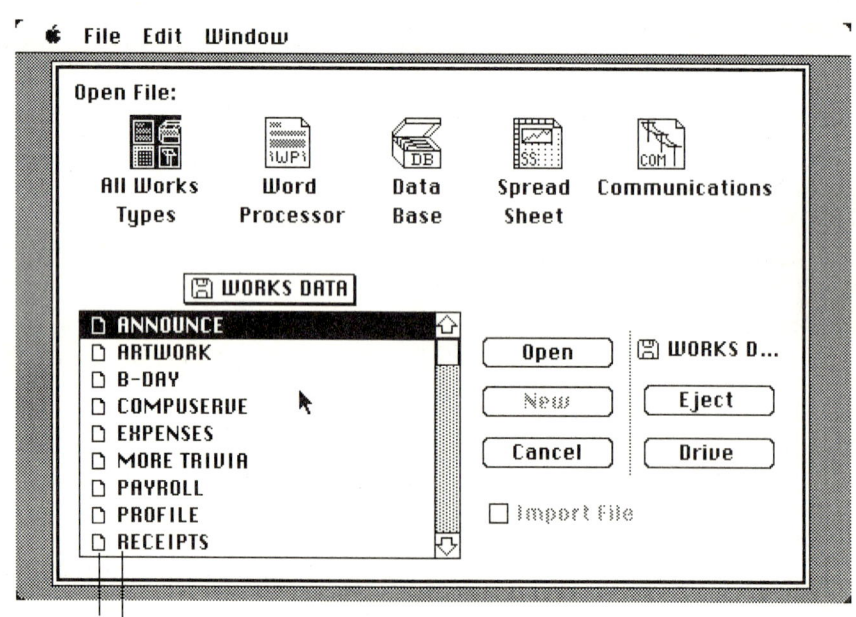

Double click on icons or filenames to load a file.

58 *Microsoft Works on the Macintosh*

Figure 5-3. The Page Setup dialog box. Note settings for Paper, Orientation, and Special Effects.

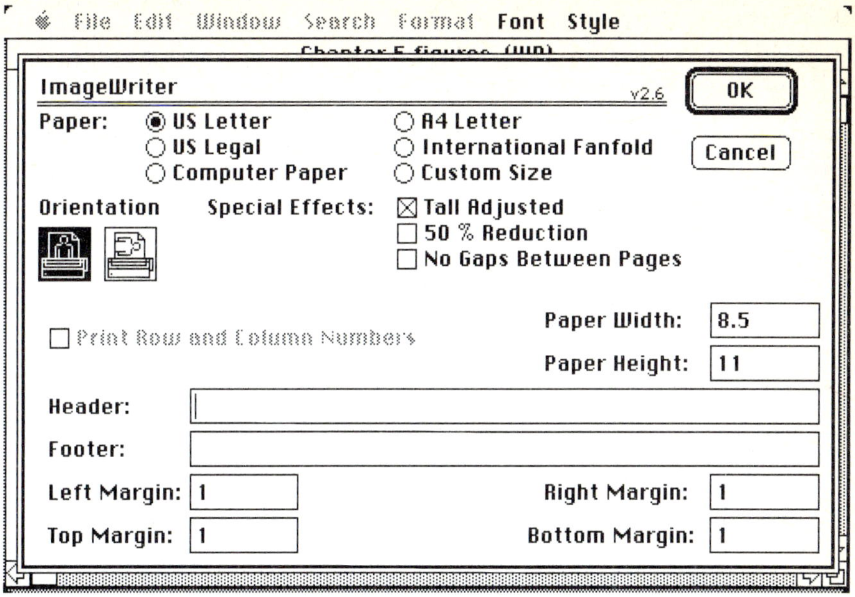

Figure 5-4. The ruler shows the left indent, the first-line indent, and left and right tabs. Read the text of the illustration carefully.

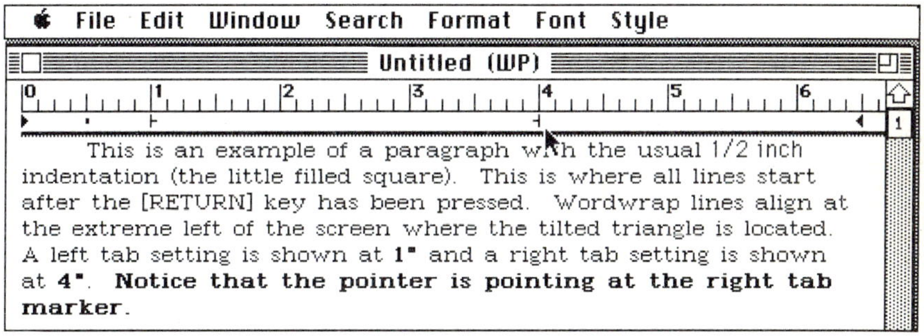

Formatting Hints

Format Menu

Four options in the Format Menu allow you to control how text is aligned.

- **Left** is the default. It prints all text flush against the left margin. Since this is the default selection, text is left-aligned unless you select a different option.

- **Center** centers the selected text.

- **Right** lines text up against the right margin.

- **Justified** evens out the left and right margins by adding spaces between words to fill in the shorter lines.

5 Word Processing: Worksheet 4   **59**

Hanging Paragraphs

In a hanging paragraph, the first line of each paragraph is "outdented" rather than "indented"—that is, the first line hangs out farther to the left than the rest of the paragraph. This accents the first line and is useful in such files as bibliographies where the last name of an author is outdented or in enumerated paragraphs where the numbers stand off to the left (as in the *Trivia* article). For more details, read the text of Figure 5-5.

Figure 5-5. An outdented paragraph

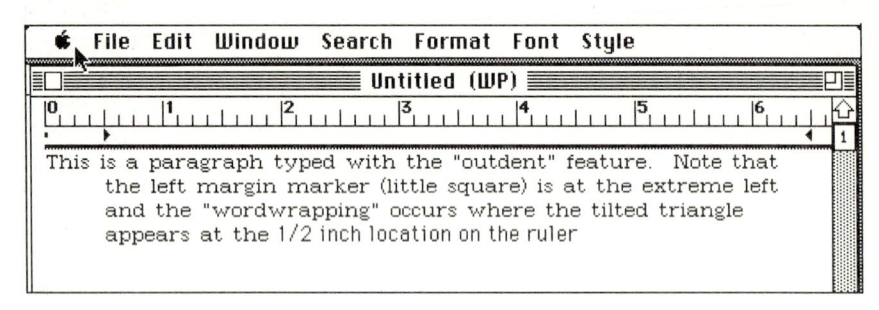

Page Breaks

As you enter text in a new file, *Works* automatically inserts page breaks according to the page length and margin settings established in the Page Setup box. The default is set for 8.5 by 11-inch paper. (Remember, you can change the defaults through the Print/Page Setup Menu.) If you insert or delete text, *Works* automatically adjusts the page breaks.

On your screen, automatic page breaks are indicated by a dotted line (....). Manual page breaks are indicated by a line of hyphens (---). If you insert a manual page break, *Works* automatically readjusts the automatic page breaks that follow.

To insert a manual page break, you must first select the line of text that you want at the top of the next page and then use the Format Menu to make the insertion, as follows:

1. **Move the insertion bar anywhere on the line that should appear at the top of the new page.**

2. **Pull down the Format Menu and select Insert Page Break.**

To delete a manual page break,

➡ 1. Click anywhere on the line immediately following the manual page break.

2. Pull down the Format Menu and select Remove Page Break.

This is the end of the word processing worksheets. You have used many of *Works*' word processing features. To learn more, select Help from the Window Menu or refer to the *Works* manual.

6 Spreadsheets Worksheet 1

Spreadsheet Background

Figure 6-1. A paper spreadsheet with rows and columns

Spreadsheet programs are immensely popular. In fact, one in four computer owners buys a spreadsheet program. Two well-known programs are *Lotus 1-2-3*™ (which has become the standard by which others are measured) and *Excel*™. As you complete these worksheets, you will discover why so many people from so many different backgrounds find spreadsheet programs useful for business or for personal projects.

What is a spreadsheet? A paper spreadsheet is a tool normally used for financial analysis. A paper spreadsheet is a large page divided into vertical **columns** and horizontal **rows**.

An *electronic* spreadsheet displays the same structure on a computer screen, but with some significant differences. For example, a paper spreadsheet is limited by the size of the paper, but an electronic spreadsheet can be hundreds of columns wide and thousands of rows long.

With a paper spreadsheet, a **cell** (the block located at the intersection of a row and a column) holds only a label or a number, but a cell in an electronic spreadsheet can hold a label, a number, a mathematical formula, or a logical instruction. If the cell holds a formula, the program displays the number resulting from the application of the formula at the cell's location in the spreadsheet. The program shows the formula in another section of the screen. The formula can be as complex as a trigonometric equation or a logical comparison, or as simple as a two-number addition.

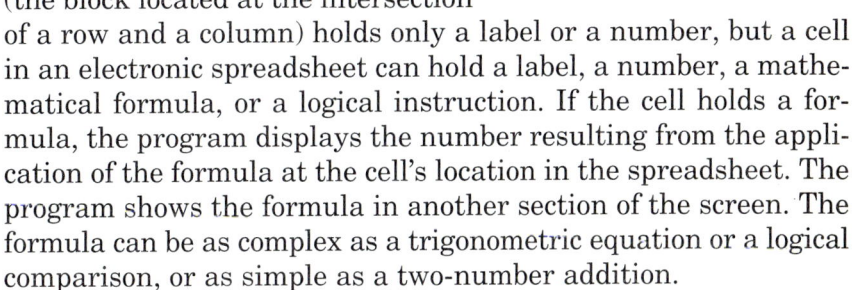

An electronic spreadsheet creates in memory an enormous grid of rows and columns (a very small portion of which can be seen on the screen at any one time). Some people create spreadsheets that take pages to print. You can, of course, use the scroll bars to scroll through a larger spreadsheet just as you scroll through a large word processor document.

Although many spreadsheet programs are available, there is much similarity between them. As a result, if you learn one program, you can easily adapt to another.

Objectives

In this worksheet, you will learn how to

- Open a spreadsheet file
- Identify rows, columns, and cells
- Select parts of a spreadsheet
- Explain the difference between labels and values *(words / #'s)*
- Enter and delete characters
- Enter and clear cells
- Change cell contents
- Delete a column — *cut*
- View formulas and functions
- Save and print a spreadsheet

Setting the Scene

In order to discover trends in the sales of various ice cream products, Chris Hughes has created a spreadsheet on which she plans to itemize sales by category for each day of the week. The spreadsheet contains formulas that will compute for each day

    Total sales
    Taxes collected
    Total receipts

The spreadsheet will also calculate the weekly sales for each category, as well as total sales, taxes collected, and total receipts for the week.

Chris wants to modify the spreadsheet and asks you to make the changes for her. Figure 6-2 shows the spreadsheet with the changes marked.

Figure 6-2. These are the changes you will make on Chris' spreadsheet.

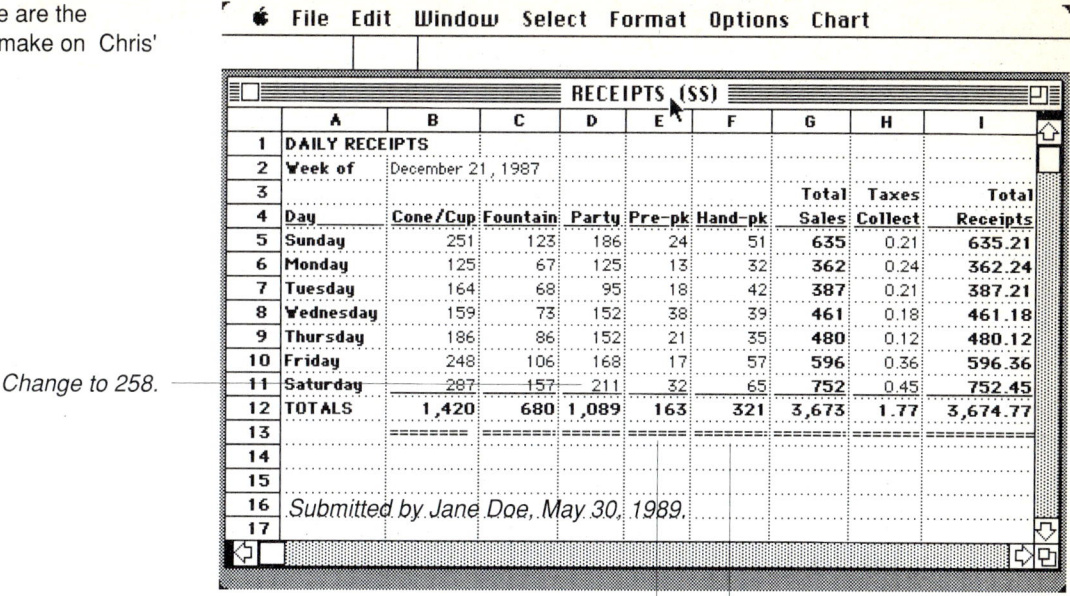

```
 ´  File  Edit  Window  Select  Format  Options  Chart
```

	A	B	C	D	E	F	G	H	I
1	DAILY RECEIPTS								
2	Week of	December 21, 1987							
3							Total	Taxes	Total
4	Day	Cone/Cup	Fountain	Party	Pre-pk	Hand-pk	Sales	Collect	Receipts
5	Sunday	251	123	186	24	51	635	0.21	635.21
6	Monday	125	67	125	13	32	362	0.24	362.24
7	Tuesday	164	68	95	18	42	387	0.21	387.21
8	Wednesday	159	73	152	38	39	461	0.18	461.18
9	Thursday	186	86	152	21	35	480	0.12	480.12
10	Friday	248	106	168	17	57	596	0.36	596.36
11	Saturday	287	157	211	32	65	752	0.45	752.45
12	TOTALS	1,420	680	1,089	163	321	3,673	1.77	3,674.77
13	========	========	======	======	========	========	========	========	==========
14									
15									
16	Submitted by Jane Doe, May 30, 1989.								
17									

Change to 258. (row 11)

Combine these two columns into one column with the heading Bulk.

Getting Started

➡ • **Turn on the Macintosh and load *Works* as described in Getting Started, Chapter 1.** You should see the Open dialog box shown in Figure 6-3.

Figure 6-3. The Open dialog box with All Works types highlighted

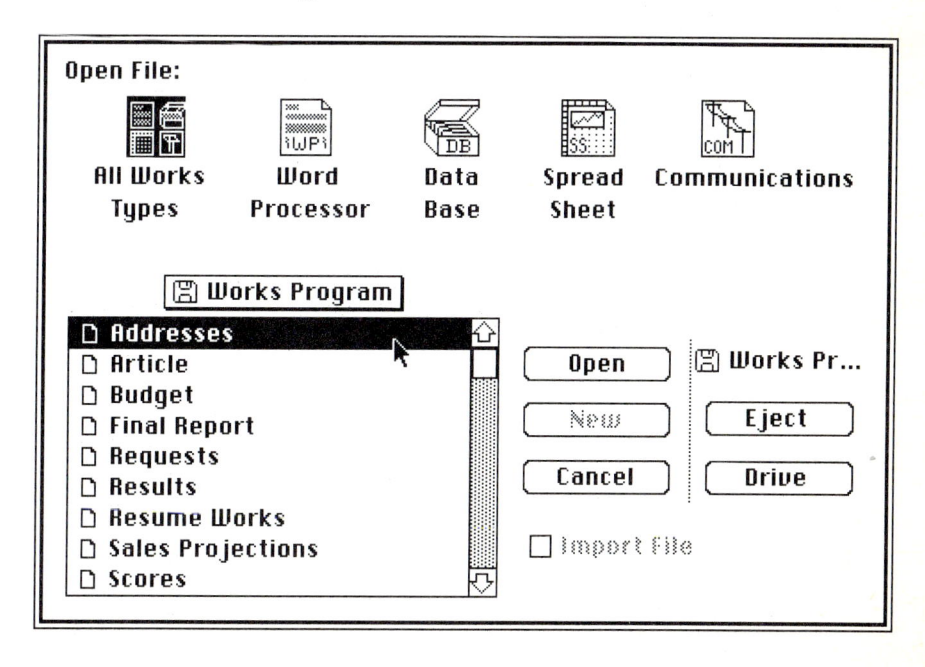

Open File:

All Works Types | Word Processor | Data Base | Spread Sheet | Communications

🖫 Works Program

- Addresses
- Article
- Budget
- Final Report
- Requests
- Results
- Resume Works
- Sales Projections
- Scores

[Open]   🖫 Works Pr...
[New]   [Eject]
[Cancel] [Drive]

☐ Import file

6 Spreadsheets: Worksheet 1   **65**

Opening a File

When you first load *Works,* you see the Open dialog box. The spreadsheet file that you saw in Figure 6-2 and on which you will work has been prepared for you and is stored on your data disk under the file name *Receipts*. Follow the steps below to open the *Receipts* file.

➡ 1. **Insert your *Works Data Disk* into the lower drive.** Your data disk should now be the active disk.

2. **Move the pointer to the Spreadsheet icon and click once.** Now only spreadsheet files are listed in the list box.

3. **Move the pointer to the filename *Receipts* and click once to select it.**

4. **Move the pointer to the Open button and click once.** You should see the spreadsheet shown in Figure 6-2. Look at Figure 6-4, page 67. Here you see the spreadsheet with some of the parts labeled. We will describe those parts as we work with *Receipts*. Especially note the areas labeled entry bar, deselect box, row, and column.

Identifying Rows, Columns, and Cells

Look at the menu bar on your screen. Note that the menus are like those in word processing. But here the screen area is also divided across the top by letters and down the left side by numbers. The letters label the vertical **columns** and the numbers label the horizontal **rows**. A column and row intersect to form a **cell**.

To refer to a cell, you use its **address**. This includes the letter of its column and the number of its row. For example, in Figure 6-4, Cell B5 (Column B, Row 5) gives the sales of cones and cups on Sunday.

When you use the mouse to click in a cell, that cell becomes highlighted to remind you that it is the **active** cell. The active cell is the one with which the spreadsheet program is ready to work. If you want to work with a different cell, you will have to change the highlighting.

You can also tell which cell is the active cell by looking at the extreme left side of the **entry bar.** In Figure 6-4, the entry bar is empty because no cell is active.

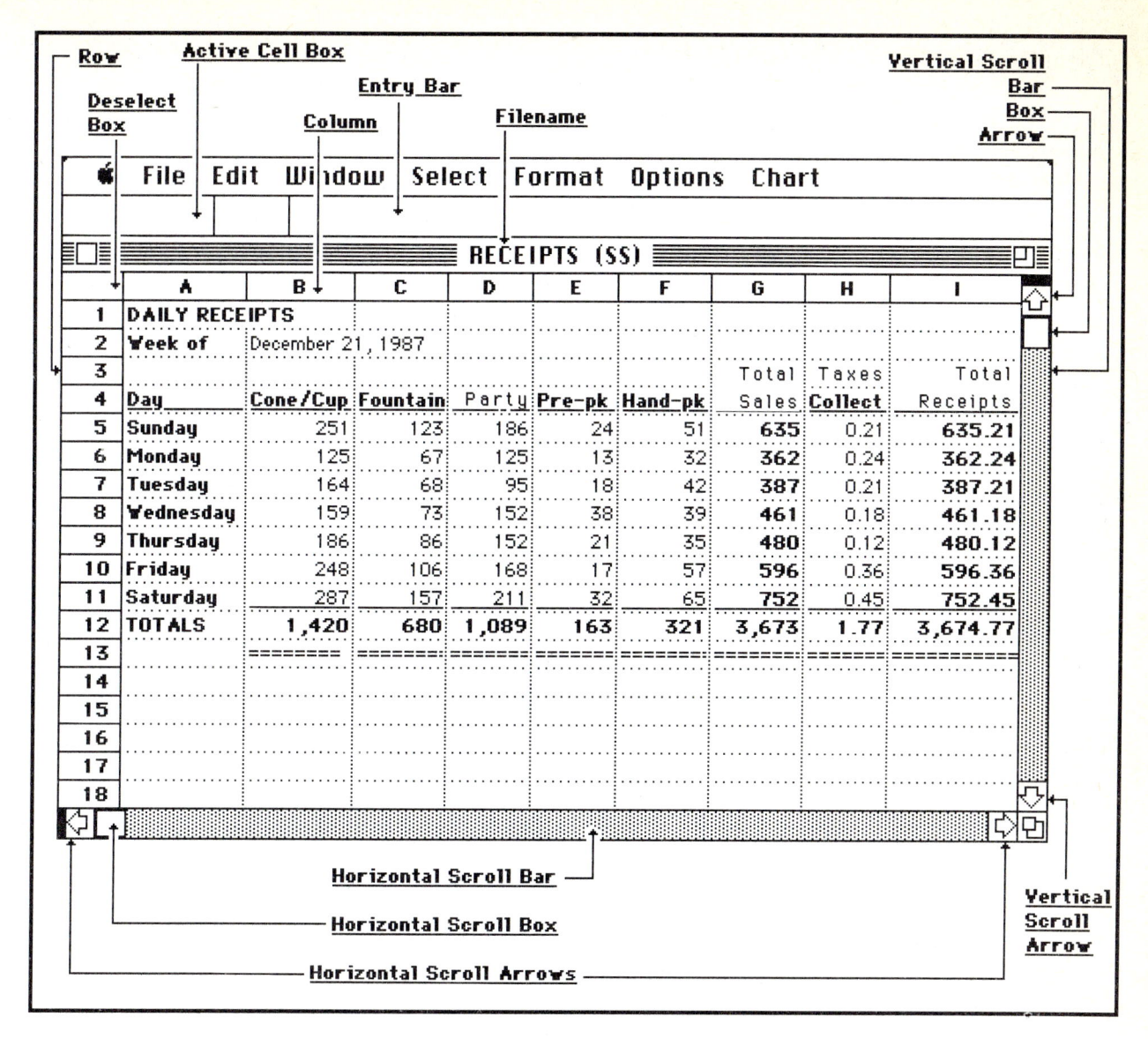

Figure 6-4

Cell Contents

In *Works,* a spreadsheet cell can hold three different types of information: a value, a formula, or a label. *Works* distinguishes one type of cell content from another by the beginning character typed into the cell.

- If the first character typed is a numeric character (0, 1, 2 ... 9), *Works* treats the cell content as a numeric *value.*

6 *Spreadsheets: Worksheet 1* **67**

- If the first character is the equals symbol (=), *Works* treats the cell content as a formula (and the formula must conform to the syntax for formulas).

- If the first character typed is a letter or any special character other than =, *Works* treats the cell content as a label. If the special character is the quotation mark ("), *Works* still treats the cell content as a label but it does not print the initial quotation mark in the cell, thus enabling you to use numbers as labels.

Labels

A label describes information in the spreadsheet. Labels make numbers and formulas easier to understand. You can use letters, numbers, or a combination of letters and numbers in labels. Labels automatically line up at the left of the cell. However, you can use the Format Menu to center or right-align labels. Column A in Figure 6-4 consists of labels.

Scrolling Through the Spreadsheet

A *Works* spreadsheet can be enormous (up to 9,999 rows and 256 columns). Obviously, you cannot see all of a large spreadsheet at one time. To move to cells not displayed, you will first use the scroll arrows shown at the ends of the scroll bars (as diagramed in Figure 6-5). To move around the spreadsheet,

Figure 6-5

1. **Move the pointer to the right horizontal scroll arrow in the lower right corner of your screen. Click the mouse until you have moved to an area where the cells are empty.** Note that the column letters advance alphabetically as you move to the right.

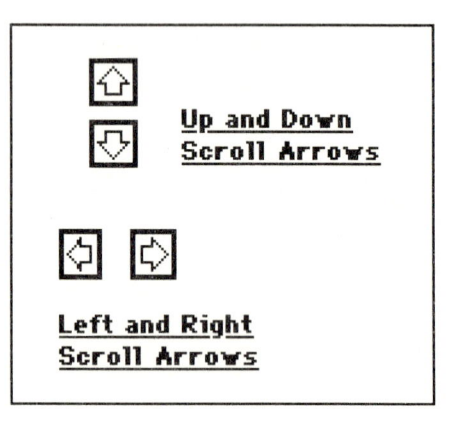

2. **Move the pointer to the left horizontal scroll arrow in the lower left corner of your screen. Click the mouse until you have moved back to the area where the cells contain labels and data.**

68   *Microsoft Works for the Macintosh*

3. **Move the pointer to the down scroll arrow in the lower right corner of your screen. Click the mouse until you have moved to an area where the cells are empty.** Note that the row numbers increase as you move down the spreadsheet.

4. **Move the pointer to the up scroll arrow in the upper right corner of your screen and click the mouse until you have moved back to the area where the spreadsheet cells contain labels and data.**

As you can probably tell, using the arrows is a rather slow way of moving long distances. You would not want to move to the bottom of a large spreadsheet using the scroll bars! Luckily you don't have to. To move long distances in the same row or same column, you can use the scroll boxes at the bottom and at the right of the screen. These boxes are shown in Figure 6-6. For example, to move quickly to the bottom of columns,

Figure 6-6. Scroll bars and scroll boxes

1. **Move the pointer to the scroll box in the vertical scroll bar on the right of your screen.**

2. **Hold down the mouse button while you drag the scroll box to the bottom of the scroll bar. Then release the mouse button.** This is called *dragging*.

Note that the row numbers increase but the column labels do not change. Do you know how to move back quickly to the top of the spreadsheet?

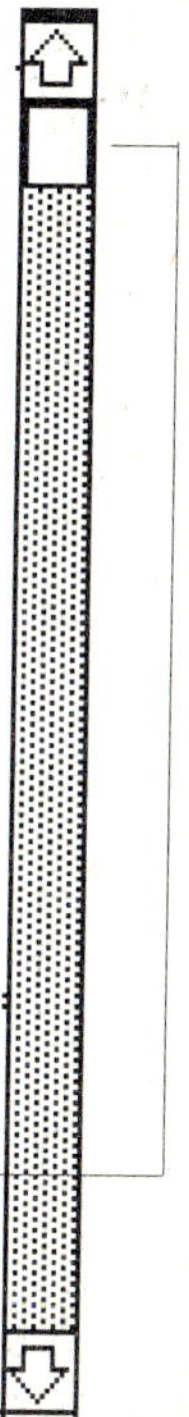

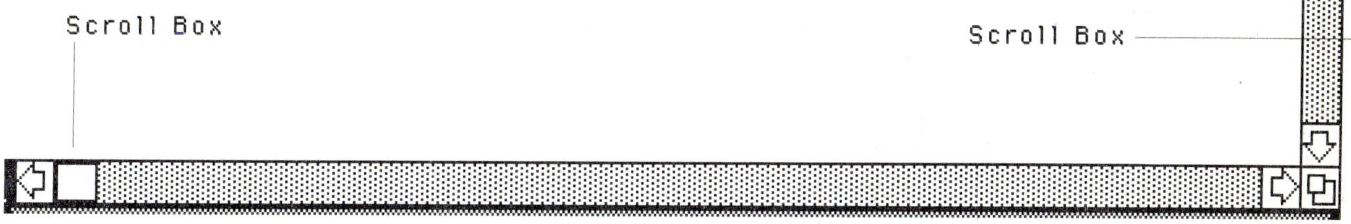

Scroll Box

Scroll Box

6 *Spreadsheets: Worksheet 1* **69**

- **Move the pointer to the scroll box at the right and drag it to the top of the scroll bar.**

If Column A is not showing on your screen, use the scroll box at the bottom of the screen to move quickly to the left.

1. **Move the pointer to the scroll box at the bottom of the screen.**

2. **Drag the box to the far right of the scroll bar.** To return to the file,

3. **Drag the box back to the far left of the scroll bar.**

Selecting Parts of a Spreadsheet

In order to work with a cell or a group of cells, you must *select* (highlight) it.

To select a **single cell**, you simply click on that cell. For example, select Cell A1 where the spreadsheet title "Daily Receipts" was typed,

- **Move the pointer to Cell A1 and click.** Cell A1 is highlighted.

To select a **block of cells**, for example, the sales amounts by category for each day of the week,

1. **Move the pointer to the cell in one corner of the block (Cell B5).**

2. **Drag to the cell in the opposite corner (Cell F11).**

Remember: to drag, press down the mouse button and hold it down until you reach the opposite corner. Then release the button. When you have selected a range of cells, the entry bar displays the content of the first cell in the selected block.

Frequently, you will want to select **entire rows** or **columns** in order to format or delete them. There is an easy way to do this. For example, to select Row 5,

- **Move the pointer to the row header 5 on the far left of the spreadsheet and click.** The entire row is selected. See Figure 6-7.

Figure 6-7. Note the pointer on the header for Row 5

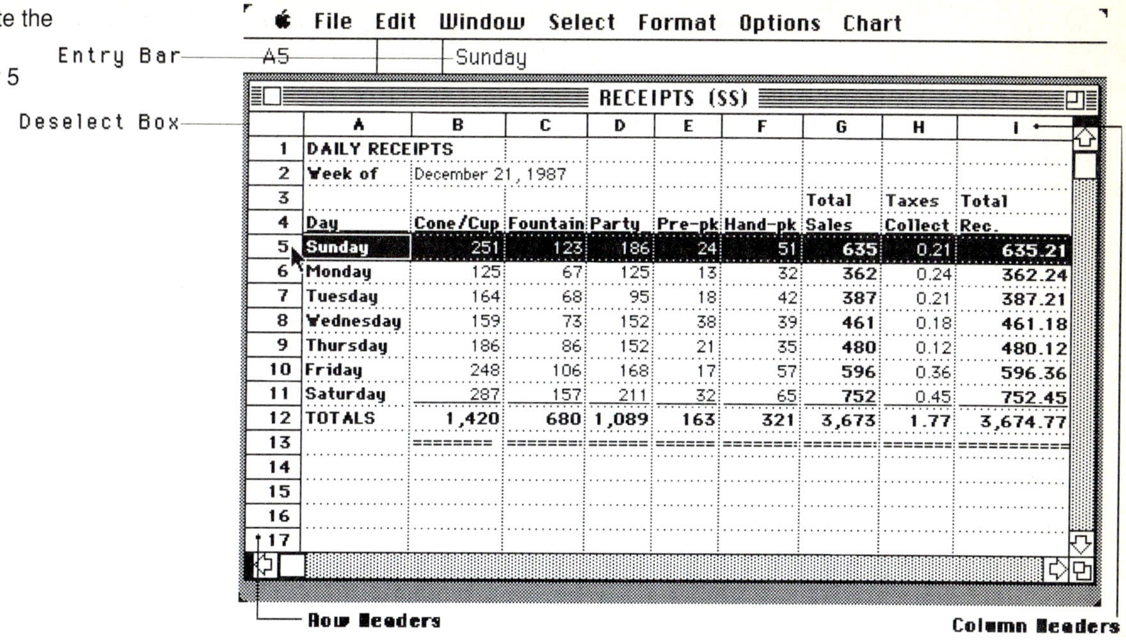

Entry Bar ── A5 ── Sunday

Deselect Box

	A	B	C	D	E	F	G	H	I
1	DAILY RECEIPTS								
2	Week of	December 21, 1987							
3							Total	Taxes	Total
4	Day	Cone/Cup	Fountain	Party	Pre-pk	Hand-pk	Sales	Collect	Rec.
5	Sunday	251	123	186	24	51	635	0.21	635.21
6	Monday	125	67	125	13	32	362	0.24	362.24
7	Tuesday	164	68	95	18	42	387	0.21	387.21
8	Wednesday	159	73	152	38	39	461	0.18	461.18
9	Thursday	186	86	152	21	35	480	0.12	480.12
10	Friday	248	106	168	17	57	596	0.36	596.36
11	Saturday	287	157	211	32	65	752	0.45	752.45
12	TOTALS	1,420	680	1,089	163	321	3,673	1.77	3,674.77

Row Headers — Column Headers

To select a **single column**, such as Column D,

- **Move the pointer to the column header D at the top of the spreadsheet and click.**

To select **Columns** B through I,

1. **Move the pointer to the column header B (the top of the column with cone/cup figures).**

2. **Drag to the header for the farthest column, Column I.** If you have forgotten how to drag, see the Reminder following selecting a block near the bottom of page 70.

To select all cells in the spreadsheet,

- **Pull down the Select Menu and select All Cells.**

To remove the highlight from the spreadsheet,

- **Click on the deselect box.** (See Figure 6-7 above.)

6 Spreadsheets: Worksheet 1   **71**

Using the Go To Method

You can move quickly to a distant cell and select it at the same time by using the Go To method. Follow the steps below to move to Cell Z1000.

➡ 1. **Pull down the Select Menu and select Find Cell.** You see a dialog box with a highlighted type-in box. You may see some data already present in the type-in box. Just ignore the data. It's the last item searched for by a previous *Works* user.

2. **Type:** Z1000

3. **Click the Find Next button**. The highlighting is now in Cell Z1000, making it the active cell. (To confirm this, look at the left side of the entry bar.)

You can also use the Go To method to search for a cell that contains a specific value. For example, to find the cell that contains the value 163.

➡ 1. **Pull down the Select Menu and select Find Cell.**

2. **Type:** 163

3. **Move the pointer to the Find Next button and click once.** The highlighting moves to Cell E12. It contains 163.

If several cells contained the value 163 and the program did not select the proper cell, you could perform Step 1 again and click on Find Next. When all occurrences have been found, you would see a message "All references to ... have been found." Click on the OK button to complete the search.

Entering Data

It is a good idea to identify each spreadsheet you create or change with your name and the date you revised it. You can simply type your name and the date at the bottom of the spreadsheet. To identify this spreadsheet,

➡ 1. **Move the pointer to Cell A14 and click to select it.** You can use either the scroll bar or the Select Menu to find Cell A14.

72   *Microsoft Works for the Macintosh*

2. Type your name and today's date.

As you can see, the information you type appears in the entry bar but not on the spreadsheet. This is because you have not yet entered any data into the cell. If you have made a typing error, you can still backspace and retype. You may also have noticed the appearance of two new items in the entry bar. These are the cancel box and the entry box. Look at Figure 6-8 and check the locations of these new boxes on your screen.

Figure 6-8

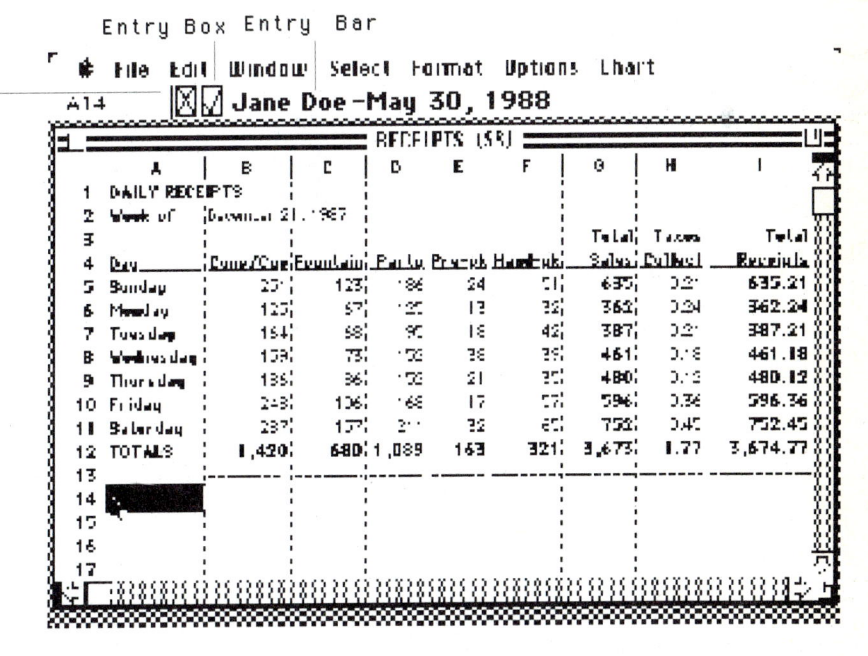

By selecting the cancel box, you can cancel the typing. By selecting the entry box, you can enter the typing into the spreadsheet. However, if you are already using the keyboard, you will normally press [RETURN] or [ENTER] to enter data into cells. When you press [RETURN], the pointer will move to the cell below. When you press [ENTER], the pointer will remain in the same cell.

To record your entry into the spreadsheet and remain in the same cell,

- **Press:** [ENTER].

Note that the name overflows into Column B. However, only Column A is considered occupied. When a cell is not wide enough to show all the characters it contains, most spreadsheet programs will display the characters until they encounter an occupied cell. Since the other cells on Row 14 are not occupied, the entire line is available for displaying the name and date stored in A14. To verify that Cell B14 is empty,

- **Move the pointer to Cell B14 and click once.** As you can see from the entry bar, Cell B14 is empty. If it contained any data, the label from A14 would not be displayed in this cell.

Correcting Errors

Look back at Figure 6-2 again. Suppose you want to erase a cell that already contains data. For example, you should have typed "Submitted by" before you typed your name! Also, since you have to make this change, why not add a little more space between the last line of the spreadsheet and your name in order to make the line look better. (Note that on Figure 6-2, your name appears in Row 16.) First, to erase your name:

1. **Select Cell A14.** This is the cell you want to erase.

2. Press: **[DELETE]** or **[BACKSPACE]**. Note that the name has been deleted from the entry bar but not from Cell A14.

3. Press: **[RETURN]** to enter the correction and move the cursor to the line below.

Cell A14 is now empty and the highlighting has advanced to Cell A15, anticipating another entry. To type your name one blank line below,

4. Press: **[RETURN]**. The pointer moves to Cell A16.

5. Type: **Submitted by** *your name, today's date.*

6. Press: **[RETURN]**.

To prepare for the next exercise,

7. **Use scroll boxes or arrows to bring Cell A1 into view.**

74 *Microsoft Works for the Macintosh*

Values and Alignments

All the cells in the area from Cell B5 through Cell I12 are **values**. Values are either simple numerics or formulas. *Works* automatically aligns a numeric value on the right side of a cell. However, as with labels, you can change the alignment by using the Format Menu.

Deleting a Column

Look back again at Figure 6-2. Chris had decided that there was no need to separate pre-packaged sales from hand-packed sales. She has asked you to combine the columns under one heading, "Bulk." So you will eliminate the Pre-pk column, adding the daily numbers and listing them under the new label Bulk (which will replace Hand-pk).

Before you begin, take a moment to check the total sales for the week and total receipts. Since you are simply combining two existing columns, these totals should not change.

Remember that you must select (highlight) cells before you tell *Works* to perform actions on those cells. Therefore, you first select the entire column and then tell *Works* to delete the cells.

➡ 1. **Move the pointer to the header E at the top of Column E and click once to select the entire column.** See Figure 6-9 to see how your screen should look.

Figure 6-9. Spreadsheet showing Column E highlighted

	A	B	C	D	E	F	G	H	I
1	DAILY RECEIPTS								
2	Week of	December 21, 1987							
3							Total	Taxes	Total
4	Day	Cone/Cup	Fountain	Party	Pre-pk	Hand-pk	Sales	Collect	Receipts
5	Sunday	251	123	186	24	51	635	0.21	635.21
6	Monday	125	67	125	13	32	362	0.24	362.24
7	Tuesday	164	68	95	18	42	387	0.21	387.21
8	Wednesday	159	73	152	38	39	461	0.18	461.18
9	Thursday	186	86	152	21	35	480	0.12	480.12
10	Friday	248	106	168	17	57	596	0.36	596.36
11	Saturday	287	157	211	32	65	752	0.45	752.45
12	TOTALS	1,420	680	1,089	163	321	3,673	1.77	3,674.77
16	Submitted by Jane Doe, May 30, 1988								

2. Pull down the Edit Menu and select Cut.

The Pre-pk column disappears. (Note that the data to the right of that column has moved in.) Now you are ready to rename the Hand-pk column and to enter the revised data for the new Bulk column.

Changing Cell Contents

Before practicing on changing a cell's contents, you will try another correction method—clearing a cell. Sometimes you may make such a mess of an entry that you want to erase the entire cell and then start over again. Clearing cells is also useful if you type data into a cell that should have left been blank. To clear Cell E4,

➡ **1. Move the pointer to Cell E4 and click.**

2. Press: **[DELETE]** or **[BACKSPACE]** to clear the entry bar.

3. Press: **[ENTER]** to enter the clear-cell correction into the spreadsheet and to leave the pointer in Cell E4.

Note that when you pressed [ENTER], the highlighting did not move. It remained in Cell E4, which is what you want since you will enter a new label into that cell. If you had pressed [RETURN], the highlighting would have moved down to the next cell, anticipating that you would be working in that direction.
You will now enter a new label into Cell E4.

4. If Cell E4 is not selected, click on it now.

5. Type: Bulk

6. Press: **[RETURN]** to enter the new label and to move to the next cell.

You are now ready to enter the new values. You don't need to clear a cell first. You can simply type the new value (and it will appear only in the entry bar) and press [RETURN]. On the spreadsheet, pressing [RETURN] replaces the old data with the new. For example, to change Sunday bulk sales to 75 (24 + 51),

Microsoft Works for the Macintosh

7. **Type:** **75** The entry bar displays the new value, but the spreadsheet still displays the old value. See Figure 6-10.

Figure 6-10. Note the 51 in Cell E5 and the 75 in the entry bar.

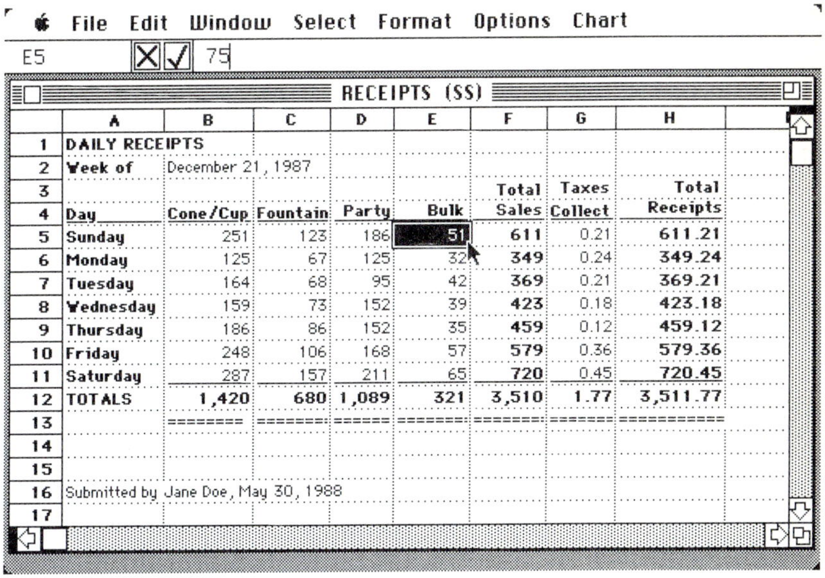
File Edit Window Select Format Options Chart

E5 75

RECEIPTS (SS)

	A	B	C	D	E	F	G	H
1	DAILY RECEIPTS							
2	Week of	December 21, 1987						
3						Total	Taxes	Total
4	Day	Cone/Cup	Fountain	Party	Bulk	Sales	Collect	Receipts
5	Sunday	251	123	186	51	611	0.21	611.21
6	Monday	125	67	125	32	349	0.24	349.24
7	Tuesday	164	68	95	42	369	0.21	369.21
8	Wednesday	159	73	152	39	423	0.18	423.18
9	Thursday	186	86	152	35	459	0.12	459.12
10	Friday	248	106	168	57	579	0.36	579.36
11	Saturday	287	157	211	65	720	0.45	720.45
12	TOTALS	1,420	680	1,089	321	3,510	1.77	3,511.77
13		========	=======	======	=======	=======	=======	===========
14								
15								
16	Submitted by Jane Doe, May 30, 1988							
17								

To enter the new value on the spreadsheet,

8. **Press:** **[RETURN].**

9. **Now follow Steps 7 and 8 to enter the remaining values into Column E:**

Monday 45	Thursday 56
Tuesday 60	Friday 74
Wednesday 77	Saturday 97

10. Compare the entries in your Total Sales and Total Receipts columns to the entries in Figure 6-9, page 75. If they are not the same, check your work to find the error and correct it.

Viewing a Formula

A formula is another kind of a value used in spreadsheets. You enter a ***formula*** in a cell and it tells the program how to calculate a numeric value to be displayed in that cell. The program displays the calculated value in the cell and the formula in the entry bar. You can write two kinds of formulas. These are called *user defined* formulas and *predefined* (or *built-in*) formulas. Pre-defined formulas are often called ***functions*** (and will be explained later). To view a formula,

- **Click on Cell H5**

Note that, unlike the cells you have worked with previously, the value displayed in the spreadsheet looks far different from the contents displayed in the entry bar. Rather than entering a number into this cell, Chris entered a formula. It appears in the entry bar. *Works* made the calculations and displayed the resulting value in the cell. Formulas consist of values and cell addresses, together with arithmetical or logical operators. The arithmetical operators are

- \+ for add
- \- for subtract
- * for multiply
- / for divide

Look again at the formula in the entry bar.

=F5+G5

As noted earlier, the equals sign before the F tells *Works* that this expression is a formula. The formula instructs *Works* to make Cell H5 (Sunday's total receipts) equal to the amount in Cell F5 (Sunday's sales) *plus* the amount in Cell G5 (Sunday's taxes).

Can you create a formula to compute the total sales for the week? Answer: =F5+F6+F7+F8+F9+F10+F11. But, as you will soon see, there is an easier way!

Using a Function

Some formulas (such as the summing formula above) are used so often that most (if not all) spreadsheet programs include them as functions so that you don't have to create a new formula. Generally speaking, functions save time when you are calculating with large numbers of adjacent cells. For example, Chris used a function to compute the total sales for the week. Let's look at it.

- **Click on Cell F12.** Your entry bar should look the same as the entry bar in Figure 6-11.

78 *Microsoft Works for the Macintosh*

Figure 6-11. Note the formula in the entry bar and the result of the formula in Cell F12.

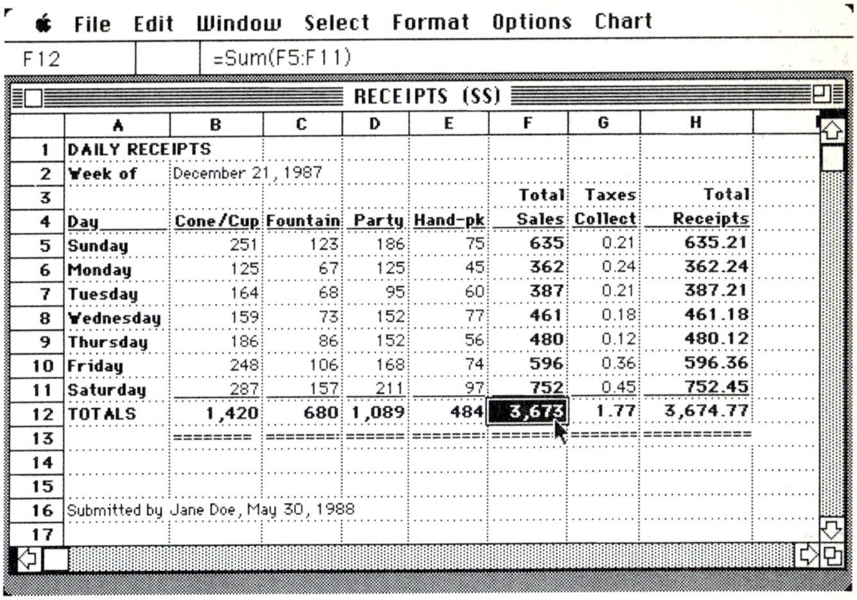

Again, compare the value displayed in Cell F12 with the content displayed in the entry bar. As you can see, the two are very different. The entry bar shows the function used to calculate the value displayed in Cell F12. The function instructs *Works* to make the amount in Cell F12 (total sales for the week) equal to the sum of all cells from F5 through F11 (daily total receipts). Each element of the function has a special meaning.

=	Signifies that a formula or function follows.
SUM	Name of a pre-defined formula (function). It adds the contents of cells.
( )	Parentheses surround the references to the cells with which the function will work.
F5	Cell F5 is the first cell to add.
:	Colon separates the first cell from the last cell in the range of cells to add.
F11	Cell F11 is the last cell to add.

6 Spreadsheets: Worksheet 1 **79**

Many other functions are available. For example, you can use

> **Mathematical functions**, such as random numbers
> **Statistical functions**, such as average value
> **Logical functions**, such as if-then-else
> **Financial functions**, such as present value

For a comprehensive listing of functions and an explanation of each, see the *Works* manual.

"What If?"

Now that you have worked with a spreadsheet, you are probably wondering if you would really save any time by using a spreadsheet rather than pencil and paper. If you use the model you develop (sometimes called a ***template***) only once, then the answer is probably "no." But if you use the model over and over again, the answer is "yes, a considerable amount of time." For example, suppose an error was made in closing on Saturday—one large, off-site $47 order for party goods was not recorded because Chris delivered it herself, took the money home, and did not discover her mistake until today.

If you were using pencil and paper to correct the weekly total for party goods (Column D), you would have to recalculate five items:

1. Saturday party sales
2. Total sales for Saturday
3. Total receipts for Saturday
4. Total sales for the week
5. Total receipts for the week.

However, to correct the electronic spreadsheet, you simply

1. **Click on Cell D11.** It contains the Saturday party sales total of $211.

2. **Type:**   258 This adds the $47 error to the previous $211 balance. As you press [RETURN] in the next step, several cells below and to the right of Cell D11 will change. Watch Cell D12, the Totals cell for the Party column. Now

3. **Press:**   **[RETURN]**. All five calculations are completed automatically!

80   *Microsoft Works for the Macintosh*

You only needed to make one calculation. Works automatically updated the other cells because those cells contain formulas that refer directly or indirectly to Cell D11. So, if you wanted to play "What if," you could change any of the daily sales amounts and watch the totals change. Thus the model becomes a tool for forecasting and writing budgets.

Your spreadsheet should now agree with Figure 6-12. You have made all the revisions Chris needed and you can now print the file.

Figure 6-12. The complete Receipts spreadsheet

	A	B	C	D	E	F	G	H
1	DAILY RECEIPTS							
2	Week of	December 21, 1987						
3						Total	Taxes	Total
4	Day	Cone/Cup	Fountain	Party	Bulk	Sales	Collect	Receipts
5	Sunday	251	123	186	75	635	0.21	635.21
6	Monday	125	67	125	45	362	0.24	362.24
7	Tuesday	164	68	95	60	387	0.21	387.21
8	Wednesday	159	73	152	77	461	0.18	461.18
9	Thursday	186	86	152	56	480	0.12	480.12
10	Friday	248	106	168	74	596	0.36	596.36
11	Saturday	287	157	258	97	799	0.45	799.45
12	TOTALS	1,420	680	1,136	484	3,720	1.77	3,721.77
13	========	========	========	========	========	========	========	============
14								
15								
16	Submitted by Jane Doe, May 30, 1988							
17								

Printing a File

Because spreadsheets are often quite wide, they sometimes do not fit on the standard 8.5 by 11-inch wide page. Although this spreadsheet would fit, you will take advantage of the Mac's ability to print sideways.

➡ 1. **Pull down File Menu and select Page Setup.**

2. **Click on the sideways image under the heading "Orientation" (as shown in Figure 6-13).**

3. **Click once in the OK box.**

6 Spreadsheets: Worksheet 1 **81**

Figure 6-13. Note the sideways highlighted icon.

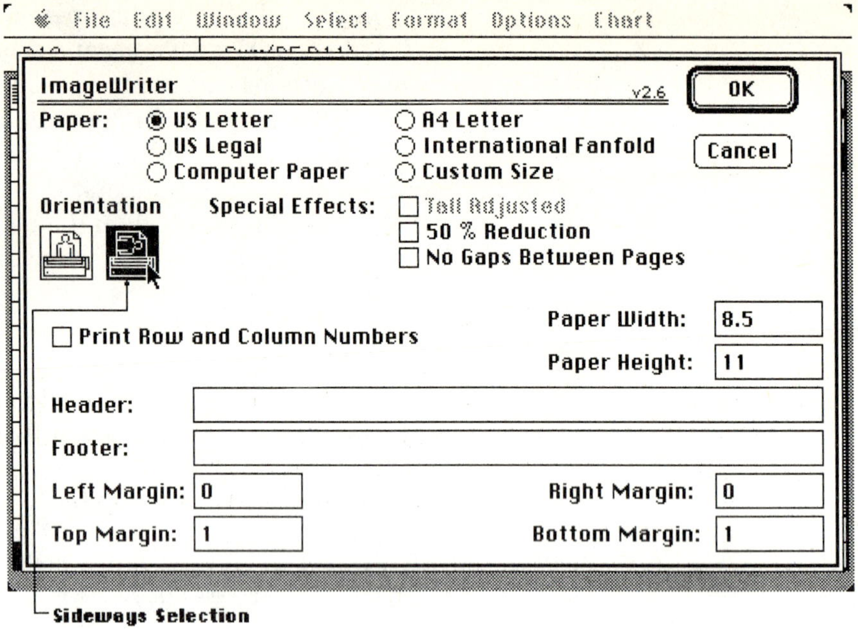

```
ImageWriter                                      v2.6      [  OK  ]
Paper:   ◉ US Letter         ○ A4 Letter
         ○ US Legal          ○ International Fanfold       [Cancel]
         ○ Computer Paper    ○ Custom Size
Orientation    Special Effects:  ☐ Tall Adjusted
                                 ☐ 50 % Reduction
                                 ☐ No Gaps Between Pages

                                          Paper Width:  8.5
☐ Print Row and Column Numbers            Paper Height: 11

Header: [                                     ]
Footer: [                                     ]
Left Margin: 0              Right Margin:  0
Top Margin:  1              Bottom Margin: 1
```

Sideways Selection

To print the worksheet,

4. **Turn on the printer and check to be certain it is ready to print.**

5. **Pull down the File Menu and select Print.** You see the Print dialog box. Since all defaults are acceptable,

6. **Click on OK.**

Saving a File Under a Different Name

The following steps tell you how to save your revised *Receipts* file on your data disk under a different name. Then, if you want to work with the original *Receipts* file again, you can.

➡ 1. **Move the pointer to the deselect box and click once.**

2. **Pull down the File Menu and select Save As.**

You see a Save dialog box with the original filename highlighted. To create a new file with a new name,

82   *Microsoft Works for the Macintosh*

3. **Check to see that your data disk is the active disk.** You should see "Works Data" next to the active disk icon. If it is not, click on the Drive button.

4. **Type:** Receipt1

5. **Click on the Save button.**

Review

If time permits, load *Receipts* again and practice with this worksheet. Add a name to the bottom of the file, use the Go To method to find a cell, delete the Pre-Packaged Sales column, change the Hand-Packed Sales column to Bulk and insert the combined sales amounts, and change some daily sales amounts and watch their impact on the cells containing formulas (as in Column H) and those containing functions (as in Column F and Row 12).

Summary

Congratulations! You've covered a lot of territory. Now you can recognize spreadsheets and identify rows, columns, and cells. You can move the highlighting around the spreadsheet, identify labels and columns, enter and delete cells, explain the difference between cell content and cell display, and identify formulas and functions.

Quitting Works

To quit *Works*,

1. **Pull down the File Menu and select Quit.** If you have forgotten to save your document, a message will appear to remind you to do it. After you click on the appropriate box,

2. **Close all open windows.**

3. **Pull down the Special Menu and select Shut Down.**

4. **Remove the disks and return them to their appropriate places.**

5. **Turn off the Macintosh.**

7 Spreadsheets Worksheet 2

Feb 21, 1990

Objectives

In this worksheet, you will learn how to

- Insert a column
- Format cells to display values accurate to two decimal places
- Format a label to center it
- Explain absolute and relative cell references
- Copy cells using the Fill Down command
- Use the Edit function key
- Change column width

Setting the Scene

The Ice Cream Factory has a number of part-time employees, mostly students. The owner, Chris Hughes, has created a spreadsheet to keep track of the payroll. (See *Payroll* Figure 7-1, page 86.) The spreadsheet lists the employees alphabetically with their pay rates (Columns A-C).

Each week Column D will be updated to include hours worked that week. The last three columns contain formulas and functions that compute each employee's gross pay, FICA (Social Security) tax deduction, and the net amount of each paycheck.

As you can see, Chris has not attempted to align headings or to display values in a standard format. Chris has delegated the spreadsheet to you and asked you to change the format of all dollar amount columns so that the amounts will be displayed accurately to two decimal points. She also wants you to insert a column for Holiday bonuses and to improve the appearance of the spreadsheet by centering the column labels.

Getting Started

1. Open*Works* as described in Getting Started, Chapter 1.

2. Insert your *Works Data Disk* into the second disk drive.

```
                                                                    
    ┌─Row Headers                        ┌─Column Headers─
    │ This spreadsheet                   │ This spreadsheet
    │ uses Rows 1 thru 17                │ uses columns A thru G
    ▼                          payroll.ss (SS)
         A          B         C      D       E       F         G        H
  1  WEEKLY PAYROLL
  2  Week of    December 14, 1987
  3
  4  Last Name  First Name  Rate   Hours   Gross    FICA*    Net Pay
  5  ---------  ---------- ------ ------- -------- -------- ----------
  6  Carlson    Roberta     4.5    22      99      7.0785    91.9215
  7  Carrillo   Angela      6      18     108      7.722    100.278
  8  Jacobsen   Russ        4.5    21      94.5    6.75675   87.74325
  9  Mansur     Gloria      5      20     100      7.15      92.85
 10  Prada      Josephine   4.5    17      76.5    5.46975   71.03025
 11  Tyler      Geoffrey    3.75   12      45      3.2175    41.7825
 12  Villarreal Raoul       4      22      88      6.292     81.708
 13  Williams   Corinne     3.75   25      93.75   6.70313   87.046875
 14  Yee        Wendy       4      26     104      7.436     96.564
 15                                -------- -------- -------- ----------
 16             TOTALS             183     808.75  57.8256  750.92438
 17                                ======== ======== ======== ==========
```

Figure 7-1: Payroll

Opening a File

When you open *Works*, you see the Open dialog box. Chris' spreadsheet is in the *Payroll* file on your data disk. To open it, follow the steps in Opening a File, Chapter 6.

Chris' spreadsheet is also shown in Figure 7-1 above. The filename *Payroll* helps you remember the type of data stored in the spreadsheet.

Inserting a Column

Sometimes you need to insert additional columns, rows, or spaces in a spreadsheet. You use the column headers across the top of the spreadsheet and row headers along the left edge of the spreadsheet. In order to insert a column for the $10 Holiday bonus that Chris plans to give each employee, first you must select (highlight) the column for the bonus entries. Don't worry if the column already has entries. When you insert a new column, the program will move the contents of the selected column to the right. To insert a new column named Bonus between Hours and Gross,

1. **Move the pointer into the column header E and click once.** You have selected (highlighted) Column E.

2. **Pull down the Edit menu and select Insert.** Column E is now empty and highlighted. The "old" Column E is now Column F. (See Figure 7-2.)

Figure 7-2

	A	B	C	D	E	F	G	H
1	WEEKLY PAYROLL							
2	Week of	December 14, 1987						
3								
4	Last Name	First Name	Rate	Hours		Gross	FICA*	Net Pay
5	---------	---------	----	-----		-----	-----	-------
6	Carlson	Roberta	4.5	22		99	7.0785	91.9215
7	Carrillo	Angela	6	18		108	7.722	100.278
8	Jacobsen	Russ	4.5	21		94.5	6.75675	87.74325
9	Mansur	Gloria	5	20		100	7.15	92.85
10	Prada	Josephine	4.5	17		76.5	5.46975	71.03025
11	Tyler	Geoffrey	3.75	12		45	3.2175	41.7825
12	Villarreal	Raoul	4	22		88	6.292	81.708
13	Williams	Corinne	3.75	25		93.75	6.70313	87.046875
14	Yee	Wendy	4	26		104	7.436	96.564
15								
16		TOTALS		183		808.75	57.8256	750.92438

To label the new column "Bonus,"

3. **Click once in Cell E4.** Here is where you want the label for the new column. Note that the rest of the column is now deselected.

4. **Type: Bonus**

5. **Press: [RETURN].** The highlighting moves down to the next cell, anticipating another entry. But before making another entry, you will decrease the width of the Bonus column.

7 Spreadsheets: Worksheet 2 **87**

Changing a Column Width

1. **Move the pointer to the line dividing column headers E and F.** The pointer becomes a two-way arrow. (See Figure 7-3.)

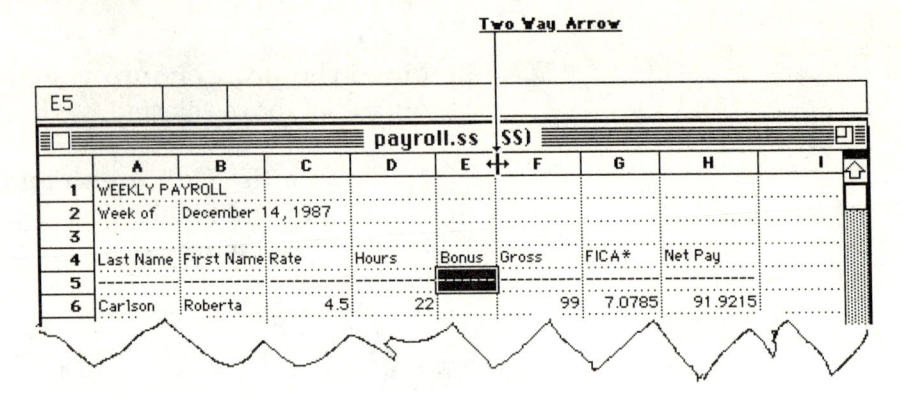

2. **Hold down the mouse button while you drag the edge of the column to the left until it is even with the last hyphen in Cell E5.** This leaves enough room for a five-character bonus entry.

3. **Release the mouse button.**

Now you need to enter and total the figures for the Bonus column. All employees will receive the same bonus. So you will type the figure once and then copy it through the other cells.

1. **Click once in Cell E6 to select it.**

2. **Type:**   10   This is the amount of the bonus.

3. **Press:**   [RETURN] to enter the amount.

Copying one cell through a range of adjacent cells is very easy. First you identify the cell you want to copy (here, E6) and the range through which you want to copy it (here, E7 through E14).

4. **Move the pointer to E6. Hold down the mouse button while you drag the mouse down to E14. Release the mouse button.**

88   *Microsoft Works for the Macintosh*

You have selected (highlighted) all the cells from E6 through E14 as shown in Figure 7-4. Note the white border around Cell E6. The white border indicates that E6 is the active cell. The program will copy it to the other selected cells.

Figure 7-4. Cells E6 through E14 are highlighted.

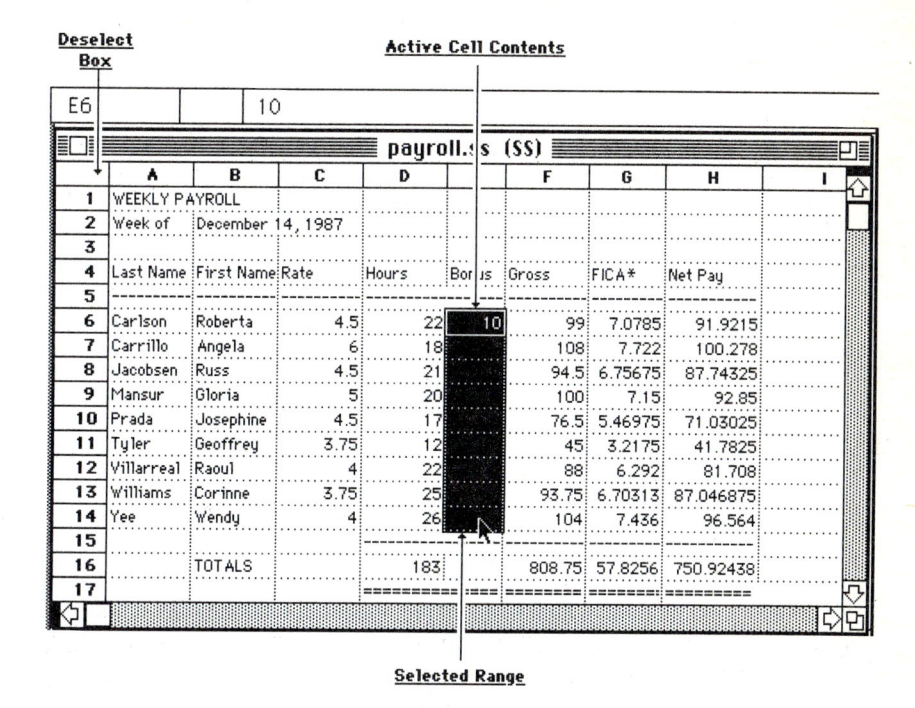

```
Deselect                    Active Cell Contents
  Box
┌──────┐         ┌──────────┐
│ E6   │         │    10    │
└──────┘         └──────────┘
```

	A	B	C	D	E	F	G	H
1	WEEKLY PAYROLL							
2	Week of	December 14, 1987						
3								
4	Last Name	First Name	Rate	Hours	Bonus	Gross	FICA*	Net Pay
5	--------	--------	----	-----	-----	-----	-----	------
6	Carlson	Roberta	4.5	22	10	99	7.0785	91.9215
7	Carrillo	Angela	6	18		108	7.722	100.278
8	Jacobsen	Russ	4.5	21		94.5	6.75675	87.74325
9	Mansur	Gloria	5	20		100	7.15	92.85
10	Prada	Josephine	4.5	17		76.5	5.46975	71.03025
11	Tyler	Geoffrey	3.75	12		45	3.2175	41.7825
12	Villarreal	Raoul	4	22		88	6.292	81.708
13	Williams	Corinne	3.75	25		93.75	6.70313	87.046875
14	Yee	Wendy	4	26		104	7.436	96.564
15								
16		TOTALS		183		808.75	57.8256	750.92438
17				=======	====	=======	=======	=======

Selected Range

5. **Pull down the Edit Menu and select Fill Down.** The copy is immediately complete.

6. **Move the pointer to the deselect box (which you can see in Figure 7-4) and click once to avoid accidentally making changes in the selected cells.**

Now you need to total the Bonus column. You can type your own formula, but an easier way is to copy the formula used to add hours in Column D. You can use the Fill Right option.

➡ 1. **Move the pointer to Cell D16 and click once.** You see the formula =SUM(D5:D15) in the entry bar, but you see the total in Column D. You can use the Fill Right option.

2. **Drag the mouse from Cell D16 to Cell E16.** Cells D6 and

7 Spreadsheets: Worksheet 2

E16 are both now highlighted. The active cell (D16) contains the formula that you will copy over to the right (E16).

3. **Pull down Edit Menu and select Fill Right.** The copy is complete.

4. **Move the pointer to the deselect box and click once.**

To understand more about how to copy formulas, read the next section about relative and absolute values. Carefully follow the spreadsheet on your screen.

Relative and Absolute Values

Copy commands are time savers and help keep errors to a minimum. So it is worth some effort to understand them. Let's consider the original formula in Cell D16. It is expressed:

=SUM(D5:D15)

What do you think the copy in Cell E16 looks like? Compare the original formula with the copy in Cell E16.

- **Move the pointer to Cell E16 and click once.** The copy is =SUM(E5:E15).

Works has changed the cell references to make them ***relative*** to the position of the cell that will contain the sum. In other words, the formula in Cell D16 adds values in Rows 5 through 15 in Column D. When you copied the formula, *Works* assumed that you wanted the formula in Cell E16 to add the values in Rows 5 through 15 in *its* column (Column E). And that's what the formula **=SUM(E5:E15)** does.

But what if you don't want cell addresses to change relative to position when you copy formulas? An example is the computation of FICA taxes (Column G). Here each employee's gross pay is multiplied by the current FICA rate. So, although the gross pay changes for each employee, the FICA rate (shown in the bottom left corner of the ***template***) does not. Now look at the FICA formula.

1. **Move pointer to Cell G6 and click once.** In this cell, FICA taxes are computed for Roberta Carlson. The formula was cop-

ied to compute taxes for all the other employees. The formula is **=F6*B18** as displayed in the entry bar. The formula looks a little difficult, but it's quite simple if you look at each part.

=	Equals sign indicates that a formula follows.
F6	Because this cell reference is not preceded by a dollar sign, the address is relative. The program will change it relative to the position of the cell to which you are copying.
*	Asterisk indicates multiplication.
$B	$ tells the program not to change the following column reference when this formula is copied. So this is an ***absolute reference.***
$18	$ tells the program that the following row number is also an absolute reference and should not be changed when this formula is copied.

Next, note that the absolute value B18 did not change when the formula was copied, but the row number in F6 was incremented by one digit each time the formula was copied.

2. Click on Cell G7 to select it and to study the changes in the formula.

3. Continue selecting and studying the cells in Column G.

A simple illustration may help you understand the difference between relative and absolute. Joe invites Mike, a new neighbor, to a party at his home, which is just up the street from Mike's. If he tells Mike to "walk north and stop at the fourth house on the right," he is giving a *relative* direction that applies only to Mike. If Joe tells him that he lives "at 125 Ocean Street," he is giving Mike an *absolute* address.

Changing a Formula

Let's go back to the bonuses. Did you happen to notice that the Net Pay totals did not change when you entered a Holiday bonus? Do you know why? How many formulas do you need to change? If you think that only the formulas in the Gross Pay column need

7 Spreadsheets: Worksheet 2

changing, you are right! The following steps will show you how to make the adjustments.

➡️ 1. **Move the pointer to Cell F6 and click once to select it.** From here on, we will simplify the direction to "Click on Cell —."

2. **Look at the entry bar.**

The formula to compute Roberta's pay is incomplete because it does not include the bonus amount. You still need to multiply C6 times D6, but you should also add E6 to compute gross pay. Follow Steps 3 and 4 below. With F6 still selected (highlighted),

3. **Type:** **=C6*D6+E6** As you complete the next step, watch the number in Net Pay (H6) change to reflect the change in the formula.

4. **Press:** **[RETURN].**

Copying a Formula

If you did not see the changes being made above, try to watch more carefully in the next sequence. To copy the formula,

➡️ 1. **Move the pointer to Cell F6. Hold down the mouse button, drag from F6 down to F14, and release the button.** From here on, we will simplify this direction to "Drag from Cell— through Cell—."

2. **Pull down the Edit Menu and select Fill Down.** Copying is now complete.

Formatting Numeric Values

Although the Payroll columns are calculated accurately, the amounts are difficult to read because they are not aligned on the decimal point and they contain from zero to five decimal places. However, you can change the appearance of the numeric values by changing the cell's format. To quickly reformat the cells in the last four columns to two decimal places,

➡️ 1. **Drag from Cell E6 through Cell H16.** See page 70 if you have forgotten how to drag to select a block.

2. **Pull down the Format Menu and select Fixed.** The fixed format displays the cell figures rounded to the nearest hundredth.

As you can see from your screen and Figure 7-5, you have many options in the Format Menu.

Figure 7-5. The Format Menu

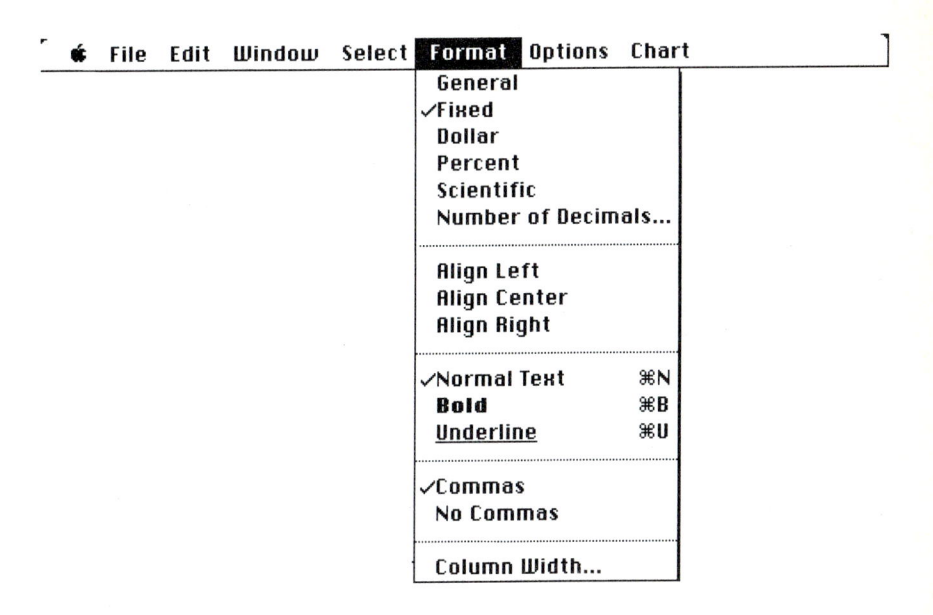

```
 File   Edit   Window   Select   Format   Options   Chart
                                 General
                                ✓Fixed
                                 Dollar
                                 Percent
                                 Scientific
                                 Number of Decimals...

                                 Align Left
                                 Align Center
                                 Align Right

                                ✓Normal Text        ⌘N
                                 Bold               ⌘B
                                 Underline          ⌘U

                                ✓Commas
                                 No Commas

                                 Column Width...
```

The formats for the General and Align Right options are defaults. Chris used these when she created the spreadsheet. The General format displays a number as accurately as possible in the space available. The Dollar format places a dollar sign before a number. This may seem like a logical format for these cells, but the dollar signs can be distracting. Since Cells E6 through H16 are still highlighted, you can see what the Dollar format would look like by trying it on those cells.

1. **Pull down Format Menu and select Dollar.** Besides the dollar signs, you may also see asterisks instead of numbers. This simply means that the column is not wide enough to accommodate the digits in a number as well as the dollar sign. But since you are not going to keep the Dollar format, you don't need to make any changes in column width. To return to the Fixed format, be sure the columns are still selected and then

7 Spreadsheets: Worksheet 2 **93**

2. Pull down Format Menu and select Fixed.

Financial worksheets are usually formatted to display values accurate to two decimal places in fixed format.

Now you need to reformat Column C so that it also displays numbers to two decimal places. See if you can remember how to do it. If you need help, follow these steps: select Cells C6 through C14, pull down the Format Menu, select Fixed, and then deselect the column.

Formatting Labels

The spreadsheet is looking much better, but some of the columnar labels (especially Rate and Hours) float away from the columns. As Chris noted, centering the labels over the amounts should help.

➡ **1. Drag from C4 through H4.** See Figure 7-6.

Figure 7-6

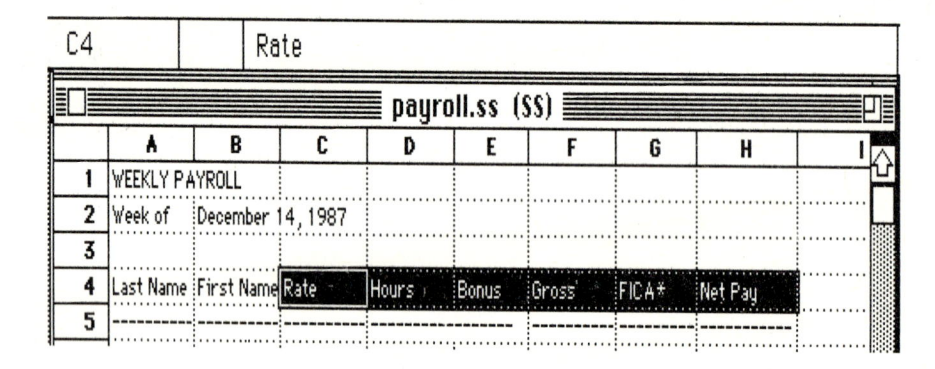

	A	B	C	D	E	F	G	H
1	WEEKLY PAYROLL							
2	Week of	December 14, 1987						
3								
4	Last Name	First Name	Rate	Hours	Bonus	Gross	FICA*	Net Pay
5	---------	---------	----	-----	-----	-----	-----	-------

C4 — Rate — payroll.ss (SS)

2. Pull down the Format Menu and select Align Center.
The labels are now centered.

Identifying Your Work

To identify yourself as the creator of this revision and to supply the date of the revision, you will type your name and the date on Row 20. Cell A20, the cell you want, does not show on the screen. The fastest way to display that part of the spreadsheet is to use the down scroll arrow in the lower right corner of the scroll bar. A few clicks on the arrow will bring Cell A20 into view.

➡ **1. Click on Cell A20.**

94 *Microsoft Works for the Macintosh*

2. **Type:** *your name* and *today's date*.

3. **Press**: [RETURN].

4. **Click on the deselect box.**

Printing a File

1. **Turn on the printer and check that it is ready to print.**

2. **Pull down File Menu and select Print.** You see the Print dialog box.

3. **Check the default selections in the Print dialog box and change them if necessary.**

4. **Click on the OK button. Printing starts in seconds.**

Saving a File Under a Different Name

Now that you have completed all the changes and the spreadsheet looks so great, you should save it with a different name.

1. **Pull down the File Menu and select Save As.** You see the Save As dialog box with the original filename highlighted. To create a new file with a new name,

2. **Check to see that your data disk is the active disk.** You should see "Works Data" displayed next to the active disk icon. If it is not active, click on the Drive button.

3. **Type:** Payroll2

4. **Click on the SAVE button.**

Review

If time permits, load *Payroll* again and practice with this worksheet.
    Insert the Bonus column
    Center the column headings
    Reformat the numeric fields
    Change the size of the bonus column
    Change relative references to absolute references
    Add your name

7 Spreadsheets: Worksheet 2

Summary

Congratulations! The *Payroll* spreadsheet is now ready to submit to Chris. You have successfully added a column, formatted a block of values, formatted labels, studied the difference between absolute and relative cell references, copied formulas, and changed column widths.

Quitting Works

To quit *Works,*

1. **Pull down the File Menu and select Quit.** If you have forgotten to save your document, a message will appear to remind you to do it. After you click in the appropriate box,

2. **Close all open windows.**

3. **Pull down the Special Menu and select Shut Down.**

4. **Remove the disks and return them to their appropriate places.**

5. **Turn off the Macintosh.**

8 Spreadsheets Worksheet 3

Objectives

In this worksheet, you will revise the spreadsheet shown in Figure 8-1. You will learn how to

- Reposition a spreadsheet title
- Insert a row
- Study the effect of adding cells at the end of a range
- Create a formula
- Copy a formula
- Align column data and their headings
- Protect cells

Setting the Scene

The Ice Cream Factory does not have space to stock more than one week's supply of ice cream at a time. To assure an efficient use of this space, Chris has drafted a spreadsheet (Figure 8-1) that standardizes the reordering process and becomes an easy-to-use reorder form. Chris has given the spreadsheet the filename *Reorder*. As with the spreadsheet in Worksheet 2, she has delegated the final version of *Reorder* to you.

Getting Started

- **Open *Works*.** Follow the instructions in Getting Started, Chapter 1.

Opening a File

Chris' spreadsheet is on your data disk under *Reorder*.

1. **Insert your *Works Data Disk* into the second disk drive.** You see "Works Data" next to the active disk icon.

2. **Click on the Spreadsheet icon.** The list box now displays only spreadsheet files.

Figure 8-1. Chris' *Reorder* spreadsheet.

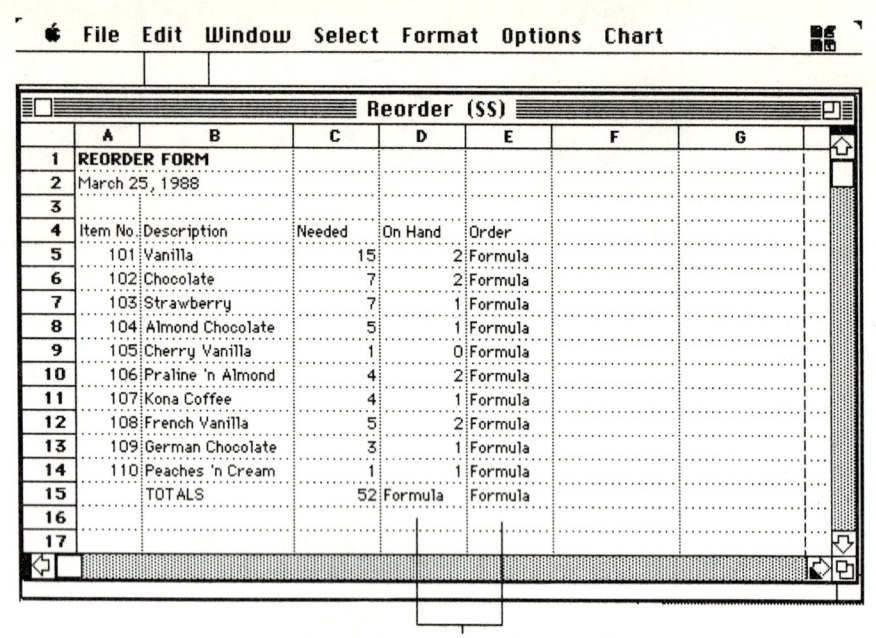

	A	B	C	D	E	F	G
1	REORDER FORM						
2	March 25, 1988						
3							
4	Item No.	Description	Needed	On Hand	Order		
5	101	Vanilla	15	2	Formula		
6	102	Chocolate	7	2	Formula		
7	103	Strawberry	7	1	Formula		
8	104	Almond Chocolate	5	1	Formula		
9	105	Cherry Vanilla	1	0	Formula		
10	106	Praline 'n Almond	4	2	Formula		
11	107	Kona Coffee	4	1	Formula		
12	108	French Vanilla	5	2	Formula		
13	109	German Chocolate	3	1	Formula		
14	110	Peaches 'n Cream	1	1	Formula		
15		TOTALS	52	Formula	Formula		

Insert formulas into these cells.

3. **Click on the *Reorder* filename.**

4. **Click on the Open button.**

Repositioning a Title

Look at the spreadsheet title "Reorder Form" on Figure 8-1. Although you cannot select a range of cells and insert a title in the middle of that range, you can perform a "quick and dirty" centering by placing the title where you think it dominates the columns even if it is not centered.

For example, to reposition the title "Reorder Form" so that it looks centered,

1. **Click on Cell A1.** It presently contains the title.

2. **Pull down the Edit Menu and select Move.**

When the dialog box asks for "destination,"

3. **Type:**   **C1** This is the approximate center of spreadsheet.

4. **Click on OK to complete the move.**

The title should now appear almost in the middle of the screen.

5. **Follow Steps 1 through 4 above to move the date (presently in Cell B2) to Cell C2.**

6. **Click on the deselect box.**

Inserting a Blank Row

To further improve the appearance of the spreadsheet, you will insert a blank row to separate the title and the date. Inserting a row is very similar to inserting a column.

1. **Click on the row header for Row 2 on the left side of the spreadsheet.** The row is highlighted. (See Figure 8-2.)

Figure 8-2

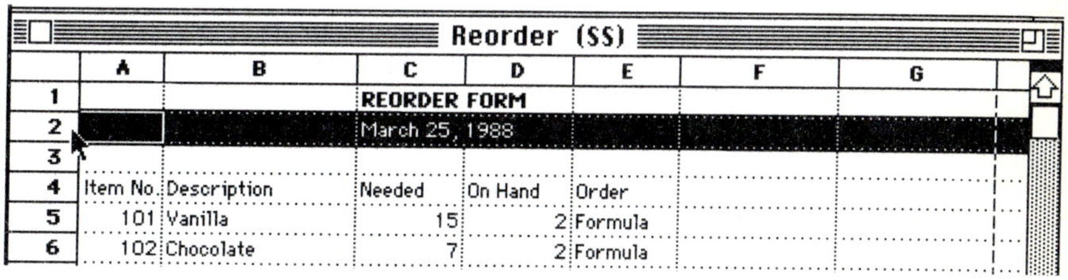

2. **Pull down the Edit Menu and select Insert.** Now you see a blank row between the title and the date.

Inserting a Row at the End of a Range

Chris plans to introduce a new flavor (Caramel Crunch) next week and she estimates that you will need three containers in your store. You must add the new flavor to your *Reorder* spreadsheet. Before you insert a new row and enter the new flavor, look at the formula in Cell C16.

1. **Click on Cell C16.** You see the formula =SUM(C6:C15) in the entry bar.

8 Spreadsheets: Worksheet 3   **99**

What do you think will happen to the formula when you add a row for the new flavor data at the end of the list? To find out, insert a row between Rows 15 and 16, as follows:

2. **Click on the row header for Row 16 on the left side of the spreadsheet.**

3. **Pull down Edit Menu and select Insert.** A new row is inserted.

4. **Click on Cell A16.** This selects the cell in which you want to enter the item number for the new flavor.

5. **Type:** 111

6. **Press:** [RIGHT ARROW] to enter the number *and* move to the cell to the right

7. **Type:** Caramel Crunch

8. **Press:** [RIGHT ARROW] to enter the label *and* move to Cell C16.

9. **Type:** 3 (the amount needed)

10. **Press:** [RIGHT ARROW] to enter the value *and* move to Cell D16. Since you do not yet have any of this new flavor in stock,

11. **Type:** 0 (the number zero)

12. **Press:** [RETURN] to complete the entry of the new flavor.

13. **Click on the deselect box.**

If you were watching your spreadsheet as you entered the 3 into Cell C16, you may have noticed that the total (now in Cell C17) reflected that change immediately. To see why,

14. **Click on Cell C17** (the total of Column C) and you will see the formula =SUM(C6:C16) in the entry bar.

Works automatically expanded the range in the formula in order to accommodate the new flavor! It is important to note that all spreadsheets do not make this adjustment. If you were using such a spreadsheet program, you would have to manually change the range in the formula.

Creating a Formula

As you can see, Column E (Order) is missing its formulas. To insert a formula that will print the difference between Columns C and D (the "Needed" number minus the "On Hand" number),

1. **Click on Cell E6**.

2. **Type:** =C6-D6 This formula will compute the number to order.

3. **Press:** [RETURN] to enter the formula. You see the difference (13) for the first item in Cell E6.

Copying a Formula

By now you probably know how to copy Cell E6 down through the entire column. In case you need help,

1. **Drag the mouse down from Cell E6 through E16.**

2. **Pull down the Edit Menu and select Fill Down.** Column E will display the correct number to reorder for each flavor.

Now you should copy the summing formula in C17 to D17 and E17.

3. **Drag from C17 through E17 to select the cell you want to copy (C17) and the range to which you want to copy it (D17 through E17).**

4. **Pull down Edit Menu and select Fill Right.** The correct totals are now displayed.

Aligning Columns of Data and Their Headings

When Chris drafted her spreadsheet, she did not format the columns. Numbers are usually right aligned for ease of reading. But since all the numbers in Column A contain three digits, you can

8 Spreadsheets: Worksheet 3 **101**

center the entire column. Centering Column A prevents it from running into Column B, which contains labels and is left aligned.

1. **Drag from Cell A5 to A16** to select the entire column, including the heading, for centering.

2. **Pull down Format Menu and select Align Center.** Both labels and amounts are now centered.

The labels for columns of numbers are frequently aligned at the right to agree with the alignment of the numbers.

To realign the headings for Columns C through E,

3. **Drag from Cell C4 through E4** to select the columns you want to realign.

4. **Pull down the Format Menu and select Align Right.**

5. **Click on the deselect box.**

Figure 8-3. The Reorder file with columnar data and headings realigned

	A	B	C	D	E	F	G
1			REORDER FORM				
2			March 25, 1988				
3							
4	Item No.	Description	Needed	On Hand	Order		
5	101	Vanilla	15	2	13		
6	102	Chocolate	7	2	5		
7	103	Strawberry	7	1	6		
8	104	Almond Chocolate	5	1	4		
9	105	Cherry Vanilla	1	0	1		
10	106	Praline 'n Almond	4	2	2		
11	107	Kona Coffee	4	1	3		
12	108	French Vanilla	5	2	3		
13	109	German Chocolate	3	1	2		
14	110	Peaches 'n Cream	1	1	0		
15	111	Caramel Crunch	3	0	3		
16		TOTALS	55	13	42		
17							

102 *Microsoft Works for the Macintosh*

Identifying Your Work

To identify yourself as the creator of this revision and to supply the date of this revision,

➤ 1. **Click on Cell A20.** Use the down scroll arrow to move the screen up if you cannot see Cell A20.

2. **Type:** *your name* and *today's date*.

3. **Press:** **[RETURN].**

4. **Click on the deselect box.**

Protecting Cells

Whenever you have data, especially formulas, that you do not want anyone to accidentally change or destroy, you should ***protect*** the cells in which they are stored. If anyone tries to enter data into a protected cell, the program will sound a warning beep and display a warning message. You and Chris probably do not want anyone tampering with your formulas in Column E and in Row 17. To protect those cells,

➤ 1. **Drag from E6 through E17.**

2. **Pull down the Options Menu and select Protected.**

3. **Repeat the process for Cells C17 and D17.**

4. **Click on the deselect box.**

Although it doesn't appear that anything has happened, now no one can enter any data into those cells unless they remove the protection by using the Options Menu. For example,

➤ 1. **Select Cell E8.**

2. **Type:** 57

Did you get the warning and a message indicating that Cell E8 is protected? As you can see, it would be difficult for someone to accidentally change the spreadsheet.

3. **Click on the OK button** to return to the spreadsheet

4. **Click the deselect box.**

8 Spreadsheets: Worksheet 3   **103**

Saving a File Under a Different Name

By now you should know how to save your spreadsheet under a different name. If you have forgotten how, see Saving a File Under a Different Name at the end of Chapter 7.

Printing a File

Print a copy of your file. If you need help, refer to Printing a File at the end of Chapter 7.

Review

If time permits, load *Reorder* again and without looking at the detailed instructions, practice with this worksheet: center the title and date lines, erase the word "Date," insert a blank line to separate the title and date, make up a new flavor and insert its name and data at the end of the list, create and copy formulas, and realign columns of data or their labels. You may want to further improve the appearance of the spreadsheet by centering the label for the flavors and drawing a line under each column above the total cells. (**Hint**: Underline the data cells in row 15.)

Summary

Congratulations! The Reorder spreadsheet is now complete and you have successfully centered a title, inserted a row, created new formulas, centered columnar data, and protected cells.

Quitting Works

1. **Pull down the File Menu and select Quit.** If you see a message that asks if you want to save changes, click on the appropriate button.

2. **Close all open windows.**

3. **Pull down the Special Menu and select Shut Down.**

4. **Remove the disks and return them to their appropriate places.**

5. **Turn off the Macintosh.**

9 Shortcuts, Charting, and Other Techniques Worksheet 4

Objectives

In this worksheet, you will learn to

- Use keyboard shortcuts
- Enter functions using the Paste Function option
- Create a pie and bar chart
- Size windows to display a spreadsheet and chart at same time
- Print a chart
- Display formulas in cells
- Print selected cells
- Explain If Statements

As with the last word processing worksheet, you will note that the instructions in this worksheet are less detailed and leave more to your imagination. Ready for the challenge?

Setting the Scene

Are you ready for some keyboard shortcuts? Or, how about creating a graph that shows Chris how expenses were distributed in January?

Shortcuts

The following keyboard shortcuts are those most commonly used in place of the menu options. The letters for the keys are listed to the right of the options on the menus.

To use a keyboard command instead of selecting an option with the pointer, hold down [Command] (⌘) and type the letter. For example, to select the Save command, hold down [⌘] and type S. The following table lists some keyboard commands. For a complete list, consult the *Works* manual.

105

Option	Key to type while you press [⌘]
Bold	**B**
Copy	**C**
Go to Cell	**G**
Insert	**I**
Normal Text	**N**
Open	**O**
Print	**P**
Quit	**Q**
Fill Right	**R**
Fill Down	**D**
Save	**S**
Underline	**U**
Undo	**Z**

Entering Functions

Works makes it easy for you to use functions when you are creating formulas even if you are a poor typist or can't remember the name of the function. You can select the function from a list and automatically insert it into your spreadsheet. This is how it works.

1. **Pull down the Edit Menu and select Paste Function.** You see a long list of functions.

2. **Scroll down the list until you find the function you want.**

3. **Click on the function.**

4. **Click on the OK button.** The list disappears, your spreadsheet screen reappears, and the function you selected appears in the entry bar with the insertion bar between the parenthesis marks. To complete the function,

5. **Type the parameters for the formula within the parentheses.** Then

6. **Press [RETURN] or [ENTER].**

Charting

Works can create two types of charts: pie charts and series charts. Pie charts help you see the proportions of a whole. Series charts show relationships between numbers. Series charts include line, bar, stack, and combination charts (bar-and-line charts).

Getting Started ➡

- See Getting Started, Chapter 1, if you need help in turning on the Macintosh and loading *Works*.

Opening a File ➡

- **Open *Receipt1*..** It's on your data disk. If you need help in opening a file, see Opening a File, Chapter 1. Your screen

Figure 9-1. The *Receipt1* spreadsheet

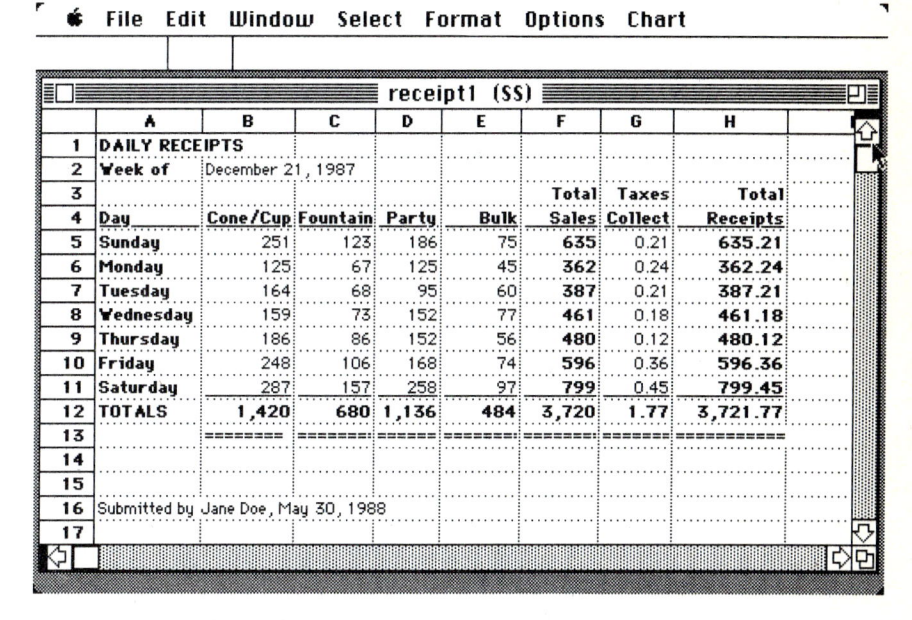

	A	B	C	D	E	F	G	H
1	DAILY RECEIPTS							
2	Week of	December 21, 1987						
3						Total	Taxes	Total
4	Day	Cone/Cup	Fountain	Party	Bulk	Sales	Collect	Receipts
5	Sunday	251	123	186	75	635	0.21	635.21
6	Monday	125	67	125	45	362	0.24	362.24
7	Tuesday	164	68	95	60	387	0.21	387.21
8	Wednesday	159	73	152	77	461	0.18	461.18
9	Thursday	186	86	152	56	480	0.12	480.12
10	Friday	248	106	168	74	596	0.36	596.36
11	Saturday	287	157	258	97	799	0.45	799.45
12	TOTALS	1,420	680	1,136	484	3,720	1.77	3,721.77
13	========	========	========	========	========	========	========	========
14								
15								
16	Submitted by Jane Doe, May 30, 1988							
17								

should display the spreadsheet in Figure 9-1.

Creating a Pie Chart

Review *Receipt1*. You will first create a pie chart in which the entire pie represents total receipts for the week of December 21, 1987. You will need to provide *Works* with some essential information:

- The **dollar** amounts. These are contained in Column H.

9 Shortcuts, Charting, and Other Techniques

- The **days**. These are contained in Rows 5 through 11.

Follow the steps to define and create this pie chart.

1. **Pull down the Chart Menu and select New Pie Chart.**
   You see The Pie Chart Definition dialog box as shown in Figure 9-2.

Figure 9-2. The Pie Chart definition box

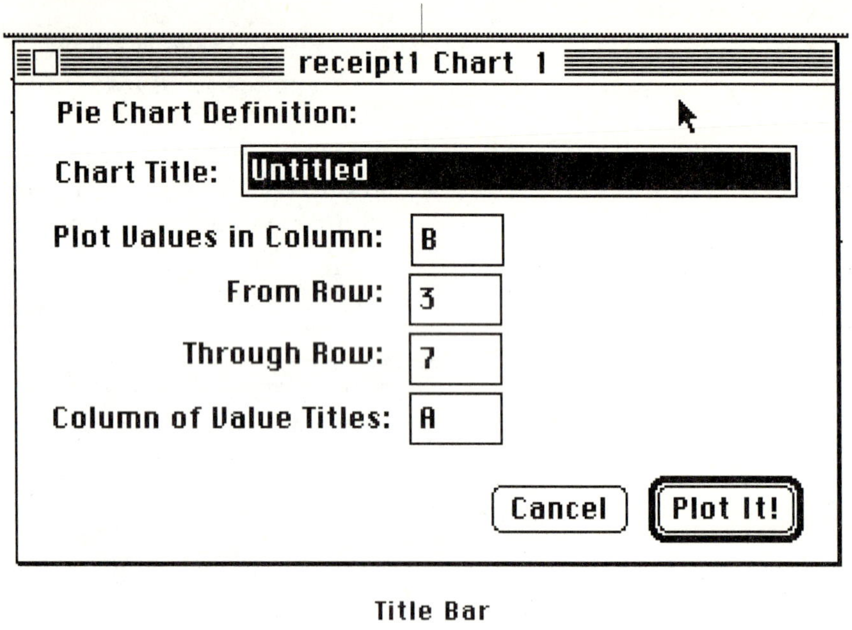

```
┌─────────────── receipt1 Chart 1 ───────────────┐
│ Pie Chart Definition:                          │
│                                                │
│ Chart Title: │Untitled                        │
│                                                │
│ Plot Values in Column:  [B]                    │
│           From Row:  [3]                       │
│        Through Row:  [7]                       │
│ Column of Value Titles: [A]                    │
│                                                │
│                         [Cancel]  [[Plot It!]] │
└────────────────────────────────────────────────┘
                    Title Bar
```

2. **If you want to look at portions of the spreadsheet while you are completing the dialog box, move the pointer to the title bar of the dialog box. Hold down the mouse button while you drag the dialog box up and down the screen. Release the mouse button when the dialog box is where you want it.**

You will note that the Chart Title: box is currently selected (highlighted). To change to a more descriptive title,

3. **Type: Daily Receipts**

From the filled-in information, you can see that *Works* has made some assumptions regarding the information you want to use from the spreadsheet. Unfortunately, those assumptions are not correct in this case. You will have to make some changes since you want to plot (draw) the values in Column H, not the data in default Column B.

Microsoft Works for the Macintosh

4. **Press** [TAB] to move the cursor to the Plot Values in Column: box.

5. **Type:** H

The expenses are in Rows 5 through 11 in Column A. So,

6. **Press** [TAB] to the From Row: box.

7. **Type:** 5

8. **Press** [TAB] to the Through Row: box.

9. **Type:** 11

Since the default Column A is correct for the Column of Value Titles: box,

10. **Move the pointer to the Plot It! button and click once.**
    You see a pie chart similar to Figure 9-3.

Figure 9-3. The pie chart *Daily Receipts* drawn from the data in the *Receipt1* spreadsheet

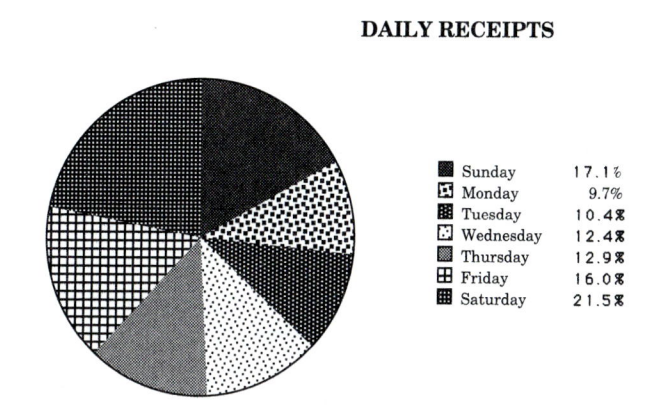

DAILY RECEIPTS

■	Sunday	17.1%
▨	Monday	9.7%
▨	Tuesday	10.4%
▨	Wednesday	12.4%
▨	Thursday	12.9%
▨	Friday	16.0%
▨	Saturday	21.5%

Sizing Windows

One of the advantages of having a chart program within a spreadsheet program is that if you change the spreadsheet, the graph will also change. Suppose you project an increase in sales on Friday. Imagine how much trouble it would be to recompute all the figures and to redraw the chart? You can easily complete this task with *Works*. Before you do, however, you will reduce the size of both windows so that both the spreadsheet and the chart are visible at the same time. This way, you can immediately see how the changes in the spreadsheet affect the chart. For an effective layout, see Figure 9-4.

Figure 9-4. Both spreadsheet and pie chart are visible on the screen at the same time.

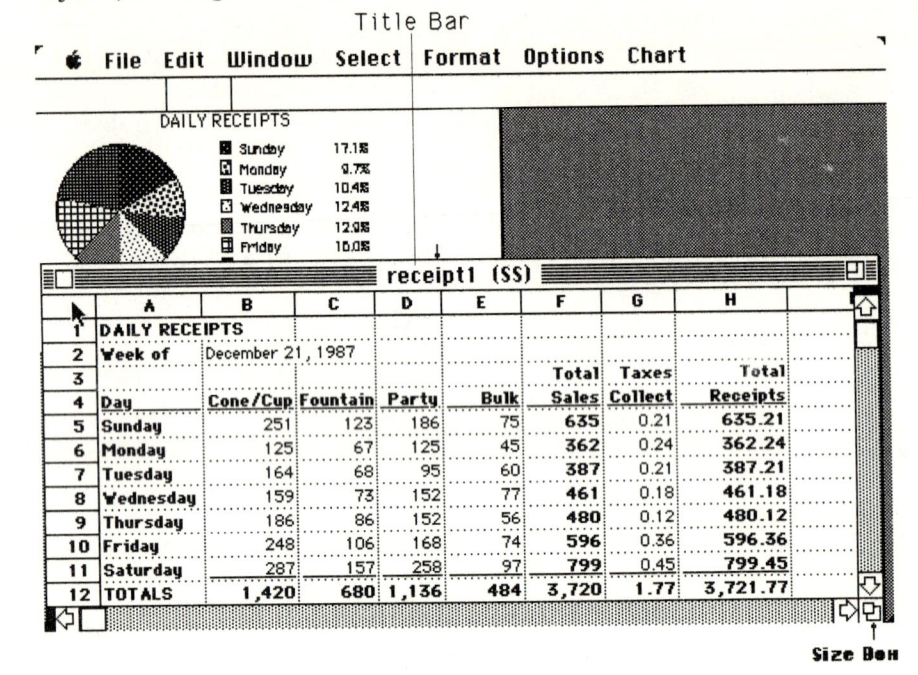

Follow the steps below to reposition the windows to resemble Figure 9-4. The pie chart should be the only window visible on your screen as you start.

1. **Move the pointer to the size box in the lower right corner of the pie chart window. Hold down the mouse button while you drag the size box up and to the left until the pointer is about in the middle of the screen.**

2. **Release the mouse button.**

When you release the mouse button, the pie chart window will shrink to about one-fourth its original size. See Figure 9-5.

You now can see part of the *Receipt1* spreadsheet behind the pie chart. To select the spreadsheet window so that you can reduce its size,

110   *Microsoft Works for the Macintosh*

Figure 9-5. Note the size box at the lower right corner of the chart window.

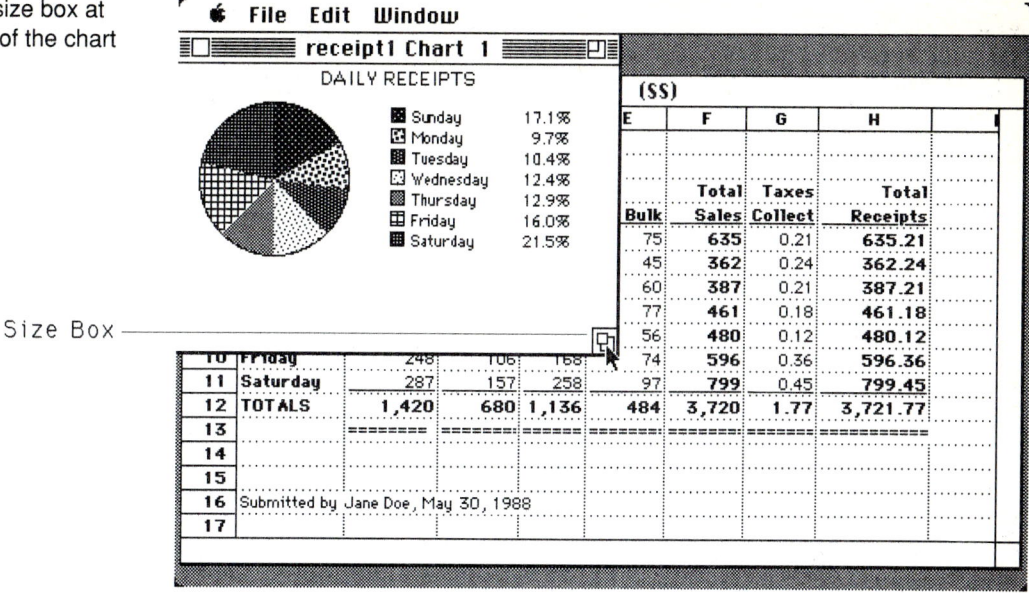

Size Box

3. **Click anywhere on the spreadsheet.**

   The spreadsheet window is now the active window. Follow the steps to shrink the spreadsheet window and move it to the bottom of the screen.

4. **Move the pointer to the size box in the lower right corner of the spreadsheet window and drag the size box up under Row 12 (the Totals line).**

5. **Release the mouse button.** The window now displays only Rows 1-12 of the spreadsheet.

6. **Move the pointer to the spreadsheet window title bar and drag it down until the spreadsheet window is in the bottom half of the screen.** Your screen should look like Figure 9-6.

   If you cannot see the entire pie chart and the spreadsheet down through the Totals line, use the title bars and size boxes to move and size the windows again. Use the scroll bar arrows if some needed data is not displayed.

9 Shortcuts, Charting, and Other Techniques **111**

Figure 9-6

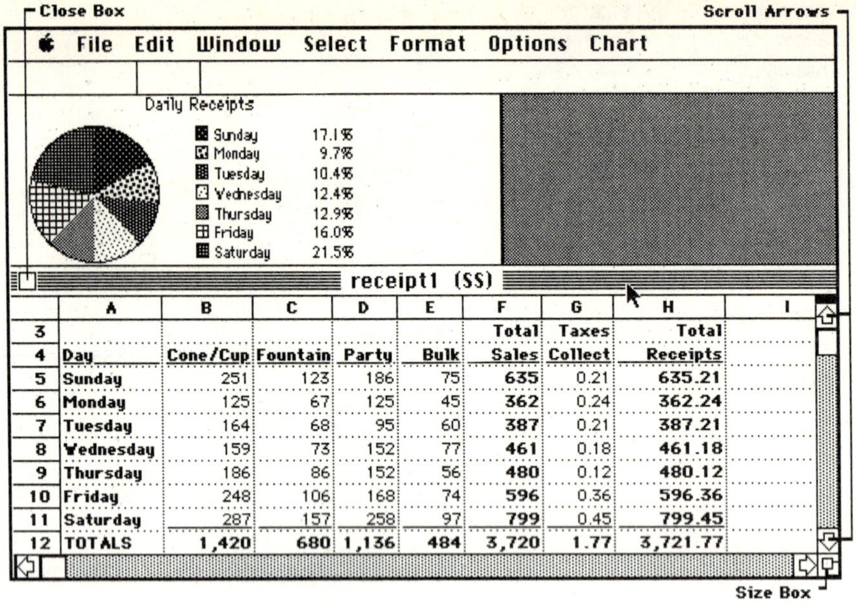
Close Box
Scroll Arrows
File Edit Window Select Format Options Chart
Daily Receipts
Sunday 17.1%
Monday 9.7%
Tuesday 10.4%
Wednesday 12.4%
Thursday 12.9%
Friday 16.0%
Saturday 21.5%
receipt1 (SS)
A B C D E F G H I
3 Total Taxes Total
4 Day Cone/Cup Fountain Party Bulk Sales Collect Receipts
5 Sunday 251 123 186 75 635 0.21 635.21
6 Monday 125 67 125 45 362 0.24 362.24
7 Tuesday 164 68 95 60 387 0.21 387.21
8 Wednesday 159 73 152 77 461 0.18 461.18
9 Thursday 186 86 152 56 480 0.12 480.12
10 Friday 248 106 168 74 596 0.36 596.36
11 Saturday 287 157 258 97 799 0.45 799.45
12 TOTALS 1,420 680 1,136 484 3,720 1.77 3,721.77
Size Box

Next you are going to record a dramatic increase in Cone/Cup sales for Saturday and see the changes automatically reflected in the pie chart.

1. **Click on Cell B11.**
2. **Type: 2000**
3. **Press: [RETURN].** Your screen should now look like Figure 9-7.

Not only did the Cone/Cup sales on the spreadsheet jump from 287 to 2,000, but the Cone/Cup segment of the chart at the same time changed from 22% to 46.2%. Because the chart is linked directly to the spreadsheet, any change in the spreadsheet is automatically reflected on the chart.

If you missed seeing the change, replace the original number (287) and watch the change in the pie chart. Then repeat Steps 1-3 to change the number back to 2,000.

Printing a Pie Chart

The Print Window command prints a copy of whatever appears in the active window. (The active window displays a title bar.) You can give the command at almost any time. You will learn more about printing charts in the Integration worksheet, Chapter 14.

Figure 9-7. Note Saturday cone/cup sales on the left side of the pie chart.

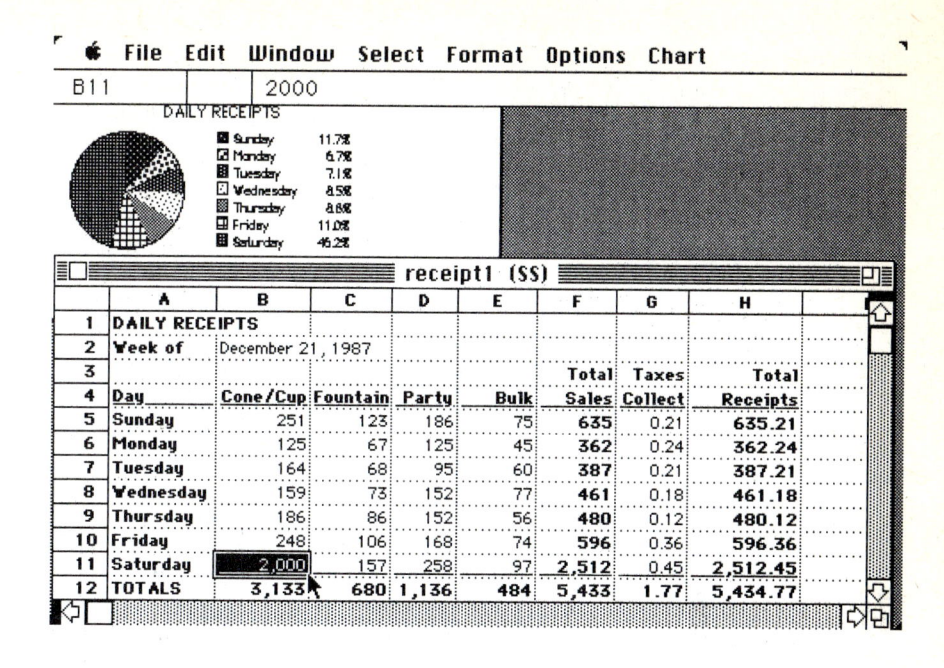

To print the pie chart,

• **Pull down File Menu and select Print Window.**

Creating a Bar Chart

How would the information that we used to create the pie chart appear in a bar chart? To find out,

1. **Close the pie chart window.** The *Receipt1* spreadsheet is now the only file open.

2. **Pull down the Chart Menu and select New Series Chart.**

You may want to rearrange the Chart Definition dialog box and the spreadsheet window so that you can see both the box and the window at the same time. Follow the steps below to guide you.

1. **Move the pointer to the dialog box title bar. (See Figure 9-8.) Drag the box down until the dialog box title bar is about in the middle of the screen.**

9 Shortcuts, Charting, and Other Techniques   **113**

Figure 9-8. Note the pointer on the title bar.

	A	B	C	D	E	F	G	H
				receipt1 (SS)				
4	Day	Cone/Cup	Fountain	Party	Bulk	Sales	Collect	Receipts
5	Sunday	251	123	186	75	635	0.21	635.21
6	Monday	125	67	125	45	362	0.24	362.24
7	Tuesday	164	68	95	60	387	0.21	387.21
8	Wednesday	159	73	152	77	461	0.18	461.18
9	Thursday	186	86	152	56	480	0.12	480.12
10	Friday	248	106	168	74	596	0.36	596.36
11	Saturday	2,000	157	258	97	2,512	0.45	2,512.45
12	TOTALS	3,133	680	1,136	484	5,433	1.77	5,434.77

receipt1 Chart 2

Type of Chart: LINE, BAR, ...
Values to be Plotted: 1st Row: 3, 2nd Row: 4, 3rd Row:, 4th Row:, From Column: B
Vertical Scale: ● Numeric ○ Semi-Logarithmic
Maximum:
Minimum: 0

2. Move the pointer anywhere within the spreadsheet and click once to select it.

3. If the spreadsheet is not already at the top of the screen, move the pointer to the spreadsheet title bar and drag it there.

4. Move the pointer anywhere within the dialog box and click once to select it.

From now on, you can drag the dialog box up, down, left, or right as necessary to view the spreadsheet or to fill in the dialog box. You can also scroll the spreadsheet window to display any needed data.

Now continue creating the bar chart. Look at Figure 9-8 again. For the purpose of initial identification, *Works* has already assigned the name "Receipt1 Chart 2" to your chart definition. But that name will not appear on your completed chart. Note that the Chart Title box is selected (highlighted). Here you can type the title that you want to appear on the chart. You will also identify yourself in the title as the creator of the chart. In the Chart Title box,

➡ 1. Type: **Receipts by *Your Name***

The next box asks for the Vertical (up and down) Scale Title, and the box after that asks for Horizontal (side to side) Scale Title. The values in Column H are dollars and the values in Rows 5, 10, 11 represent days. (Remember that you can move the dialog box around to see unexposed parts of the spreadsheet.) So,

2. Press   [TAB] to select the Vertical Scale Title: box.

3. Type: **Dollars**

4. Press   [TAB] to select the Horizontal Scale Title: box.

5. Type: **Days**

For type of chart (in the upper left corner of the dialog box), select Bar.

6. **Move the pointer to the Bar icon or its button and click once.**

Works again tries to help you by inserting some assumed information in the upper middle boxes of the dialog box window. Unfortunately, most of these values are incorrect for your graph. So, first of all, type in the rows and columns for the values you want to plot.

7. Press: [TAB] to move the 1st Row: box.

8. Type: **10** (the row for Friday)

9. Press: [TAB].

10. Type: **11**

11. Press: [TAB].

12. Type: **5**

13. Press: [TAB] until you reach the From Column: box.

9 Shortcuts, Charting, and Other Techniques   **115**

14. **Type:** H

15. **Press:** [TAB] until the cursor is in the To Column: box. Now, since you want only Column H ("Total Receipts"),

16. **Type:** H

Because the data is in normal numeric format, and because you need no maximum or minimum values for your scale, and because you want a grid (lines) and labels to appear, you do not have to enter any more specifications into the dialog box. Your screen should look like Figure 9-9.

Figure 9-9. Chart dialog box with arrow on the title bar

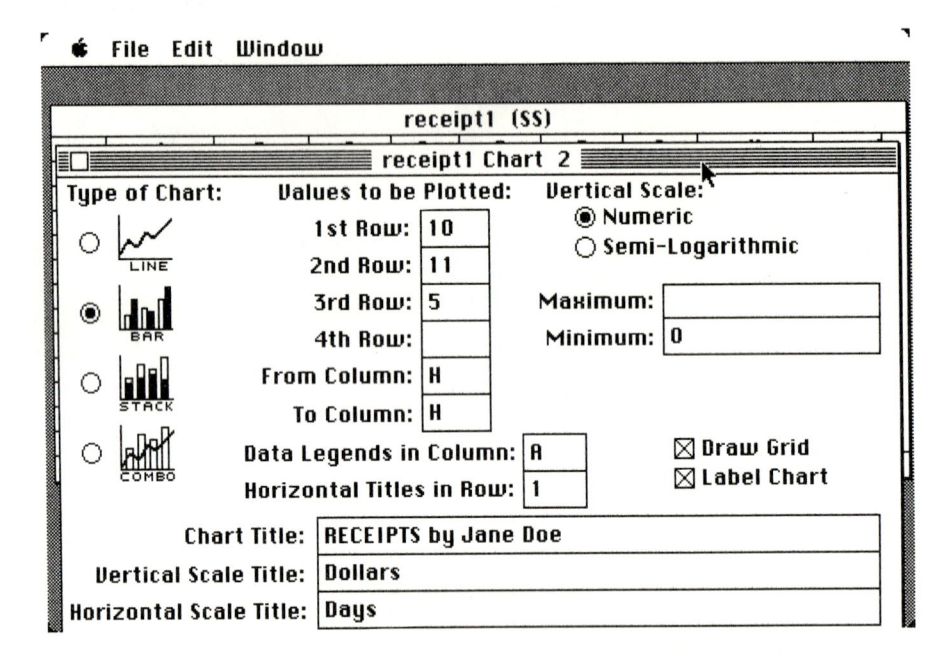

17. **Drag the dialog box up to the top of the screen and click Plot It!** You will see a bar chart similar to the one in Figure 9-10.

Printing a Chart

1. **Turn on the printer and check to be certain it is ready to print.**

2. **If the chart window is not active, move the pointer anywhere within the chart window and click once.**

116 *Microsoft Works for the Macintosh*

Figure 9-10. Bar chart

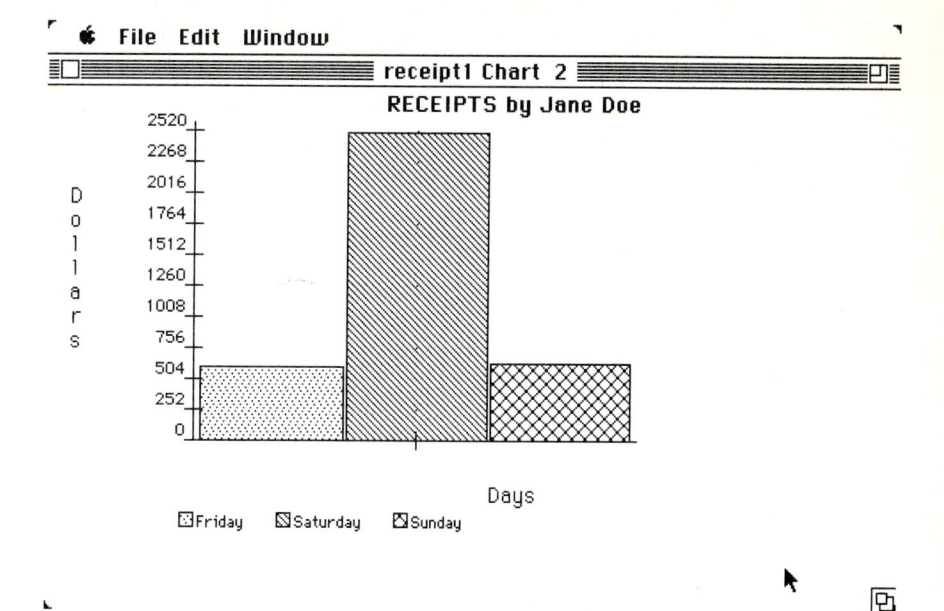

To print a chart, you use the Print Window command. It prints a copy of whatever appears in the active window.

3. Pull down the File Menu and select Print Window.

You can use the Print Window command at almost any time. (You will learn more about printing charts in the Integration worksheet, Chapter 14.) Now close the chart window.

4. Pull down the File Menu and select Close. You see the spreadsheet window, which was behind the chart window.

Saving a Chart

In *Works,* the **specifications** (not the charts) are automatically stored with the spreadsheet whenever you close the chart window. As a result, if you change a spreadsheet figure that has been plotted in a graph, the graph will also change the next time you recall it. The program does not erase the specifications unless you tell it to.

To save this spreadsheet and the specifications for your two charts under a different name and to leave the present file, *Receipt1,* untouched for future use, complete the following steps.

9 Shortcuts, Charting, and Other Techniques **117**

➡ 1. **Pull down the File Menu and select Save As.**

2. **If your data disk is not the active disk, click on the Drive button.**

3. **Type: Receipt2**

4. **Click on the Save button.**

To check to see that the file contains the chart specifications,

➡ 1. **Pull down the Chart Menu and select Select Definition.**

You see the Select Chart dialog box. It lists your chart definitions by using *Work's* assigned Chart Definition titles. If you want to see the definition for either chart, simply select it. To cancel the selection,

2. **Click on the Cancel button.**

Showing Formula(s)

It is always desirable to print the spreadsheet formulas in order to check their accuracy.

➡ • **Pull down the Option Menu and select Show Formulas.**

The formula(s) will show in place of the figures. You may have to use the two-way arrow to change the width of the cells in order to see the complete formulas. (For the arrow, see Figure 9-11.)

Printing Options

At times you may want to print only a portion of a spreadsheet. You can by following the steps below.

➡ 1. **Drag to select the portion you want to print.**

2. **Pull down File Menu and select Print.**

3. **Click the appropriate options.**

4. **Click the OK button.**

Figure 9-11. Two-way arrow appears between Columns F and G

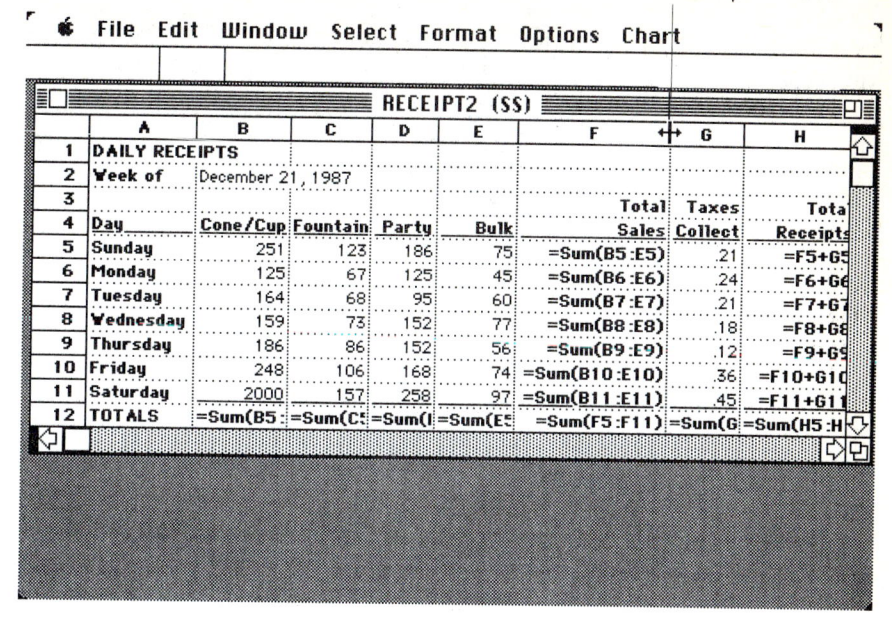

	A	B	C	D	E	F	G	H
1	DAILY RECEIPTS							
2	Week of	December 21, 1987						
3								
4	Day	Cone/Cup	Fountain	Party	Bulk	Total Sales	Taxes Collect	Total Receipts
5	Sunday	251	123	186	75	=Sum(B5:E5)	.21	=F5+G5
6	Monday	125	67	125	45	=Sum(B6:E6)	.24	=F6+G6
7	Tuesday	164	68	95	60	=Sum(B7:E7)	.21	=F7+G7
8	Wednesday	159	73	152	77	=Sum(B8:E8)	.18	=F8+G8
9	Thursday	186	86	152	56	=Sum(B9:E9)	.12	=F9+G9
10	Friday	248	106	168	74	=Sum(B10:E10)	.36	=F10+G10
11	Saturday	2000	157	258	97	=Sum(B11:E11)	.45	=F11+G11
12	TOTALS	=Sum(B5:	=Sum(C5:	=Sum(D5:	=Sum(E5:	=Sum(F5:F11)	=Sum(G5:	=Sum(H5:H

If Statement

You can use the **If Statement** in situations where a cell's content is contingent upon the content of another cell. For example, look at Figure 9-12. It shows an If Statement on the *Reorder* spreadsheet.

Figure 9-12

AS STORED IN MEMORY:

	A	B	C	D	E
1			REORDER FORM		
2					
3	ITEM	NEEDED	ON HAND	DIFFERENCE	ORDER
4					
5	Vanilla	5	2	=B5-C5	=If(D5>1,D5,0)
6	Chocolate	4	3	=B6-C6	=If(D6>1,D6,0)

AS DISPLAYED ON SCREEN:

	A	B	C	D	E
1			REORDER FORM		
2					
3	ITEM	NEEDED	ON HAND	DIFFERENCE	ORDER
4					
5	Vanilla	5	2	3	3
6	Chocolate	4	3	1	0

9 Shortcuts, Charting, and Other Techniques

As you can see, the formulas in Column D subtract the supply of containers "on hand" from the "needed" amount. However, suppose that you did not want to reorder an item unless you had used *more* than one container of that item. The If Statement in Column E makes that calculation for you. The If Statement

$$=IF\ D5>1,D5,0$$

translates as follows: "If the content of Cell D5 is greater than 1, then the program will display the content of Cell D5. If the content of Cell D5 is not greater than 1, then the program will display 0 in Cell E5.

Summary

This is the end of the spreadsheet worksheets. You have been introduced to many of the tools available when using spreadsheets. To learn more, pull down the Window Menu and select Help or refer to the *Works* manual.

Quitting Works

1. **Pull down the File Menu and select Quit.** If you have forgotten to save your document, a message will appear to remind you to do it. After you click in the appropriate box,

2. **Pull down the Special Menu and select Shut Down.**

3. **Remove the disks and return them to their appropriate places.**

4. **Turn off the Macintosh.**

10 Database Worksheet 1

Database Background

The term *database* is broadly applied to any large collections of related information (data). For example, two familiar manual databases are the telephone directory (a collection of names with addresses and phone numbers) and a recipe file (a collection of recipe titles with the ingredients and instructions for preparation).

Databases are made up of ***records***. One record describes one entry (or single item) in the collection. In a telephone directory, a record is the data about one subscriber. For the recipe file, a record is the data for one recipe.

Each record is composed of ***fields***. For example, a record in the telephone directory has a name field, address field, and phone-number field. A record in a recipe file has a category field, ingredients field, and an instructions field.

Obviously, the manner in which records are organized has a major effect on how easily you can find a specific record. For example, in searching the telephone directory, you know the name of a person or company and you want the telephone number. For that reason, the telephone database is organized alphabetically by name.

Suppose, however, that you do not know a name—that all you know is a telephone number and what you really want is to find out the name of the person or company that belongs to the number. Or suppose you have scribbled an address on a scratch pad and forgotten the name of the company it belongs to. Can you find the company in a traditional telephone book? No, you cannot.

However, when a database is stored on a computer by a database program, you are not limited to just one search method. For example, you can search by name, address, or phone number. You can also view the database as individual records on the screen or as a list that displays all records (or just selected records). In some cases, you can move the database records into *Works* word processor documents and thus create more informative reports. *Works* can also perform calculations using some of the fields.

Besides *Works*, three popular database programs are *dBase III*™, *Filemaker*™, and *RBase*™.

In the following worksheets, you will use *Works* to retrieve a database file from your *Works Data Disk*, change the database, and then create a new database file. After you have completed the exercises, you should be able to create a simple database of your own.

Objectives

In this worksheet, you will learn how to

- Recognize fields and records
- View a file as a list and as a form
- Select records
- Search records
- Sort records
- Enter new data
- Add fields to a record
- Add a record to a database

Setting the Scene

In order to more efficiently manage The Ice Cream Factory, Chris Hughes has created a simple database of information about the employees. As well as keeping track of addresses and phone numbers, Chris plans to use it to create work schedules and identify employees in line for raises. As the manager of your branch of The Ice Cream Factory, you will update and revise the database and learn how to use it to keep Chris informed.

Getting Started

- **Open *Works*** as described in Getting Started, Chapter 1. You see the Open dialog box on your screen.

Opening a File

The database file with which you will work is already stored on your *Works Data Disk* under the filename *Profile*. To open the file,

1. **Insert the *Works Data Disk* into the second disk drive**.

2. **If necessary, click on the Drive button to change drives until the data disk is the active disk.**

3. **Move the pointer to the Database icon and click once.**
   Now you see only database files in the list box.

4. **Move the pointer to the filename *Profile* and click once.**

5. **Move the pointer to the Open button and click once.** A file similar to Figure 10-1, page 124, will appear.

Viewing a Database File As a List

Study Figure 10-1. Note that the menu bar is similar to the word processor and spreadsheet menu bar. The ***entry bar*** is similar to the spreadsheet entry bar. You use it to enter data and to edit the contents of the active cell.

You can organize and review the information in a database as a list in a list window or a form in a form window (which you will learn more about later). In a ***list*** window, each ***record*** (here, information relating to each employee) occupies one line in the list and the records are listed one under the other. The ***field*** names (here, the labels for each item of information for each employee) are strung across the top of the window. (For example, you see "LAST NAME," "FIRST NAME," etc.).

The list window lets you work with a database much as you did with spreadsheets in the last worksheets. Viewing your database as a list enables you to see many records at one time. It is therefore very handy when making comparisons or trying to get an overall picture of what records are in the database.

If you would like to see the rest of the database in the list window, you can use the scroll bars. Try it.

1. **Move the pointer to the right arrow in the horizontal scroll bar at the bottom of the screen. Cick the mouse button until you reach the last field in the record (Time Available).** To move back to the first field (Last Name),

2. **Move the pointer to the left arrow in the horizontal scroll bar at the bottom of the screen. Click the mouse button until you reach the first field in the record** (Last Name).

10 Database: Worksheet 1 **123**

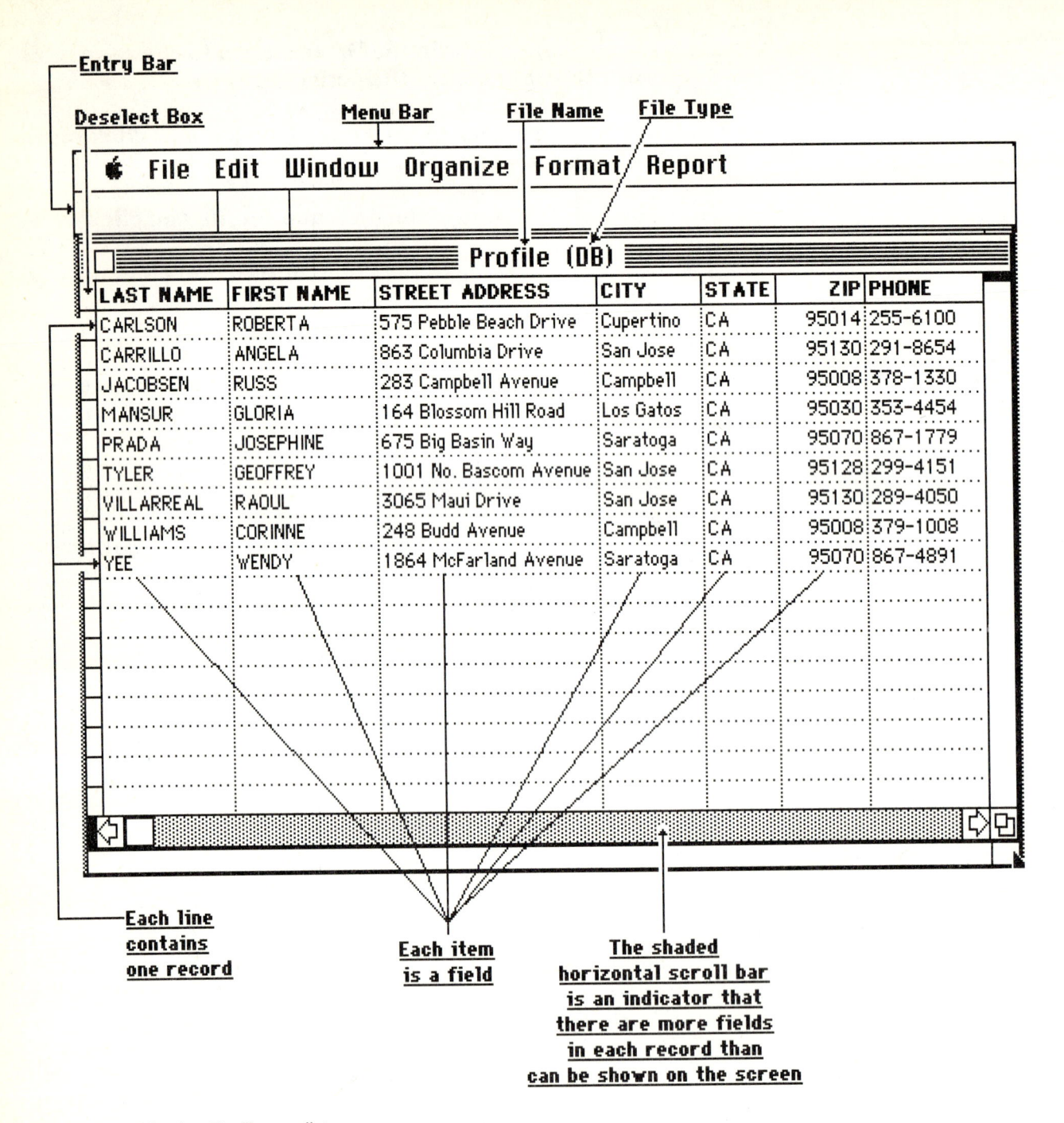

— Entry Bar
Deselect Box   Menu Bar   File Name   File Type

| | File | Edit | Window | Organize | Format | Report |

Profile (DB)

LAST NAME	FIRST NAME	STREET ADDRESS	CITY	STATE	ZIP	PHONE
CARLSON	ROBERTA	575 Pebble Beach Drive	Cupertino	CA	95014	255-6100
CARRILLO	ANGELA	863 Columbia Drive	San Jose	CA	95130	291-8654
JACOBSEN	RUSS	283 Campbell Avenue	Campbell	CA	95008	378-1330
MANSUR	GLORIA	164 Blossom Hill Road	Los Gatos	CA	95030	353-4454
PRADA	JOSEPHINE	675 Big Basin Way	Saratoga	CA	95070	867-1779
TYLER	GEOFFREY	1001 No. Bascom Avenue	San Jose	CA	95128	299-4151
VILLARREAL	RAOUL	3065 Maui Drive	San Jose	CA	95130	289-4050
WILLIAMS	CORINNE	248 Budd Avenue	Campbell	CA	95008	379-1008
YEE	WENDY	1864 McFarland Avenue	Saratoga	CA	95070	867-4891

— Each line contains one record

Each item is a field

The shaded horizontal scroll bar is an indicator that there are more fields in each record than can be shown on the screen

Figure 10-1. Viewing *Profile* as a list

124   *Microsoft Works for the Macintosh*

Viewing a Database File As a Form

The list window is rather awkward when the database has a large number of fields that take more than one screen to display or when you want to analyze all the field entries relating to one record and the fields extend beyond the screen. *Profile* has 12 fields (or 12 columns in the list window). To see all the information about one person, it is easier to view the record as a **Form** in the form window, which can display the entire record for each person. (The form was designed by the person who created the file.) To display the form view for Profile,

➡ 1. **Pull down the Format Menu and select Show Form.** You see a layout of fields and entries similar to Figure 10-2.

Figure 10-2. Viewing *Profile* As a form

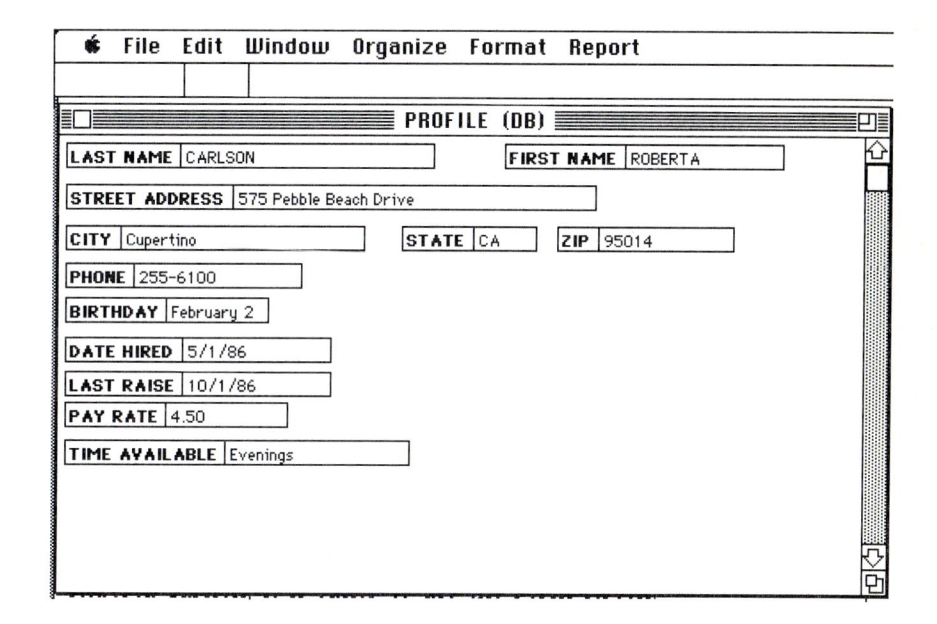

The information in the form is the same as the information in the list. The two formats are just arranged differently. In general, the list-format record is more like the telephone-book entry. The form-format record is more like a recipe card. To return to the list,

2. **Pull down the Format Menu and select Show List.**

Selecting Records

When you set up record-selection rules (criteria), *Works* can find specific records. For example, look at the database. Suppose Angela Carrillo, who works in the afternoons, calls in sick. You

10 Database: Worksheet 1   **125**

can find all the employees who are available to work the afternoon shift. You can use the Record Selection dialog box. See Figure 10-3.

➡ 1. **Pull down the Organize Menu and choose Record Selection.**

Figure 10-3. The Record Selection dialog box and the Record Selection Field Name box

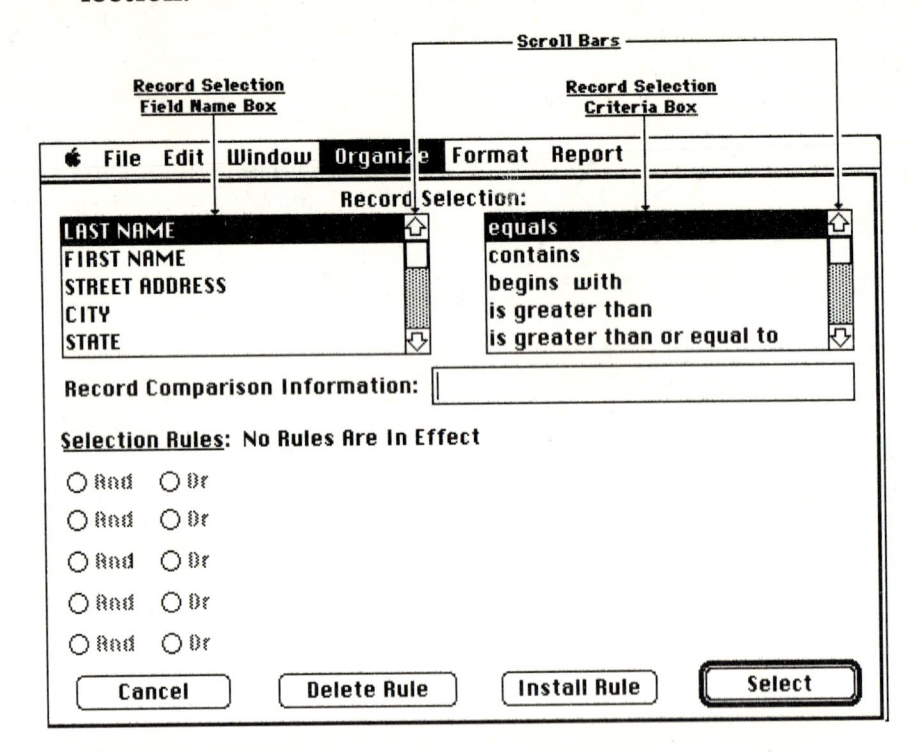

[Screenshot of Record Selection dialog box showing the Record Selection Field Name Box on the left containing LAST NAME, FIRST NAME, STREET ADDRESS, CITY, STATE; the Record Selection Criteria Box on the right containing equals, contains, begins with, is greater than, is greater than or equal to; with Scroll Bars labeled; a Record Comparison Information field; Selection Rules: No Rules Are In Effect with And/Or radio buttons; and Cancel, Delete Rule, Install Rule, Select buttons.]

The field name you want is not visible in the Record Selection Field Name box. You will have to scroll down.

2. **Move the pointer to the scroll bar to the right of the box containing the field names. Click below the scroll box until you see "Time Available."**

3. **Click once on Time Available field to select it.**

4. **Click once on the word "contains" in the Record Selection Criteria box.**

The blinking insertion point is in the Record Comparison Information box. This is where you will identify the rest of your criteria

126   *Microsoft Works for the Macintosh*

for the search. To complete the selection criteria for "Time Available Contains,"

5. **Type: afternoons** Double check the spelling. If you misspell, the program cannot find the correct records. Since there is no other criterion,

6. **Click on the Install Rule button.** To apply this selection rule,

7. **Click on the Select button.**

Works will now find all the records that contain "Afternoons" in the Time Available field. You will now see a list of the employees who can work in the afternoons. Because the Time Available field is the last field and therefore does not show on the screen, check the accuracy of this search by scrolling to the right.

8. **Click to the right of the scroll box in the horizontal scroll bar until the Time Available field is visible.** Now you can see that all the listed employees are available in the afternoons. To view all records in the database again,

9. **Pull down the Organize Menu and select Show All Records.**

10. **Drag the scroll box in the horizontal scroll bar back to the left side of the scroll bar to bring the names into view again.**

Entering New Data

A new employee has been hired recently and you need to add her record to the database. You can add a new record in either the list or form window. Since you have only one record to add, you can insert it into the correct alphabetical position. However, if you have many new records to add, you can simply type them at the end of the list and then have *Works* sort the entire list alphabetically.

For the sake of learning the technique, you will let *Works* insert the new record alphabetically so that you may see how easy it would be if there were numerous new entries. While the list window is still open,

➡️ 1. **Click once on the blank field under the last name, YEE.** This puts you in position to add a new-employee record. Now move to the form window.

2. **Pull down the Format Menu and select Show Form.** You see a blank form with the Last Name field selected.

3. **Type: HIRVONEN**

As you can see, HIRVONEN appears in the entry bar but not on the form itself. If you make a typing mistake at this point, you can still use [DEL] or [BACKSPACE] to erase errors. Now that you know how to correct typos,

4. **Press: [TAB].** This accomplishes two things. First, you insert the name into the field. Second, you get ready to insert an entry into the next field.

5. **Type   PIA** To insert this first name and to move to the Street Address field,

6. **Press: [TAB].**

If you notice a mistake in a field after you have pressed the tab key and continued on to the next field, you can return to the previous field to correct your mistake by pressing [SHIFT]-[TAB] until the field you want to correct is selected. Use the following data to complete filling in the form.

STREET ADDRESS:	823 Barcelona Drive
CITY:	San Jose
STATE:	CA
ZIP:	95130
PHONE:	298-8489
BIRTHDAY:	August 23
DATE HIRED:	10/2/87
LAST RAISE:	
PAY RATE:	4.00
TIME AVAILABLE:	Evenings

When you have entered all the information correctly,

7. **Press: [ENTER]** to record the last field and stay on form.

128   *Microsoft Works for the Macintosh*

Sorting a Database

Works can sort a database file in alphabetical, numerical, or chronological order, either backwards or forwards. It can sort on any field, in either the form or list window.

Works can also sort in succession on different fields so that you can group your records just the way you want them. You control each sort individually by repeatedly selecting the Sort command. (If you want more information on sorting, consult your *Works* manual.) For this exercise, we will do a simple alphabetical sort from the list window.

➡ 1. **Pull down the Format Menu and select Show List.**

2. **Click in the box labeled "Last Name."** The entire column is selected.

3. **Pull down the Organize Menu and select Sort.** When the Sort dialog box appears (as in Figure 10-4), you will notice that the field name "Last Name" is already selected for you and *Works* has assumed that you want an alphabetical sort from A to Z.

To confirm the selections in the dialog box,

Figure 10-4. The Sort dialog box

4. **Click the OK button.** If you want to sort in a different sequence, you would simply click once on the appropriate option.

The records are now in alphabetical order by last name.

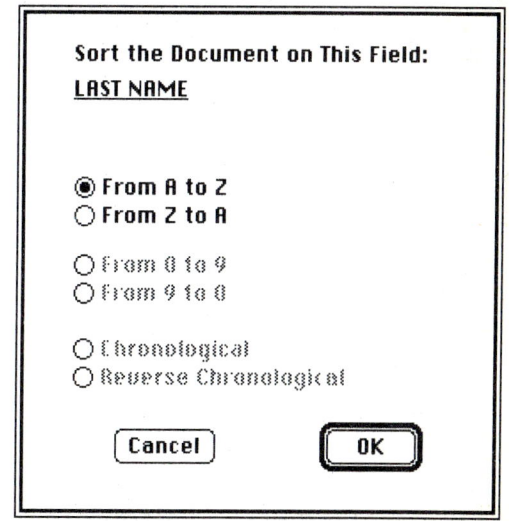

Modifying a Form

Because he plans to return to school as a full-time student, Raoul Villarreal resigned from work on December 18. To keep track of resignations and the reasons for them, you decide to add two new fields (Termination and Comments) and to fill in those fields for Raoul's record.

10 Database: Worksheet 1 **129**

First, you need to use the form window to modify the design of the existing form.

➡ 1. **Pull down the Format Menu and select Show Form.**

2. **Pull down the Edit Menu and select Add New Field.** You see the Field Name dialog box.

3. **Type:		TERMINATION**

4. **Click on Add Field.** Note that *Works* has added the new field below the last item on the form. You can move it to a different location later. To add the next new field,

5. **Pull down Edit Menu again and select Add New Field.**

6. **Type:		COMMENTS**

7. **Click on Add Field button.**

To move the Termination field next to the Time Available field,

8. **Move the pointer to the Termination field until the pointer becomes a hand.**

9. **Hold down the mouse button and drag the outline of the Termination field to the new position. Release the mouse button.** (See Figure 10-5, page 131.)

To move the Comments field up closer to the Time Available field,

10. **Move the pointer to Comments field until the pointer becomes a hand.**

11. **Hold down the mouse button and drag the outline of the Comments field up. Release the mouse button.**

The space for comments is too short. To allow more space for that field on all records in the file,

12. **Move the pointer to the right edge of the rectangle until the pointer becomes a two-way arrow.**

Microsoft Works for the Macintosh

Figure 10-5. New fields added

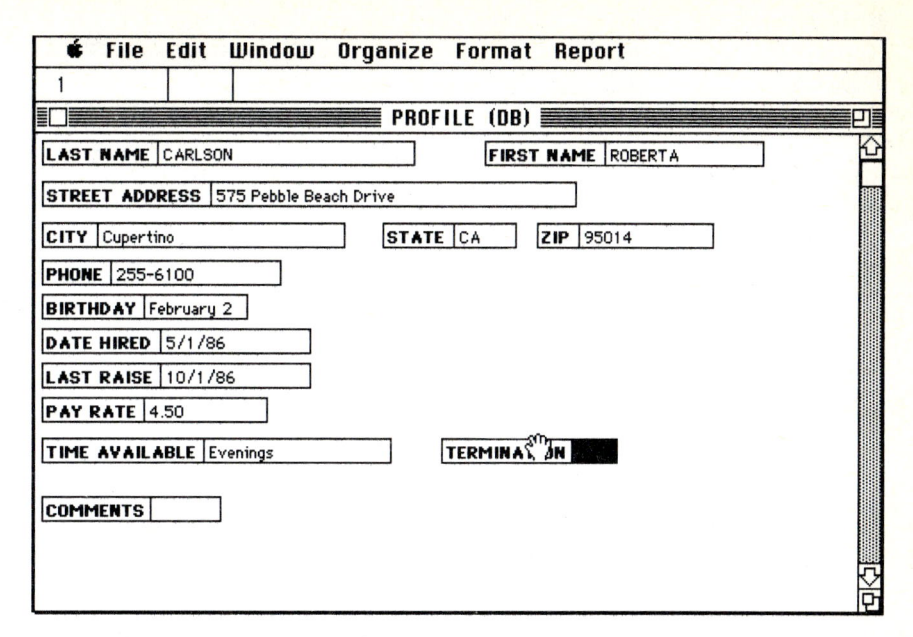

```
     File   Edit   Window   Organize   Format   Report
 1
═══════════════════════ PROFILE (DB) ═══════════════════════
 LAST NAME | CARLSON            FIRST NAME | ROBERTA
 STREET ADDRESS | 575 Pebble Beach Drive
 CITY | Cupertino         STATE | CA     ZIP | 95014
 PHONE | 255-6100
 BIRTHDAY | February 2
 DATE HIRED | 5/1/86
 LAST RAISE | 10/1/86
 PAY RATE | 4.50
 TIME AVAILABLE | Evenings     TERMINATION
 COMMENTS |
```

13. **Hold down the mouse button and drag the mouse to the end of the line. Release the mouse button.** Your Comments field is now long enough to accommodate a sentence.

14. **Repeat Steps 12-14 to increase the size of the Termination field.**

You are now ready to enter Raoul's resignation. First you need to find Raoul's record.

Searching a Database

To locate Raoul's record, you use a *Works* search feature that is similar to the Find feature in the the word processor.

➤ 1. **Pull down the Organize Menu and select Find Field.** In the dialog box, you see the blinking cursor in the Find Next Field That Contains: box.

2. **Type: VILLARREAL** Your screen should look like Figure 10-6.

The Search Text Fields Only box should be marked as illustrated in Figure 10-6. If it is not, move the pointer to the box and click once.

10 Database: Worksheet 1   **131**

Figure 10-6. The Find Next Field dialog box

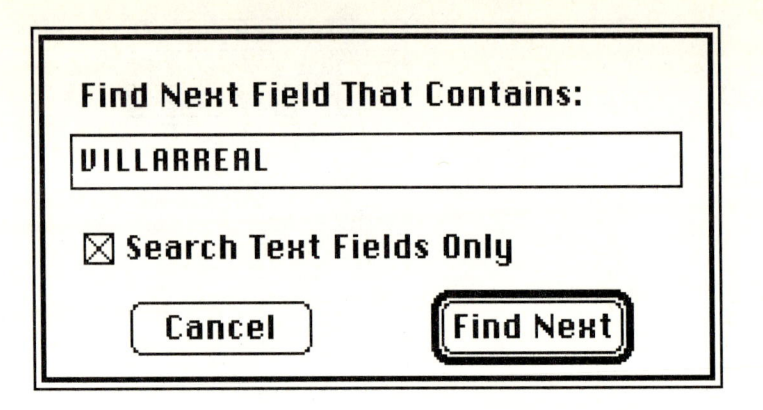

```
Find Next Field That Contains:
[ VILLARREAL                    ]

☒ Search Text Fields Only

[ Cancel ]        [[ Find Next ]]
```

3. **Move the pointer to the Find Next button and click once.** The form window reappears with VILLARREAL highlighted.

4. **Click on the Termination field to select it.**

5. **Type:**   **12/18/87**

6. **Press:**   **[RETURN].** The date is now entered on his record.

7. **Click on the Comments field to select it.**

8. **Type:**   **Returned to school full-time**

9. **Press:**   **[RETURN].** This completes the entry.

Raoul's record is now up to date.

Saving a File

Since you have revised your Profile database, you should save it. Ordinarily, you would *not* save it under a new name. However, if you want to practice on this worksheet again, you will need to keep the original *Profile* in its original state. To save this revised *Profile* as a new document,

1. **Pull down the File Menu and select Save As.** A dialog box will appear with the original file name highlighted.

132   *Microsoft Works for the Macintosh*

2. **Check to see that your data disk is the active disk.**
   "Data Disk" should appear next to the active disk icon.

3. **Type: Profile2**

4. **Click on the Save button.**

Review

If time permits, display *Profile* again, and without looking at the step-by-step instructions, try to make the revisions on your own.
   View records as a list and as forms.
   Add yourself as a new employee.
   Sort the records alphabetically.
   Add comments and termination fields to the forms.
   Search the database for your record.

Think About It

Congratulations! You have learned some basic database terms (records and fields) and performed basic database tasks (such as searching, sorting, adding fields to records, and adding a record to a file). Now you are ready for more general and useful database activities.

Quitting Works

1. **Pull down File Menu and select Quit.** You may receive a message asking whether or not you want to save your document. Answer appropriately.

2. **Close all windows.**

3. **Pull down the Special Menu and select Shut Down.**

4. **Remove the disks from the Macintosh and return them to their appropriate places.**

5. **Turn off the Macintosh.**

11 Database Worksheet 2

Objectives

In this worksheet, you will learn how to

- Create a simple database
- Design a form
- Change the size and location of fields in the Form view
- Change the size of a column (field) in the List view
- Add records
- Sort records
- Save your database

Setting the Scene

Remember the Birthday Club letter that you composed with the word processor? (If you want to review the sample letter, see page 51.) In this worksheet, you will create a simple database of Birthday Club members to go with the letter. Once you have the database, you can use *Works* to create personalized letters from your standard letter.

Getting Started

- **Open *Works*** as described in Getting Started, Chapter 1. You see the Open dialog box on your screen.

Creating a New Database File

As in Worksheet 1, the database *Profile* is already stored on your *Works Data Disk*. To open your data disk,

1. **Insert your data disk into the second disk drive**.

2. **If necessary, click on the Drive button to change drives until the data disk is the active disk.**

3. **Move the pointer to the Database icon and click once.**

135

Now you see the database files in the list box. Since you are creating a new database file,

4. **Click on the database icon.**

5. **Click on the New button.** You see the Field Name dialog box. (See Figure 11-1.)

Figure 11-1. The Field Name dialog box

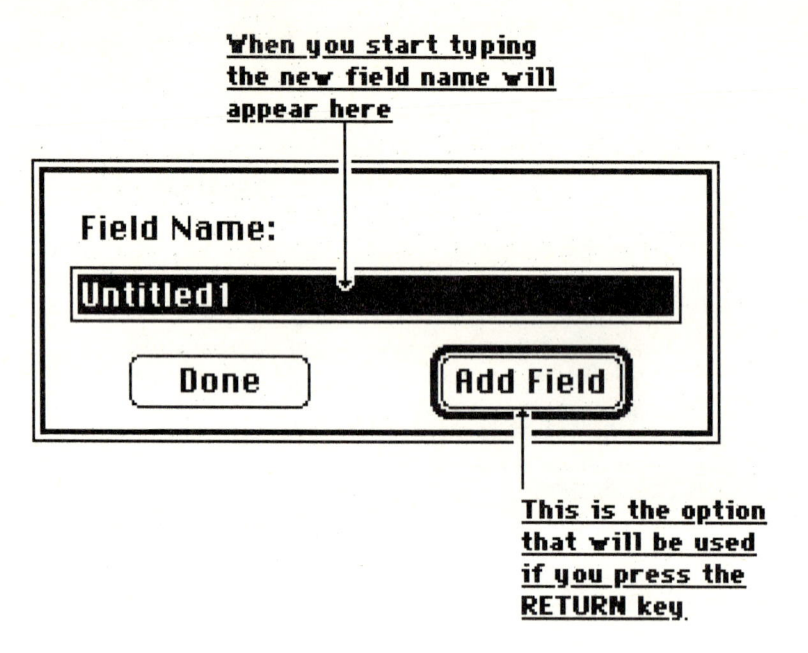

When you start typing the new field name will appear here

Field Name:

Untitled1

Done   Add Field

This is the option that will be used if you press the RETURN key.

Creating a Form

After you have clicked on the New button, *Works* displays the Field Name dialog box shown in Figure 11-1. You use this dialog box to create the various fields in a form.

You are going to create a simple database with names. To create a field for last name,

1. **Type:** **Last Name** You did not have to move the pointer to select the field because the Field Name box was already highlighted. Be sure to check the spelling of the field names before you press [RETURN]. If you make a typing mistake, you can delete the unwanted letters and retype them.

2. **Press:** **[RETURN].** This accepts the selected option. Instead of pressing [RETURN], you could have used the mouse

to click on the Add Field button. However, using the keyboard is faster and more convenient because the Add Field option is already selected. As soon as you pressed [RETURN], *Works* placed the field name at the beginning of the top line of the screen and displayed another Field Name dialog box for the "Untitled 2" field name. For this field,

3. **Type: First Name**

4. **Press: [RETURN].**

5. **Continue by using Steps 3 and 4 to enter the following five field names:**

   Street Address
   City
   State
   ZIP
   Birth Month

To indicate that you are through adding fields,

6. **Click on the Done button.**

Changing the Size and Location of Fields

You now have an opportunity to use the skills you learned in the previous worksheet to decrease or increase the length of fields and to reposition some of the fields so that they will look similar to those shown in Figure 11-2 on page 138.

Look at the fields carefully in terms of length. Some of them may seem long enough, but others may seem too large or too short. To lengthen or shorten fields, follow these steps:

1. **Position the pointer on the right edge of a field until the pointer becomes a two-way arrow.**

2. **Hold down the mouse button and drag the outline to the right or left until the field reaches the length you want. Release the mouse.**

To move a field to a new location,

```
  File   Edit   Window   Organize   Format   Report
```

```
┌─────────────────────── Untitled (DB) ───────────────────────┐
│ Last Name [          ]     First Name [          ]          │
│ Street Address [                    ]                       │
│ City [              ]   State [    ]   ZIP [    ]           │
│ Birth Month [        ]                                      │
│                                                             │
└─────────────────────────────────────────────────────────────┘
```

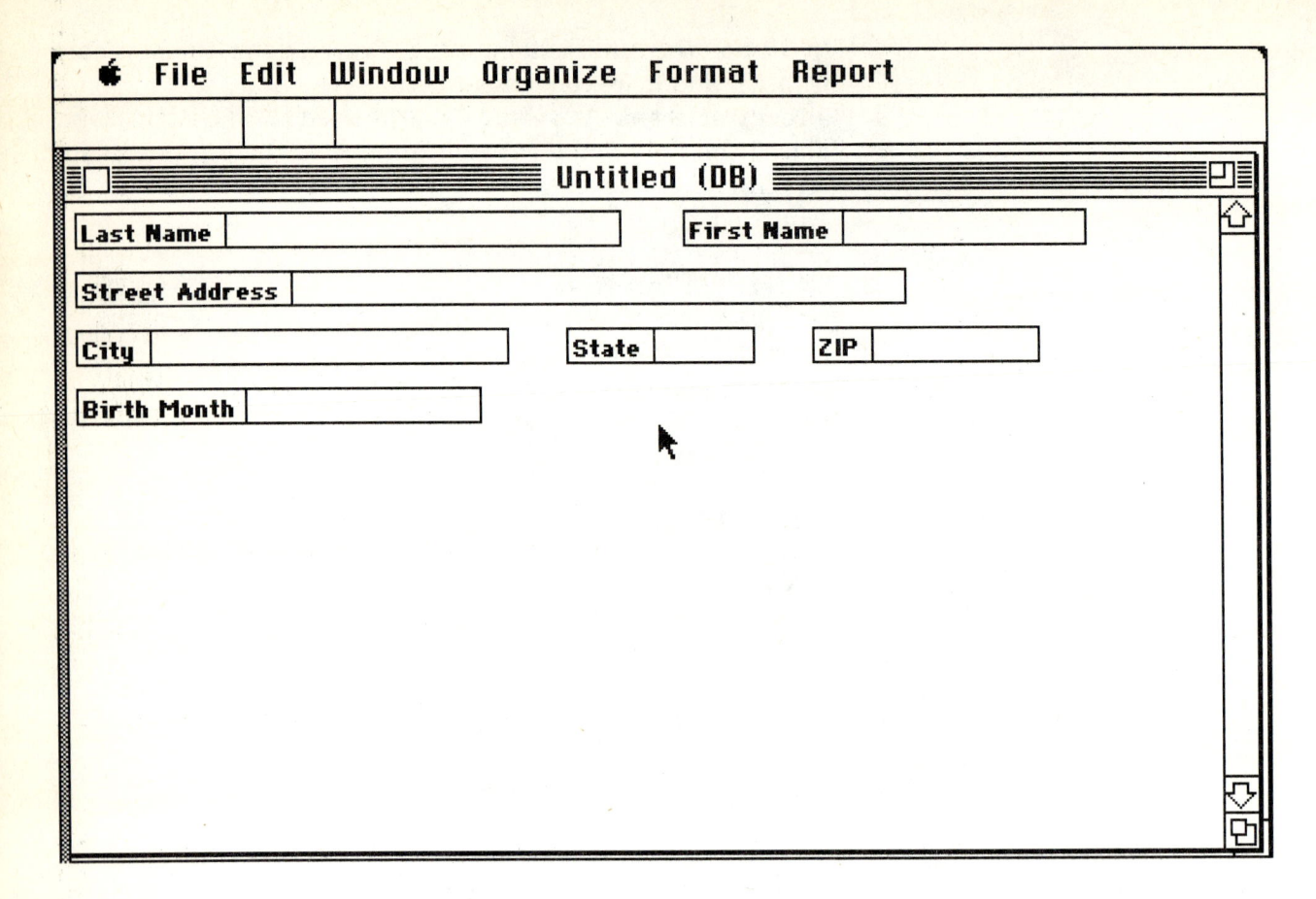

Figure 11-2. The completed form

 4. **Move the pointer to the field name you want to move. The pointer becomes a hand when it is in position.**

 5. **Hold down the mouse button and drag the field name outline to the position you want. Release the mouse button.**

Repeat Steps 4 and 5 to change the location of the First Name, State, and ZIP fields. Then using the same technique, move the field names to position them vertically so that the spaces between them are fairly equal.

Entering New Data

Now enter the following Club members into your new database. If you need help, follow the directions given in steps 1-15. If you do *not* need help, rejoin us at the heading Changing the Size of a Column, page 141.

You can enter data in either the form window or list window, but you will probably prefer the form window where you can see an entire record.

➡ 1. **Click in the first field (Last Name).**

2. **Type:**   **McNamara**

3. **Press**:   **[TAB]** to enter the last name and move to the First Name field.

4. **Type**:   **Jane**

5. **Press**:   **[TAB]** to enter and move to the Street Address field.

6. **Type**:   **719 Morse St.**

7. **Press**:   **[TAB]** to enter and move to the City field.

8. **Type**:   **San Jose**

9. **Press**:   **[TAB]** to enter and move to the State field.

10. **Type**:   **CA**

11. **Press**:   **[TAB]** to enter and move to the ZIP field.

12. **Type**:   **95128**

13. **Press**:   **[TAB]** to enter and move to the Birth Month field.

14. **Type**:   **February**

15. **Press**:   **[TAB]**.

Note that pressing [TAB] this last time moved you to the next record. (See the "2" displayed in the upper left corner. It indicates that you are in the second record of this file.) Repeat steps 1-15 to enter the data for the remaining club members.

A List of Birthday Club Members

Last Name: Kline First Name: Calvin
Street Address: 21 St. John St.
City: San Jose State: CA ZIP: 95130
Birth Month: May

Last Name: Boyle First Name: Lance
Street Address: 415 Forest Ave.
City: San Jose State: CA ZIP: 95128
Birth Month: January

Last Name: Pang First Name: Alice
Street Address: 21 Saratoga Ave.
City: Saratoga State: CA ZIP: 95070
Birth Month: September

Last Name: Montague First Name: Charles
Street Address: 3715 Bascom Ave.
City: Los Gatos State: CA ZIP: 95030
Birth Month: January

Last Name: Sakamoto First Name: Sachi
Street Address: 87 Rocky Lane
City: San Jose State: CA ZIP: 95130
Birth Month: August

Last Name: Wong First Name: Mohammed
Street Address: 711 Campbell Ave.
City: Campbell State: CA ZIP: 95008
Birth Month: March

Last Name: Mock First Name: Cherry
Street Address: 6516 Esmeralda Ct.
City: Campbell State: CA ZIP: 95008
Birth Month: April

Last Name: Piccolo First Name: Sal
Street Address: 988 Latimer Ave.
City: San Jose State: CA ZIP: 95117
Birth Month: January

Last Name: Zachary First Name: Scot
Street Address: 104 DeAnza Blvd.
City: Cupertino State: CA ZIP: 95014
Birth Month: November

Changing the Size of a Column

If you used the form window to enter the names, change now to display your database in the list window.

➡ **1. Pull down the Format Menu and select Show List.**

2. Click in the deselect box

As you can see, some of the columns are unnecessarily wide, and consequently, you are not able to see the entire record. To change the size of the columns for City, State, and ZIP,

3. Position the pointer on the right edge of the column marker between "City" and "State." When you are in position, the pointer becomes a two-way arrow. Your screen will be similar to Figure 11-3.

Figure 11-3. Note the two-way arrow between the City and State columns.

4. Hold down the mouse button and slowly drag the mouse to the left. Release the mouse button when the column nears the end of the longest city name. Note that as you narrowed the column, more of the columns on the right moved into view.

To narrow the State and ZIP columns, follow Steps 3 and 4. You may have to change the width of more than three columns to get the width of the entire database on the screen. Keep working with the column widths until all seven columns are visible on the screen.

Sorting a File

One of the many benefits of a database program is that you can use it to sort a file in different ways. For example, you can sort by ZIP code for mailing purposes or by birth date for your birthday letters. Now that you have entered data for the Birthday Club members, you can alphabetize the list for clarity and so that you can find any duplicated entries. (You don't want one person to get more than one letter.)

If you have a database with duplicated last names, you can do a multi-level sort. For example, if you want to sort names by last name and first name, you first sort on the field in which you are least interested (in this case, the first name). Then you would sort on the last name. For each level of a multi-sort, *Works* retains the order of all previous sorts. But since there are no duplicated last names, you will just sort on the Last Name field.

➡ 1. **Move the pointer to the label portion of the Last Name field** (the pointer becomes a hand when it is in proper position) **and click once.** The Last Name field of all the records is highlighted. See Figure 11-4.

Figure 11-4. Note the hand at the top of the Last Name column.

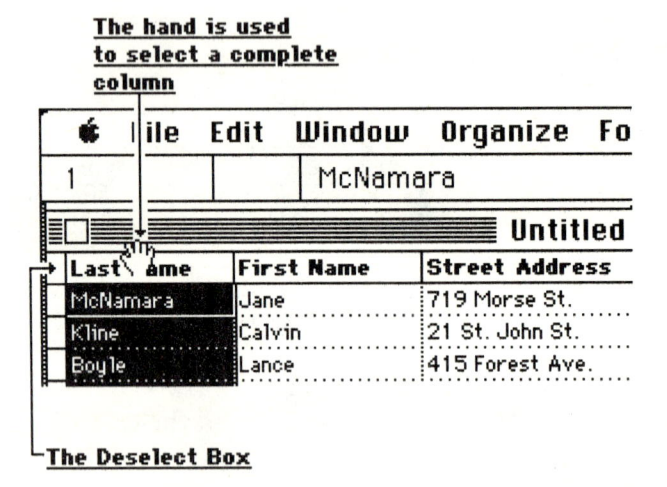

Figure 11-5. The Sort dialog box

2. **Pull down the Organize Menu and select Sort.**

You see the Sort dialog box. (Compare with Figure 11-5.) The program once again assumes that you want to sort on the selected Last Name field in *ascending* order (from A to Z). Since that is the sort you want,

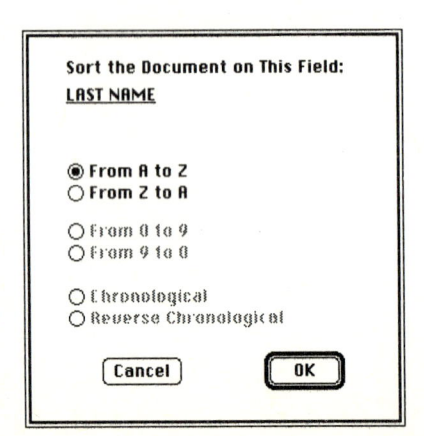

142 Microsoft Works for the Macintosh

3. **Click the OK button.** The records are now listed in alphabetical order.

4. **Move the pointer to the deselect box and click once to remove the highlighting.**

Saving a File

You have created a new file that you will use again in a later worksheet. Therefore, save it under an appropriate title.

1. **Pull down the File Menu and select Save As.** When the Save As dialog box appears,

2. **Type: Members** Check now to see if your data disk is the active disk. If it is not, click on the Drive button until you see the name of your data disk to the right of the active disk icon.

3. **Click on the Save button.** Your file reappears with its new title. See final copy in Figure 11-6.

Figure 11-6. Completed database file showing new title *Members* in the title bar

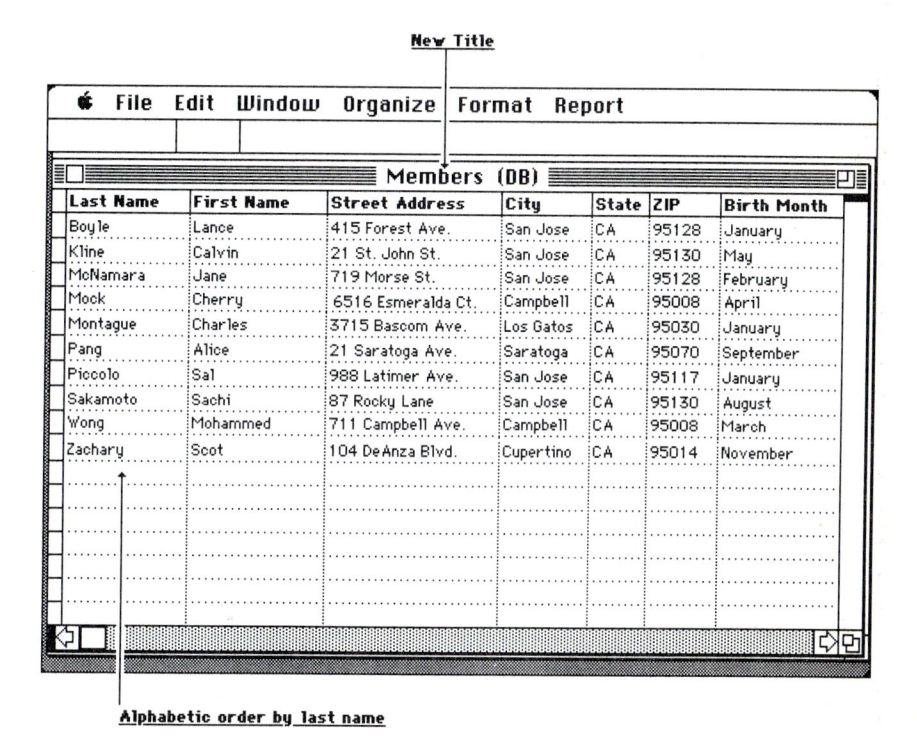

Last Name	First Name	Street Address	City	State	ZIP	Birth Month
Boyle	Lance	415 Forest Ave.	San Jose	CA	95128	January
Kline	Calvin	21 St. John St.	San Jose	CA	95130	May
McNamara	Jane	719 Morse St.	San Jose	CA	95128	February
Mock	Cherry	6516 Esmeralda Ct.	Campbell	CA	95008	April
Montague	Charles	3715 Bascom Ave.	Los Gatos	CA	95030	January
Pang	Alice	21 Saratoga Ave.	Saratoga	CA	95070	September
Piccolo	Sal	988 Latimer Ave.	San Jose	CA	95117	January
Sakamoto	Sachi	87 Rocky Lane	San Jose	CA	95130	August
Wong	Mohammed	711 Campbell Ave.	Campbell	CA	95008	March
Zachary	Scot	104 DeAnza Blvd.	Cupertino	CA	95014	November

Window title: **Members (DB)** — New Title

Alphabetic order by last name

11 Database: Worksheet 2

Review

If time permits, create a database of friends' names, addresses, and telephone numbers. Try not to look at the step-by-step instructions.

    Create a new database file.
    Design a form.
    Change the size of the fields to conform to the expected size.
    Move fields as needed.
    Add data to create several records.
    Sort the database alphabetically.
    Save the file.

Summary

Congratulations! You have learned and practiced some basic database operations, such as creating, sorting, and formatting a file. As you can probably tell from the options in the menu bar, the database application is complex and powerful. In the next worksheet, you will learn how to create special reports from your database.

Quitting Works

1. **Pull down File Menu and select Quit.**

2. **You may receive a message asking whether or not you want to save your document. Answer appropriately.**

3. **Close all windows.**

4. **Pull down Special Menu and select Quit.**

5. **Remove the disks from the Macintosh and return them to their appropriate places.**

6. **Turn off the Macintosh.**

12 Database Worksheet 3

Objectives

In this worksheet, you will learn how to

- Create a database report
- Select fields for the report
- Sort records in the report
- Add titles to the report
- Format the report
- Print the report

Setting the Scene

It is the beginning of a hot summer weekend, and The Ice Cream Factory expects a brisk business. But one of your employees calls in sick. You need a replacement who can work the same hours. What do you do? Your database contains all the data you need about all your employees. However, you now want to reorganize the data and get a report of all employees available to work at the hours scheduled for the sick employee.

In this worksheet, you will create and print a simple, easy-to-read database report that gives the name of each employee according to hours of availability. So that you can see what you are working toward, the finished report is shown in Figure 12-1.

Getting Started

- **Open *Works*** as described in Geting Started, Chapter 1. You see the Open dialog box on your screen.

Opening a File

If you finished the database Worksheet 2, then the database file with which you will work is already stored on your *Works Data Disk* under the filename *Profile2*. To open the file,

145

```
AVAILABILITY LIST        January 6, 1988                    Jane Doe

LAST NAME      FIRST NAME     PHONE        TIME AVAILABLE
CARRILLO       ANGELA         291-8654     Afternoons
JACOBSEN       RUSS           378-1330     Afternoons
PRADA          JOSEPHINE      867-1779     Afternoons
TYLER          GEOFFREY       299-4151     Afternoons
CARLSON        ROBERTA        255-6100     Evenings
HIRVONEN       PIA            298-8489     Evenings
VILLARREAL     RAOUL          289-4050     Evenings
YEE            WENDY          867-4891     Evenings
MANSUR         GLORIA         353-4454     Mornings
WILLIAMS       CORINNE        379-1008     Mornings
```

Figure 12-1. The finished database report

➤ 1. **Insert the data disk into the second disk drive.**

2. **Click on the filename *Profile2*.** If you do not see the name of the file you want, use the scroll bar at the right to see the rest of the file names.

3. **Click on the Open button.** Now you see the *Profile2* database on the screen.

Sorting Fields in a Report

You will first sort the *Profile2* database by the Time Available field in order to group the records so that the time factor is easy to read. If your database is in a form window, change to the list window by pulling down the Format Menu and selecting Show List. (It's easier to observe sorting when your database is in the list window.) If you forgot how to sort, follow these steps.

➤ 1. **Scroll to the right until you see the Time Available field.**

2. **Position the pointer on the Time Available field name** (the pointer becomes a hand when it is in the proper position) **and click to select that column.**

3. **Pull down the Organize Menu and select Sort.** You will see a Sort dialog box. Look at the example in Figure 12-2. Note that a field and an option are already selected.

Since "Time Available" is the field you want and "From A to Z" is the sequence you want,

Figure 12-2. The Sort dialog box

4. **Click on the OK button.** Your database now alphabetically lists the employees with the names of those who work in the afternoon first, the evening next, and the morning last.

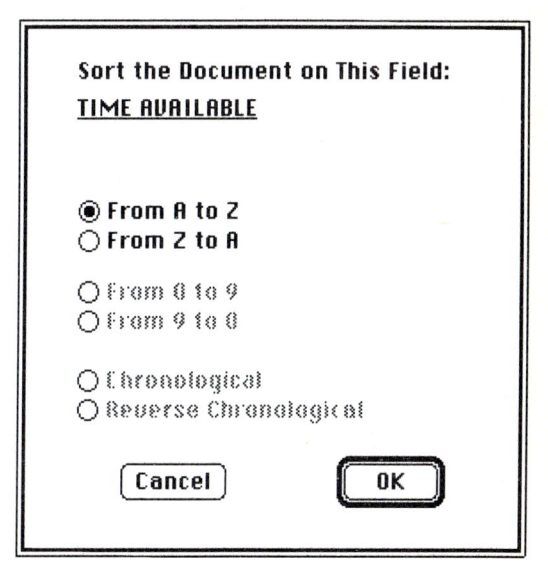

Creating a New Report

The first step in creating the report is to define it. In database jargon, creating and defining a report simply means selecting the fields to include in the report, arranging the selected fields in an efficient and pleasing layout, and printing them on paper. To begin,

➡ • **Pull down the Report Menu and select New Report.**

You see a report window screen similar to Figure 12-3. Note the title bar and the fact that "no rules are in effect." When you are working in a report window, you see only the first few records. The upside-down triangle above the Last Name field name marks the left edge of the report's print area. You can see the right-edge

12 Database: Worksheet 3 **147**

Figure 12-3. Report window

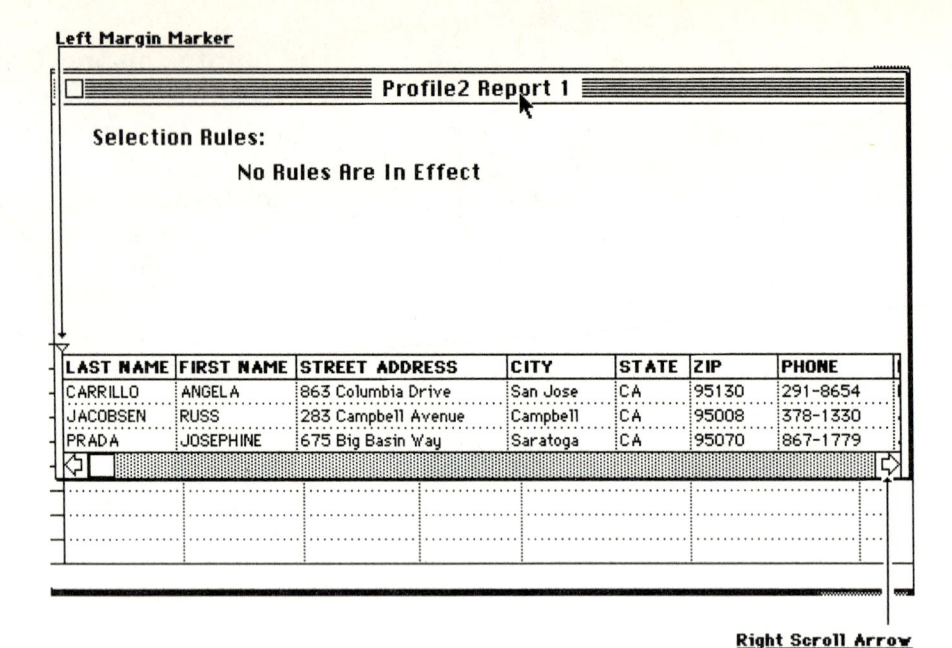

Left Margin Marker

```
┌─────────────────────────────────────────────┐
│ □         Profile2 Report 1                 │
│   Selection Rules:                          │
│              No Rules Are In Effect         │
│                                             │
│                                             │
│                                             │
│                                             │
│                                             │
│ LAST NAME │FIRST NAME│STREET ADDRESS │CITY     │STATE│ZIP  │PHONE    │
│ CARRILLO  │ANGELA    │863 Columbia Drive│San Jose│CA │95130│291-8654 │
│ JACOBSEN  │RUSS      │283 Campbell Avenue│Campbell│CA│95008│378-1330 │
│ PRADA     │JOSEPHINE │675 Big Basin Way│Saratoga │CA │95070│867-1779 │
│ ⇦                                                                    ⇨│
└─────────────────────────────────────────────┘
```

Right Scroll Arrow

marker by clicking on the right arrow in the horizontal scroll bar. Try it.

➡ • **Use the horizontal scroll bar arrow to scroll right until you see the right-edge marker.** You use the right-edge marker to remove fields from the report. The program will not print a field that is to the right (or partially to the right) of the right-edge marker.

Look at the top section of the screen. This is used for giving Selection Rules when you want to prepare a report that does not include every record in the database. In that event, you create record-selection rules (as you did in Chapter 10). You don't need record-selection rules for this report because you want to include *all* the records in the report.

Selecting Fields for a Report

Since you want a report that contains only the names of your employees, their phone numbers, and the times they are available to work, you must exclude from the print area all the other fields. As you exclude fields, remember that *you are only excluding them from the report you are creating.* You are *not* deleting them from the database.

148 *Microsoft Works for the Macintosh*

All you need for the report are the

Last Name
First Name
Phone
Time Available

fields. You must move the columns labeled by those fields into the print area between the left-edge and right-edge markers and leave all the other columns outside the print area. Follow these steps.

1. **Move the pointer to the Phone field name.** The pointer becomes a hand when it is in the proper position.

2. **Hold down the mouse button and drag the field to the left until the Street Address field name is highlighted.** The column you are moving (Phone field) will be inserted immediately before the highlighted street address column.

3. **Release the mouse button.** The first three columns of your report are now in proper sequence. Your screen should look something like Figure 12-4.

Figure 12-4. Highlighted column after first move

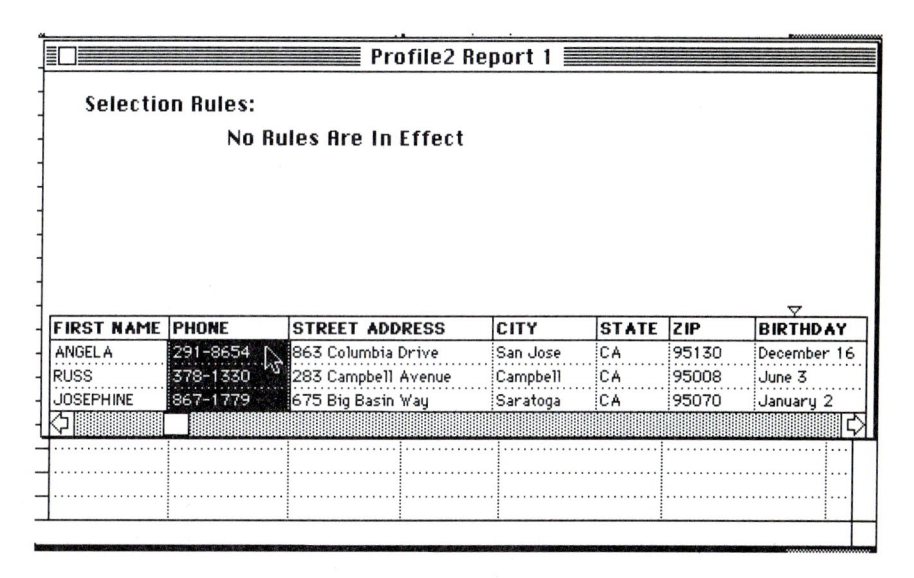

To move the column for the Time Available field into position,

12 Database: Worksheet 3 **149**

4. **Click on the right scroll arrow until you see the Time Available field.**

5. **Move the pointer to the Time Available field name.** The pointer becomes a hand when it is in the proper position.

6. **Hold down the mouse button and drag the field column to the left until the Street Address field name is again highlighted.** This is tricky because the Street Address column does not show on the screen when you start. Don't worry, just push the hand over against the left side of the screen and the columns will automatically scroll into view. (See the hand in Figure 12-5.)

Figure 12-5. Dragging the Time Available field

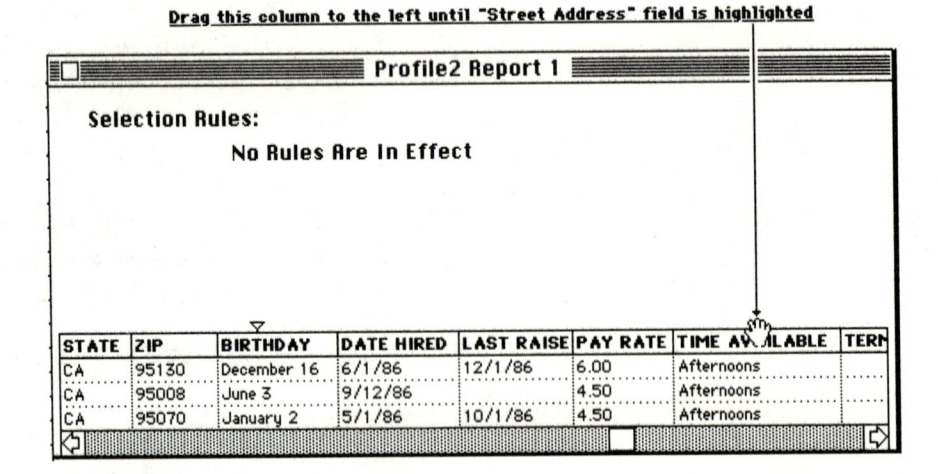

7. **Release the mouse button.** You should now have the four fields (Last Name, First Name, Phone, Time Available) that you need for your report in the printing area and in the proper sequence.

Widening Margins

Because you only have four fields in this report, it will look much better with wider side margins. So,

1. **Pull down the File Menu and select Page Setup.** You see a Page Setup dialog box as in Figure 12-6.

2. **Click the pointer immediately after the 1 in the Left Margin box.**

150 *Microsoft Works for the Macintosh*

Figure 12-6. The Print dialog box

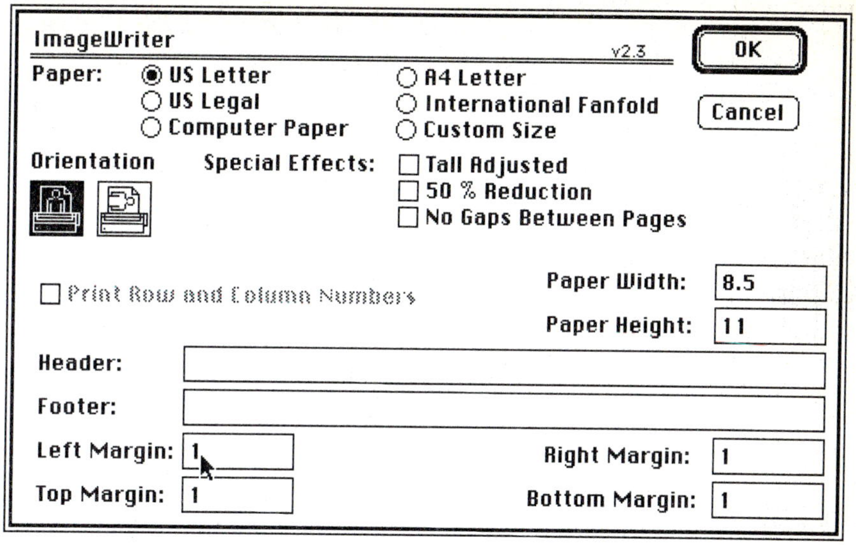

3. **Type:** **.25** to increase the left margin to 1.25 inches.

4. **Click the pointer immediately after the 1 in the Right Margin box.**

5. **Type:** **.25** to increase the right margin to 1.25 inches.

6. **Click on the OK button.**

You now have the opportunity to increase the attractiveness of this short report by widening the columns.

Widening Columns

As you may recall, the program will not print a field (a column) that is fully or partially to the right of the right-edge marker. So if you print the report now, it will include more than the four columns you want. (See Figure 12-7.) To widen the columns and eliminate the unwanted columns from the print area,

1. **Scroll to the left** if the Last Name column does not show on the screen.

2. **Position the pointer on the right edge of the Last Name field name.** The pointer becomes a two-way arrow when you are in the proper position. (See Figure 12-8, page 152.)

12 Database: Worksheet 3 **151**

Figure 12-7. Note the right-edge marker

These are the fields which should appear in the report

Right Edge Marker

Figure 12-8. Note the two-way arrow between Last Name and First Name columns.

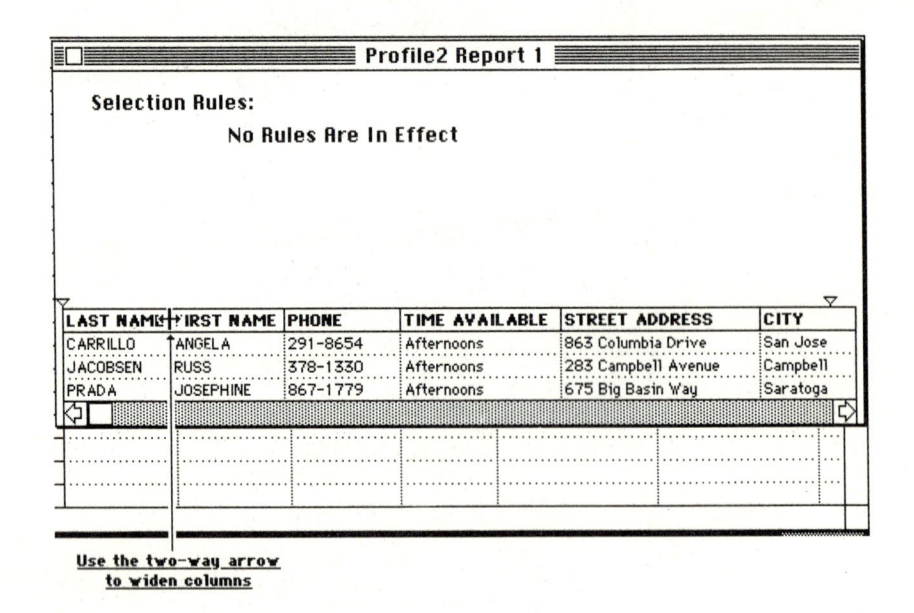

Use the two-way arrow to widen columns

152 *Microsoft Works for the Macintosh*

3. **Hold down the mouse button and drag the edge of the field to the right about a half inch.**

Use the same steps to widen the other three columns until the right-edge marker is positioned somewhere within the Street Address column. If the right-edge marker is anywhere over the Street Address field name, the address will not print in the report. See Figure 12-9. It shows the result of widening all four columns.

Figure 12-9

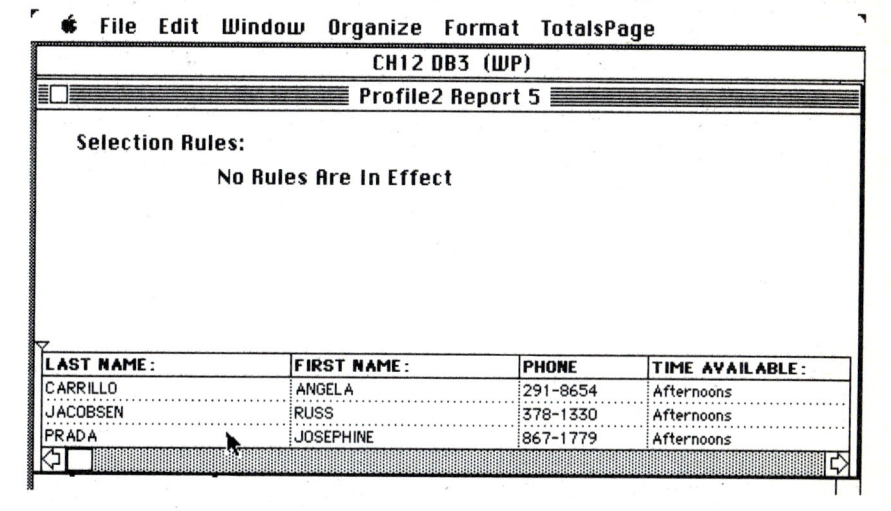

Using a Report Header (Title)

Your report now has all the data you need, but it would be a more effective report if you added a heading to identify its purpose. For example, the header "Availability List" in bold type with today's date on the left and your name as the report preparer on the right would look nice.

1. **Pull down the File Menu and select Page Setup.** The insertion point is blinking in the Header box. To tell *Works* what to print in the header, you can use the following formatting commands.

   &L = Align the following characters at the left margin.
   &C = Center the following characters.
   &R = Align the following characters at the right margin.
   &D = Print the current date. *Works* will look up today's date!
   &B = Print the following characters in bold.

12 Database: Worksheet 3   **153**

To establish the header:

2. Type: &L&BAVAILABILITY LIST&C&D&R*Your Name* The notation breaks down as follows:

&L&BAVAILABILITY LIST	=	At the <u>L</u>eft margin in <u>B</u>old, print AVAILABILITY LIST
&C&D	=	At the <u>C</u>enter of the line, print the <u>D</u>ate
&R*Your Name*	=	At the <u>R</u>ight margin, print *Your Name*

3. Click on the OK button.

The header will not show up on your screen, but it will print on your report.

Printing Without Lines

Before you print the report, there is one more thing you will probably want to do. *Works* will print the report with or without displaying the **grid** (the dotted lines that separate the rows and columns). If you do not instruct the program to eliminate the lines, it will print them. In a report such as this, the lines can distract the reader. Use the following instructions to print the report without the grid.

➡ • **Pull down the Format Menu and select No Grid.**

That's it! Now it's time to print the report and see how it looks.

Printing a Report

To print, you should still be in the report window. Check to see that the printer is on and the paper is properly positioned.

➡ 1. **Pull down the File Menu and select Print.** You see a Print dialog box similar to Figure 12-10. If the settings in your dialog box are not the same as those in Figure 12-10, click the options to match them. When you are ready to begin printing,

2. **Click on the OK button.** Printing should begin shortly. Your finished report should resemble Figure 12-1 (at the beginning of this worksheet).

Figure 12-10. The Print dialog box

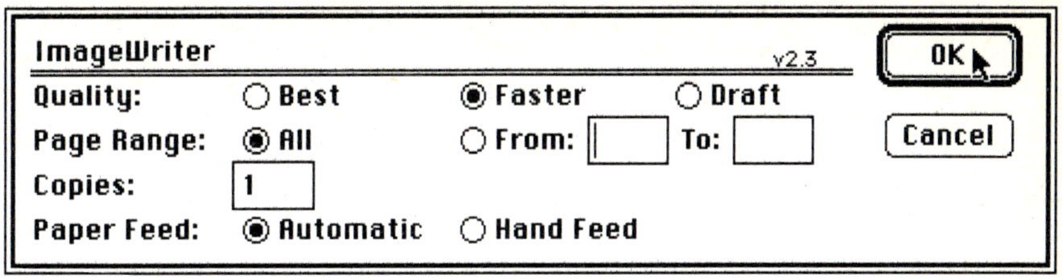

Renaming a Report

Note that in the title bar the program has automatically assigned a non-descriptive name to your file definition (the instructions to create this report). If you create several reports from this one database, you would have problems remembering the content of each report. So rename the file to link the contents to a more descriptive filename.

➤ 1. **Pull down the Edit Menu and select Change Report Title.**

2. **Type:** Availability

3. **Click on the OK button.** You see the new name on the report's title bar.

Saving a Report

When you close the report window after printing a report, *Works* stores the report definition with the database document from which it retrieved the information.

When you later save the database document, *Works* saves the report definition along with it. To save the *Profile2* together with the Availability report definition,

➤ 1. **Move the pointer to the close box in the upper left corner of the Availability report window and click once.** You see *Profile2*.

2. **Pull down the File Menu and select Save.** This replaces your old *Profile2* file with your new file containing the report.

Review

If time permits, create another report that contains only the names and addresses of all employees. Then apply to it some of the skills you have learned in this worksheet.

12 Database: Worksheet 3 **155**

Create a new database report.
Select only the names and addresses for the report.
Widen the columns.
Print the report.

Summary

Congratulations! You have learned how to prepare special purpose reports using one database. You have developed many of the skills you need to begin exploring that powerful function.

Quitting Works

1. **Pull down the File Menu and select Quit.** You may receive a message asking whether or not you want to save your document. Answer appropriately.

2. **Pull down the Special Menu and select Shut Down.**

3. **Remove the disks from the Macintosh and return them to their appropriate places.**

4. **Turn off the computer.**

13 Database Shortcuts & Other Techniques Worksheet 4

Objectives

In this worksheet, you will learn how to

- Use keyboard shortcuts (commands)
- Copy within and between documents
- Use calculated fields
- Divide a window into panes

Setting the Scene

Now that you have worked with your employee database in the last worksheet, you can probably think of modifications that you would have made if *you* had designed it. Use this worksheet to guide you in making the file more meaningful. Or, if you feel confident, design a completely different database!

This worksheet gives you an opportunity to explore the *Works* database application on your own. You will notice that the instructions in this worksheet are less precise and leave more to your imagination. See how much of what you have learned you can apply to one project.

Database Shortcuts

As with *Works* word processing and spreadsheets, you can invoke many options by commands from the keyboard. To give a command from the keyboard, hold down [COMMAND] (⌘) and type the letter corresponding to the command. For example, to give the Quit command, hold down [COMMAND] and type the letter Q.

The following table lists some of the more frequently used keyboard shortcuts. The list is not complete. Consult your *Works* manual for more information.

157

To	Press [⌘] and type
Open File	O
Print File	P
Quit Program	Q
Save File	S
Undo previous action	Z
Find Field	F
Switch between list and form windows	L
Copy selection	C

You may also move between the list and form windows by clicking the mouse.

- **To move from a form window to a list window, double click anywhere on the screen outside of the existing fields.**

- **To move from a List window to a Form window, double click in the Record Selector box at the left of any existing record.** See Figure 13-1a.

Copying Information

You can copy within and between documents. Copying saves re-typing the same information when you need it in more than one place. You can copy a record, field, or entry, or block of records, fields, or entries. Although you can copy in both list and form windows, copying is easier in a list window because you can then copy multiple records at one time.

To copy a record within the same database,

1. **Make sure you are in a list window.**

2. **Click on the Record Selector box at the left of the record you want to copy.** (See Figure 13-1b.) The entire record is highlighted.

3. **Select Copy from the Edit Menu or press [⌘] - [C].**

4. **Select the field where you want the copying to begin.**

158   *Microsoft Works for the Macintosh*

Figure 13-1a. Form window

```
  File   Edit   Window   Organize   Format   Report
≡▭≡≡≡≡≡≡≡≡≡≡≡≡≡≡ PROFILE (DB) ≡≡≡≡≡≡≡≡≡≡≡≡≡≡≡≡
 LAST NAME  CARRILLO              FIRST NAME  ANGELA
 STREET ADDRESS  863 Columbia Drive
 CITY  San Jose          STATE  CA     ZIP  95130
 PHONE  291-8654
 BIRTHDAY  December 16
 DATE HIRED  6/1/86
 LAST RAISE  12/1/86
 PAY RATE  6.00
 TIME AVAILABLE  Afternoons
```

<u>Double Clicking here or anywhere in the white space will switch to the LIST view</u>

Figure 13-1b. List window

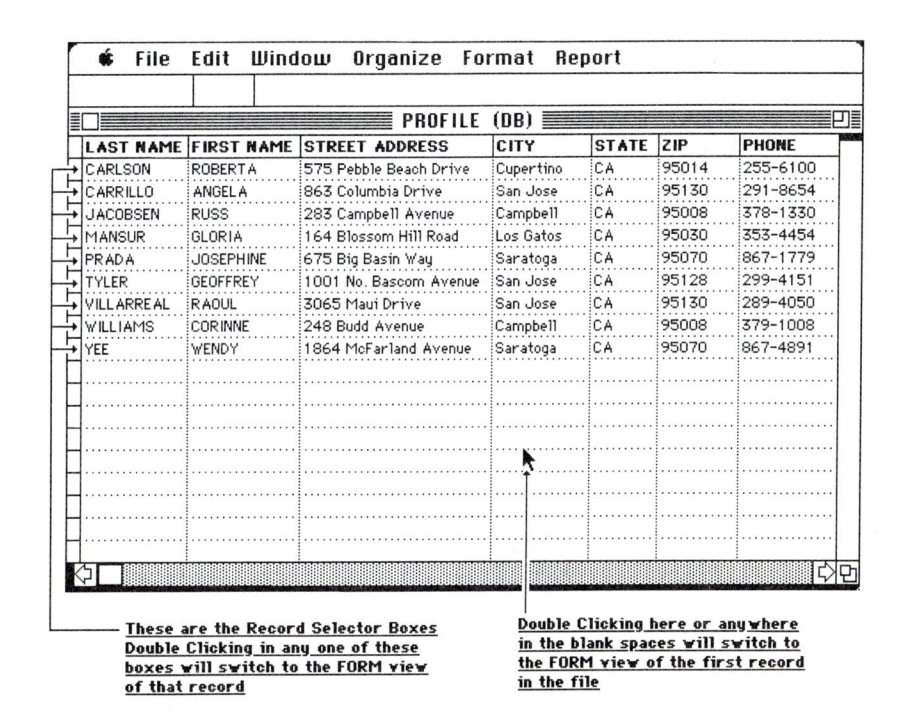

LAST NAME	FIRST NAME	STREET ADDRESS	CITY	STATE	ZIP	PHONE
CARLSON	ROBERTA	575 Pebble Beach Drive	Cupertino	CA	95014	255-6100
CARRILLO	ANGELA	863 Columbia Drive	San Jose	CA	95130	291-8654
JACOBSEN	RUSS	283 Campbell Avenue	Campbell	CA	95008	378-1330
MANSUR	GLORIA	164 Blossom Hill Road	Los Gatos	CA	95030	353-4454
PRADA	JOSEPHINE	675 Big Basin Way	Saratoga	CA	95070	867-1779
TYLER	GEOFFREY	1001 No. Bascom Avenue	San Jose	CA	95128	299-4151
VILLARREAL	RAOUL	3065 Maui Drive	San Jose	CA	95130	289-4050
WILLIAMS	CORINNE	248 Budd Avenue	Campbell	CA	95008	379-1008
YEE	WENDY	1864 McFarland Avenue	Saratoga	CA	95070	867-4891

<u>These are the Record Selector Boxes Double Clicking in any one of these boxes will switch to the FORM view of that record</u>

<u>Double Clicking here or anywhere in the blank spaces will switch to the FORM view of the first record in the file</u>

13 Shortcuts and Other Techniques: Worksheet 4

Remember that because you are copying an entire record, the receiving fields must match the sending fields.

5. Select Paste from the Edit Menu or press [⌘] - [V]

A few command-key shortcuts are not shown on the menus. One of these allows you to copy a single entry into the same field of the next record,

➡ **1. Select the field below the one you want to copy.**

2. Press: **[⌘]-[QUOTATION MARK].** *Works* displays the copied information in the entry bar.

3. Click on the enter box or press [RETURN].

To copy a block of adjacent fields,

➡ **1. Make sure you are in the list window.**

2. Select the fields you want to copy by dragging until they are all highlighted.

3. Select Copy from the Edit Menu or press [⌘] - [C].

4. Select the fields that are to receive the copy.

5. Select Paste from the Edit Menu or press [⌘] - [V].

To copy a file format:

If the database you are creating is similar to another existing database, you can use the old one to create the new one. For example, suppose you needed a vendor mailing list. You could copy the format of your old *Members* file and then modify it to suit the needs of your new *Vendors* file, as follows

➡ **1. Open the *Members* file.**

2. Pull down the Edit Menu and select Select All.

3. Pull down the Edit Menu and select Clear. You have erased the data in each record.

4. Move the pointer to the box containing "Last Name" and click once.

5. Pull down the Edit Menu and select Change Field Name.

6. Type: Vendor's Name.

7. Click in the OK box.

8. If necessary, widen the first column so that the screen can display the entire field name.

9. Click on the box containing "First Name."

10. Pull down the Edit Menu and select Delete Field.

11. Click on the Birth Month box to select that column.

12. Pull down the Edit Menu and select Delete Field.

13. **Widen the first three columns** (Vendor's Name, Street Address, and City) so that the State and ZIP columns move to the far right of the screen.

14. Pull down the File Menu and select Save As.

15. Type the title **VENDORS** into the File Name box.

16. Click on Save.

You can now enter information into your new database.

Using Calculated Fields

The data you can enter into a database are not limited to simple text and numbers. You can also enter formulas or equations in fields that reference other fields in the record. A field that contains a formula is called a *calculated field*. A field may also use functions (like those used in spreadsheets): for example, SUM or AVG.

Look, for example, at Figure 13-2. The active Cell E2 shows an equation in the formula bar, but the cell displays the result of the formula. The formula contains references to two other fields in the record (Number and Cost). The asterisk * means multiply.

Figure 13-2. Note the formula in the formula bar and the value in the active cell.

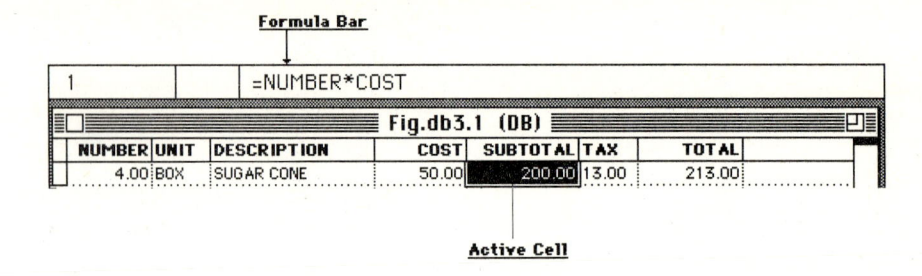

```
Formula Bar
      ↓
1            =NUMBER*COST

               Fig.db3.1 (DB)
NUMBER UNIT  DESCRIPTION   COST  SUBTOTAL TAX    TOTAL
  4.00 BOX   SUGAR CONE   50.00    200.00 13.00  213.00
                                      ↑
                                  Active Cell
```

Dividing a List Window Into Panes

Sometimes a database has so many fields that comparing information in far removed fields becomes difficult. To make it easier, you can divide a list window into side-by-side or top-and-bottom panes.

Dividing a window into panes allows you to hold one pane stationary while you scroll through another pane to find a particular bit of information. For example, suppose you want to see the phone numbers for your employees. You can split the list window vertically and hold the names stationary while you scroll the other fields horizontally until the phone numbers are in view next to the names.

To create a vertical split,

1. **Open the database file *Profile* and change to the list window.**

2. **Position the pointer on the vertical split bar.** Look in the lower left-hand corner of the screen to the left of the left scroll arrow for the vertical split bar. Check against Figure 13-3. When positioned correctly over that line, the pointer becomes a two-way arrow.

3. **Press down the mouse button and drag the split bar until it lines up with the right edge of the First Name field.**

4. **Release the mouse button.** The program divides the list window into two panes. (See Figure 13-4.)

Figure 13-3. Note the location of the vertical split bar.

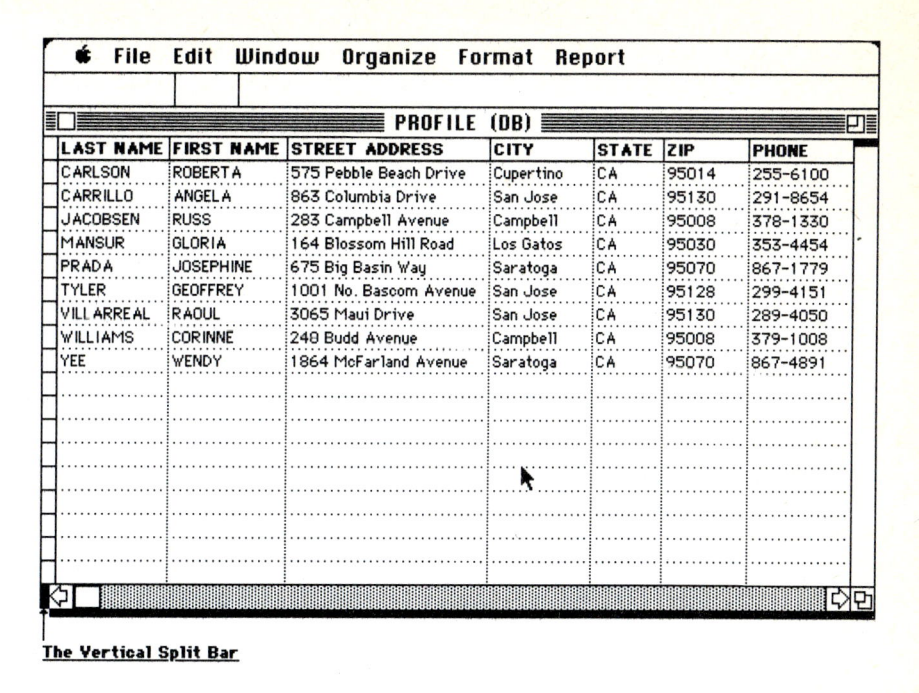

Figure 13-4. Note the location of the horizontal split bar.

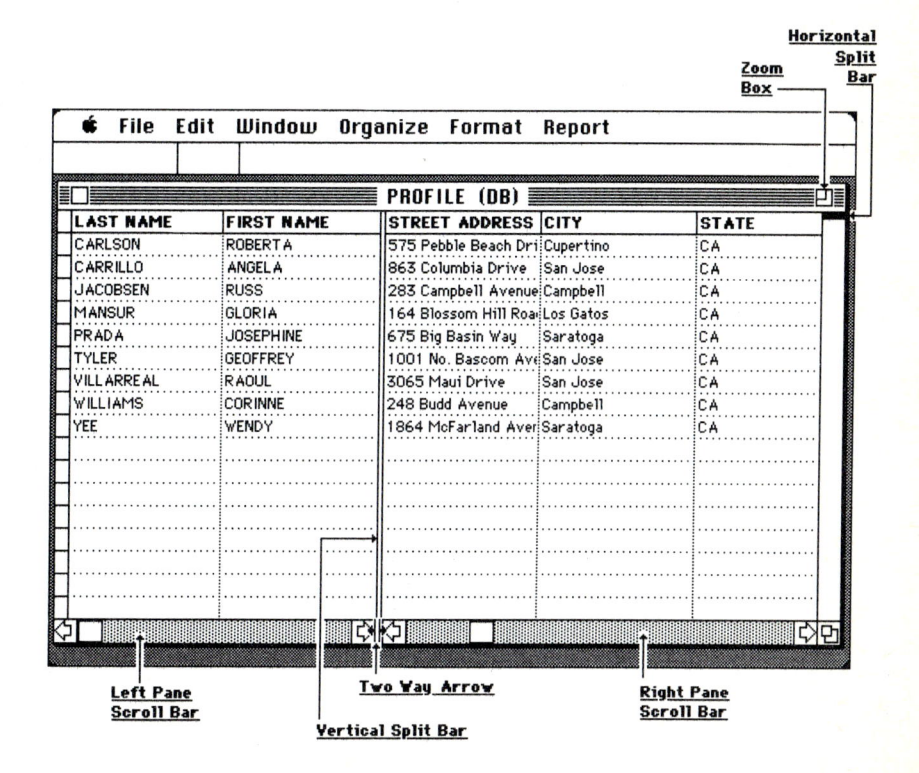

13 Shortcuts and Other Techniques: Worksheet 4

5. **Click on the right scroll arrow of the horizontal scroll bar in the right half of the divided screen until the Phone field is next to the First Name field.**

You can also divide the screen horizontally by using the horizontal split bar located in the upper right-hand corner of the screen right below the zoom box. You can even create four panes by using both the vertical and the horizontal split bars.

To close a pane,

- **Drag the split bar back to its original position in the far left or upper edge of the scroll bars.**

Summary

As you can see, there are many possibilities for using a database. You can use it to compile and manipulate lists of any kind of information. You can use it to calculate new data and to provide a basis for more databases. You can use it as a research and report tool. In short, a database offers the best foundation for good management and efficient data flows. For more information, select Help from the Window Menu or refer to the *Works* manual.

Quitting Works

1. **Pull down the File Menu and select Quit.** You may receive a message asking whether or not you want to save your document. Answer appropriately. (You should not save the changes you made to *Profile*.)

2. **Pull down the Special Menu and select Shut Down.**

3. **Remove the disks from the Macintosh and return them to their appropriate places.**

4. **Turn off the Macintosh.**

14 Integration Worksheet

Sometimes you want to combine the capabilities of one application with those of another. If you use *separate* word processor, spreadsheet, and database programs, you cannot easily produce a document that includes output from each of them. With an integrated program such as *Works*, however, you can quickly and easily develop a report that combines material generated by each *Works* application. The unifying application is the word processor. You can import data from a spreadsheet document and/or a database document into any word processor document.

Objectives

In this worksheet, you will learn how to

- Prepare a word processor document for merging with a database
- Copy and paste pictures into a word processor document
- Prepare a word processor document containing a printout of a spreadsheet
- Use the drawing tool in a word processor document
- Work with more than one document at a time in memory
- Print merged documents

Setting the Scene

Remember the letter you wrote inviting Birthday Club members to come in for a free ice cream cone in the month of their birthday? Well, it is time to print a copy for each member who has a birthday next month. You will personalize each letter by inserting the member's name and address from the *Members* database that you also created earlier. Figures 14-1a-c outline the steps from standard letter to personalized letter.

You will also use the word processor to write a memo to Chris presenting the sales figures for last week. That memo will include material taken from a spreadsheet file. Figure 14-2, page 167 shows the finished memo with the spreadsheet figures included.

Figure 14-1a. The standard Birthday Club letter

```
December 20, 1988




Dear Birthday Club Member:

HAPPY BIRTHDAY!

To help celebrate your birthday next month, we are enclosing 2 coupons
that can be exchanged for free ice cream cones.

We have many of your favorite flavors and some you would probably like to
try in the future.

We are looking forward to seeing you next month!

Yours truly,

THE ICE CREAM FACTORY



(Your Name), Manager

Enclosures

P.S. Please tell your friends about our Birthday Club. Just have them drop
by our shop and pick up an application form.
```

Figure 14-1b. The *Members* database

Last Name	First Name	Street Address	City	State	ZIP	Birth Month
McNamara	Jane	719 Morse St.	San Jose	CA	95128	February
Kline	Calvin	21 St. John St.	San Jose	CA	95130	May
Boyle	Lance	415 Forest Ave.	San Jose	CA	95128	January
Pang	Alice	21 Saratoga Ave.	Saratoga	CA	95070	September
Montague	Charles	3715 Bascom Ave.	Los Gatos	CA	95030	January
Sakamoto	Sachi	87 Rocky Lane	San Jose	CA	95130	August
Wong	Mohammed	711 Campbell Ave.	Campbell	CA	95008	March
Mock	Cherry	6516 Esmeralda Ct.	Campbell	CA	95008	April
Piccolo	Sal	988 Latimer Ave.	San Jose	CA	95117	January
Zachary	Scot	104 DeAnza Blvd.	Cupertino	CA	95014	November

Microsoft Works for the Macintosh

Figure 14-1c. The personalized letter. Note the address and salutation.

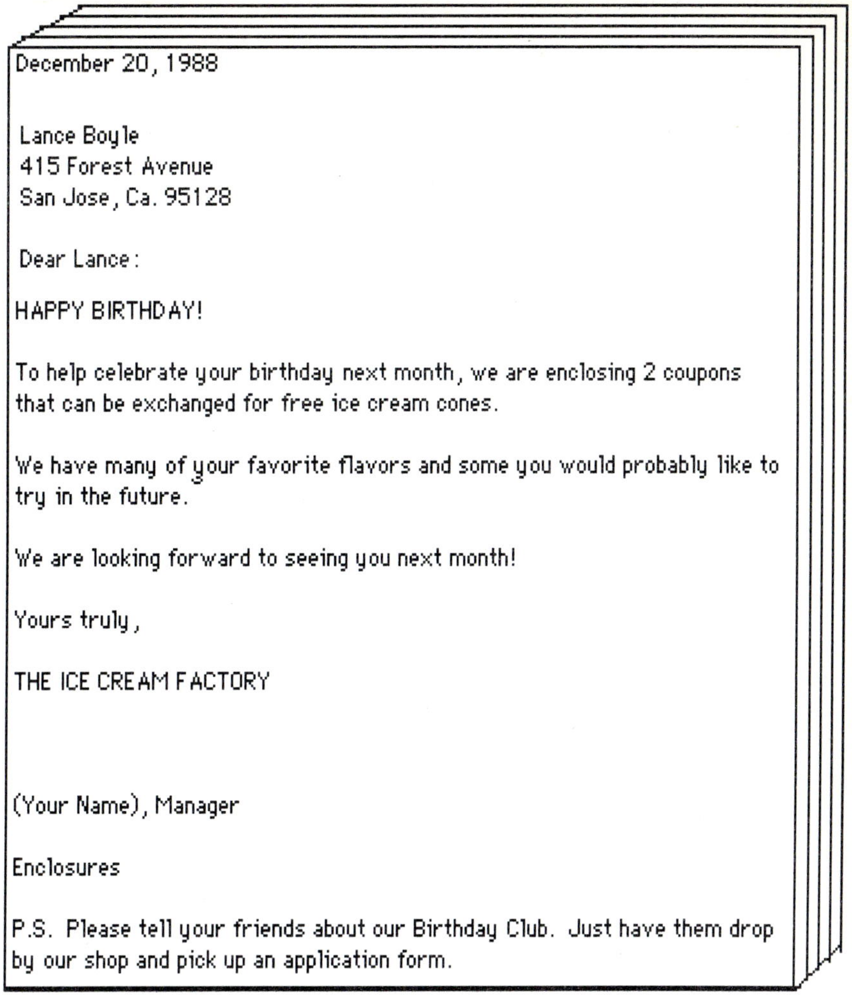

```
December 20, 1988

Lance Boyle
415 Forest Avenue
San Jose, Ca. 95128

Dear Lance:

HAPPY BIRTHDAY!

To help celebrate your birthday next month, we are enclosing 2 coupons
that can be exchanged for free ice cream cones.

We have many of your favorite flavors and some you would probably like to
try in the future.

We are looking forward to seeing you next month!

Yours truly,

THE ICE CREAM FACTORY



(Your Name), Manager

Enclosures

P.S. Please tell your friends about our Birthday Club. Just have them drop
by our shop and pick up an application form.
```

Opening Two Files

You can use both the database and the word processing applications at the same time.

➡ 1. **Open *Works*** as described in Getting Started, Chapter 1. You see the Open dialog box.

So that *Works* will have the membership records available in memory, first open the database file, *Members*.

2. **Insert your *Works Data Disk* into the second disk drive.**

14 Integration **167**

Figure 14-2. Memo created in word processing. It contains data from a spreadsheet file.

```
Memo to:    Chris Hughes
From:       Your Name
Date:       December 21, 1987
Subject:    Income Statement

Do you see any more improvements you would like made in the statement
template? I've checked the accuracy of the formulas and protected cells
as you requested.

                        INCOME STATEMENT
                         November, 1987

  SALES:                                              19079.00

  EXPENSES:
        Payroll                     1529.44
        Ice Cream Products          7982.00
        Other Food Products         2322.00
        Rent                        1000.00
        Utilities                    525.00
        Insurance                    120.00
        Payroll Tax                  148.36
        Advertising                   50.00
        Supplies                      85.00
        Miscellaneous                 50.00
        Total                                         12811.80

  NET INCOME                                           6267.20
```

3. **If your data disk is not shown as the active disk, click on the Drive button** to change the active disk drive to your data disk.

4. **Select *Members* from the Open dialog box list of files.**

5. **Click on the Open button.** The database is open on the desktop. Now open the word processor file, *Birthday,* that you typed in Chapter 4, as follows.

6. **Pull down File Menu and select Open.** When you see the Open dialog box,

7. **Select *Birthday*.**

8. **Click on the Open button.** Now the letter is also open on the desktop.

168   *Microsoft Works for the Macintosh*

Viewing the Open Documents

You now have two documents (two windows) open on the desktop. Depending on the size of the documents, you can have up to ten windows open at a time. To select a file,

➡ 1. **Pull down the Window Menu.** The bottom block lists the open files. (See Figure 14-3.) To work directly with the *Members* database file,

2. **Select** *Members* **from the Window Menu.**

Figure 14-3. Window Menu showing names of files now open

```
  File   Edit   Window   Search   Format   Font   Style
                Full Window    ⌘W

                Show Clipboard

                Help

                Birthday (WP)  3K
                Members  (DB)  1K
```

3. **Release the mouse.**

4. **Return to the** *Birthday* **word processor file** by following Steps 1 through 3 again, but this time select *Birthday* from the Windows Menu.

In order to insert names and addresses into your standard letter, you will create a merge document from the Birthday file. It will add information from the database document to the word processor document. In this exercise, you will direct *Works* to insert the recipient's name and address on the fourth line below the date.

To indicate where to insert information, you use **placeholders.** These contain the name of the database and the field containing the data you want to print at that place. You use the Prepare to Merge command to insert the placeholder. Then you use the Print Merge command to print the personalized copies of the word processor document.

➡ 1. **Place the insertion point on the line immediately above the salutation line.** (The line reads "Dear Birthday Club Member.")

Figure 14-4

You will insert the name and address beginning on this line →

```
December 20, 1988




Dear Birthday Club Member:

HAPPY BIRTHDAY!

To help celebrate your birthday next month, we are enclosing 2 coupons
that can be exchanged for free ice cream cones.

We have many of your favorite flavors and some you would probably like to
try in the future.

We are looking forward to seeing you next month!

Yours truly,

THE ICE CREAM FACTORY



(Your Name), Manager

Enclosures

P.S. Please tell your friends about our Birthday Club. Just have them drop
by our shop and pick up an application form.
```

2. **Pull down the Edit Menu and select Prepare to Merge.**
   The Prepare to Merge dialog box should resemble Figure 14-5.

Figure 14-5. The Prepare to Merge dialog box

Works has already selected (highlighted) the *Members* database in the left box. If you had more than one database file open, you would have to click on

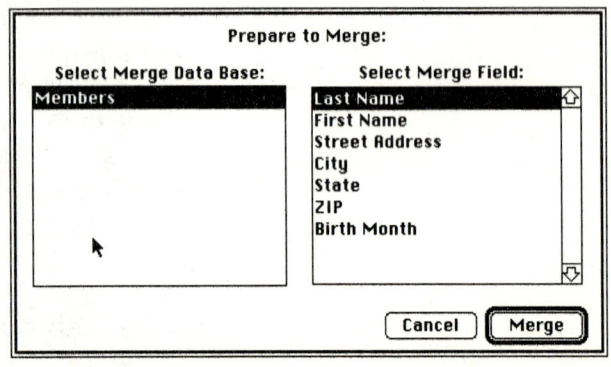

```
                    Prepare to Merge:
Select Merge Data Base:      Select Merge Field:
Members                      Last Name
                             First Name
                             Street Address
                             City
                             State
                             ZIP
                             Birth Month

                                  Cancel   Merge
```

170   *Microsoft Works for the Macintosh*

the file you wanted. In the right box, *Works* has selected the first field. Since First Name, not Last Name, is the field you want for starting the address portion of your letter,

3. **Click on First Name.**

4. **Click on the Merge button.** The program inserts the First Name field name into your letter with the name of the database document and the field name enclosed in a rectangle. Since we want to leave a space between the first name and last names,

5. **Press: [SPACEBAR] once.**

6. **Pull down the Edit Menu and select Prepare to Merge.**

7. **Click on Last Name.**

8. **Click on the Merge button.** The first line of the address is now complete. To enter the remaining lines,

9. **Press: [RETURN].**

10. **Pull down the Edit Menu and select Prepare to Merge.**

11. **Select Street Address.**

12. **Click on the Merge button.**

13. **Press: [RETURN].** The last line will contain three placeholders separated by a space or a punctuation mark.

14. **Pull down the Edit Menu and select Prepare to Merge.**

15. **Select City.**

16. **Click on the Merge button.** Since a comma follows the city,

17. **Type: ,** A space follows the comma. So,

18. **Press: [SPACEBAR] once.** The City, State, and ZIP field names go on the same line with a space between them. See if

14 Integration   **171**

you can position the last two placeholders yourself. When you are through,

19. **Press:** [RETURN]. Your screen should look like Figure 14-6.

Figure 14-6. Birthday Club letter with placeholders for data from the *Members* database

```
December 20, 1988


|Members:First Name| |Members:Last Name|
|Members:Street Address|
|Members:City|, |Members:State| |Members:ZIP|
Dear Birthday Club Member:

HAPPY BIRTHDAY!

To help celebrate your birthday next month, we are enclosing 2 coupons
that can be exchanged for free ice cream cones.

We have many of your favorite flavors and some you would probably like to
try in the future.

We are looking forward to seeing you next month!

Yours truly,

THE ICE CREAM FACTORY



(Your Name), Manager

Enclosures

P.S. Please tell your friends about our Birthday Club. Just have them drop
by our shop and pick up an application form.
```

Changing Text (the Salutation)

To change the text of the salutation to include the recipient's name rather than the impersonal "Dear Birthday Club Member," you can erase the old salutation and then follow the same procedure as above to insert a different salutation. If you need a reminder,

172   *Microsoft Works for the Macintosh*

1. **Select the words "Birthday Club Member" by dragging across them.** Do not highlight the colon.

2. **Press:** [DELETE] or [BACKSPACE].

3. **Pull down the Edit Menu and select Prepare to Merge.**

4. **Select First Name.**

5. **Click on the Merge button.**

The form letter will now include the first name of each recipient.

Selecting Data (January Birthdays)

You are almost ready to print the letters. First you must search the records in the database for Birthday Club members who have a birthday in January.

1. **Pull down the Window Menu and select *Members*.**

2. **Pull down the Organize Menu and select the Match Records command.** You see a dialog box like Figure 14-7.

Figure 14-7. The Match Records dialog box

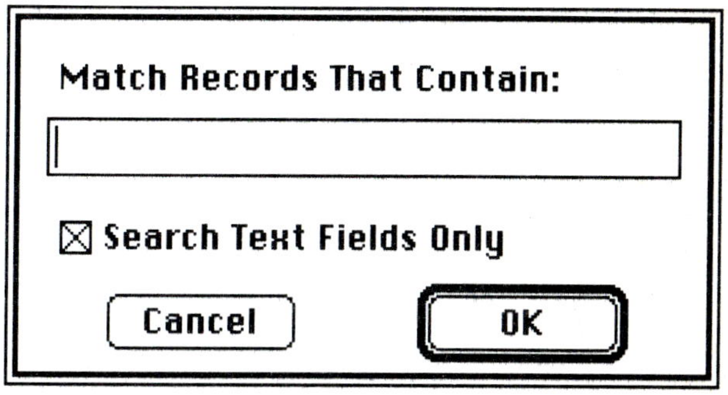

3. **Type: January**

4. **Click once on the OK button.** The program displays records for those members with a birthday in January.

```
┌─────────────────────────────────┐
│ Match Records That Contain:     │
│ ┌─────────────────────────────┐ │
│ │|                            │ │
│ └─────────────────────────────┘ │
│ ☒ Search Text Fields Only       │
│ ( Cancel )        (    OK    )  │
└─────────────────────────────────┘
```

Adding a Picture

Chris has collected some clip art drawings that you might want to incorporate into documents. The drawings have been saved in a *Works* word processor document called *Artwork*. To add a drawing (picture) to the upper right corner of the letter,

14 Integration **173**

➡️ 1. **Pull down the File Menu and select Open.** The Open dialog box appears.

2. **Select Artwork from the list box.**

3. **Click the Open button.** Chris has included three pictures. (See Figure 14-8.)

Figure 14-8. The pictures in the *Artwork* file

4. **Click once on any picture.** The cursor will appear at the extreme left margin of the screen. To select and copy one of the pictures,

5. **Press:** [⌘] and type **A** (or pull down the Edit Menu and select Select Picture). You have selected the ice cream cone.

6. **Press:** [⌘] and type **A again.** You have selected the next picture (balloons) placed horizontally on the line.

7. **Press:** [⌘] and type **A again.** You have selected the last picture (birthday cake).

8. **Press [⌘] and type A until you have selected the picture you want.** You can copy the picture onto the clipboard and then paste it into a document just as you do with text. To copy the selected picture onto the clipboard,

9. **Pull down the Edit Menu and select Copy.** To return to the letter window to paste the picture,

10. **Pull down the Window Menu and select Birthday.**

11. **Scroll to the top of the letter.**

12. **Place the insertion bar at the top of the letter.** It does not have to be in position horizontally. To paste in the picture from the clipboard,

13. **Pull down the Edit Menu and select Paste.**

The picture may not appear in the proper area, but before you move it, review Figure 14-9 to see how the insertion bar changes its shape to perform different functions when it gets near or on a highlighted picture.

Figure 14-9. Different shapes taken by the insertion bar

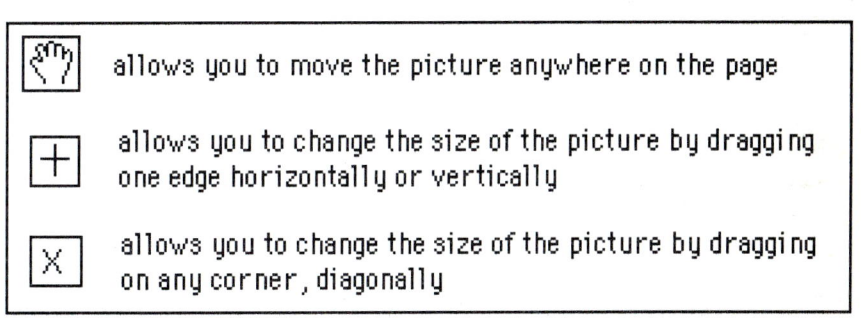

🖐	allows you to move the picture anywhere on the page
✛	allows you to change the size of the picture by dragging one edge horizontally or vertically
✕	allows you to change the size of the picture by dragging on any corner, diagonally

14. **Use the hand-shaped pointer to drag the picture.** If the picture is too large or too small for the area,

15. **Move the pointer to the lower right corner of the highlighted picture until it changes to an X.**

16. **Drag on the picture to increase or decrease its size.**

17. **To deselect the picture, click anywhere outside of the highlighted area.**

14 Integration **175**

Printing a Merged Document (The Letter)

To print a letter to each member selected from the database,

1. **Pull down the File Menu and select Page Setup.** Except for the top margin, leave all the settings as given. To add a few more lines to the top margin so that the letter will be better balanced vertically.

2. **Press:** [TAB] to Top Margin box.

3. **Type:** 1.5 (Your top margin now reads 1.5.)

4. **Click on the OK button.**

5. **Pull down the File Menu and select Print Merge.**

6. **Click on the OK button.** Printing starts shortly.

More Scene Setting

In order to keep track of profits, Chris has used the Works spreadsheet application to develop an income statement. She wants you to evaluate and make any changes you think useful. Before you submit it to Chris for her approval, you will write a brief introduction and explanation of the changes. You will use the word processor to create this memo and combine it with the spreadsheet.

Opening a New Word Processor Document

1. **Pull down File Menu and select New.** You see a message that asks you what type of document you want to create. Since you want WP (word processing) and it is already highlighted,

2. **Click on the OK button.** A blank screen appears. You will use this screen to create your memo to Chris.

Typing the Memo

You are now ready to type the memo to Chris. First you want to set a tab one inch from the left margin.

1. **Move the pointer to the 1-inch mark on the ruler and click.** (See Figure 14-10.)

176   *Microsoft Works for the Macintosh*

Figure 14-10. Note the tab stop at 1 inch

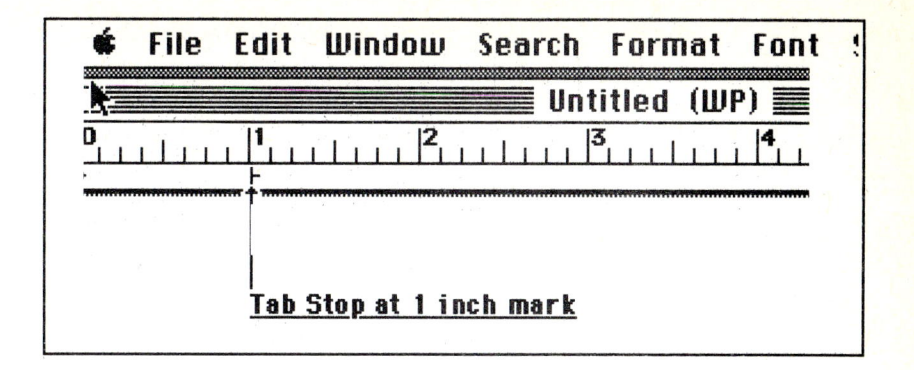

```
 🍎   File   Edit   Window   Search   Format   Font
═══════════════════════════════════════════════════
══════════════════════════ Untitled (WP) ══════════
 0         |1         |2         |3         |4
 ┬┬┬┬┬┬┬┬┬┬┬┬┬┬┬┬┬┬┬┬┬┬┬┬┬┬┬┬┬┬┬┬┬┬┬┬┬┬┬┬┬┬
             ┼
═══════════════════════════════════════════════════

         Tab Stop at 1 inch mark
```

2. **Type the following memo.** Make the substitutions indicated by the italicized words. Press [TAB] after the colon to line up items. Because your line of typing is longer than the illustration below, you line endings will not be the same.

> Memo to: Chris Hughes
> From: *Your Name*
> Date: *Today's date*
> Subject: Income Statement
>
> Do you see any more improvements you would like made in the statement template? I've checked the accuracy of the formulas and protected the cells as you requested.

3. **Press: [RETURN] two times.** This positions the insertion bar to where the spreadsheet document will be placed.

Opening the Spreadsheet Document

Before you can make a copy from a file, the original must reside in the Macintosh's memory. Therefore, you must open the spreadsheet file *Statement*. (This is Chris' income statement.)

➡ 1. **Pull down the File Menu and select Open.**

2. **Select *Statement*.**

3. **Click on the Open button.** Since you want to place this entire file in your memo,

4. **Pull down the Select Menu and select All Cells.**

14 Integration **177**

5. **Pull down the Edit Menu and select Copy.** A copy of the statement is now on the clipboard. To return to the memo,

6. **Pull down the Window Menu and select the filename *Untitled* (WP).** Since you have not saved your memo yet, *Works* has temporarily named it in memory *"Untitled."* You will give it your own file name when you save it. The blinking cursor is where you last left it—two lines below the text of the memo. To insert the income statement at that point,

7. **Pull down the Edit Menu and select Paste.** The spreadsheet appears below the memo. The final copy should look like Figure 14-2 on page 168.

Drawing a Frame

Now for more fun! *Works* has some drawing capabilities. You can draw a frame or border around the statement.

1. **Pull down the Edit Menu and select Draw.**

You see a dialog box similar to Figure 14-11. Use it to select a pattern for the frame.

Figure 14-11. The Select Draw Pattern dialog box

2. **Click on the bottom rounded-corner rectangle to select it.**

3. **Click on the OK button.** The pointer becomes a crosshair.

4. **Use the arrows in the scroll bar on the right of the screen to position the statement so that only the statement shows on the screen.** Before you draw the border around the statement, look at Figure 14-12. It shows you how to drag the crosshair. Then continue with Step 5.

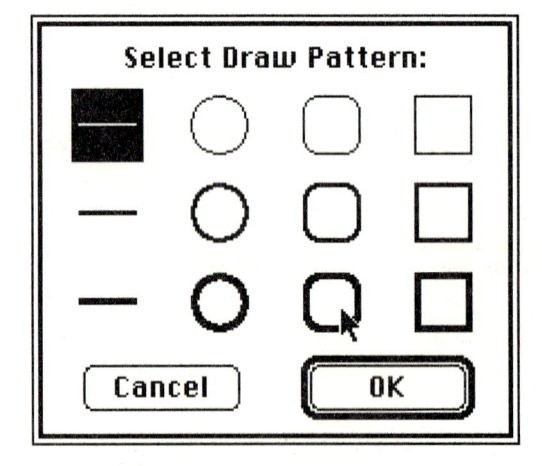

178 *Microsoft Works for the Macintosh*

5. **Position the crosshair above and to the left of the first line of the statement.**

6. **Drag the marker diagonally down and to the right** as shown in Figure 14-12.

7. **Release the mouse button** when the crosshair gets to the lower right of the statement.

Figure 14-12. Drawing a frame around the income statement

<u>**Start here**</u>

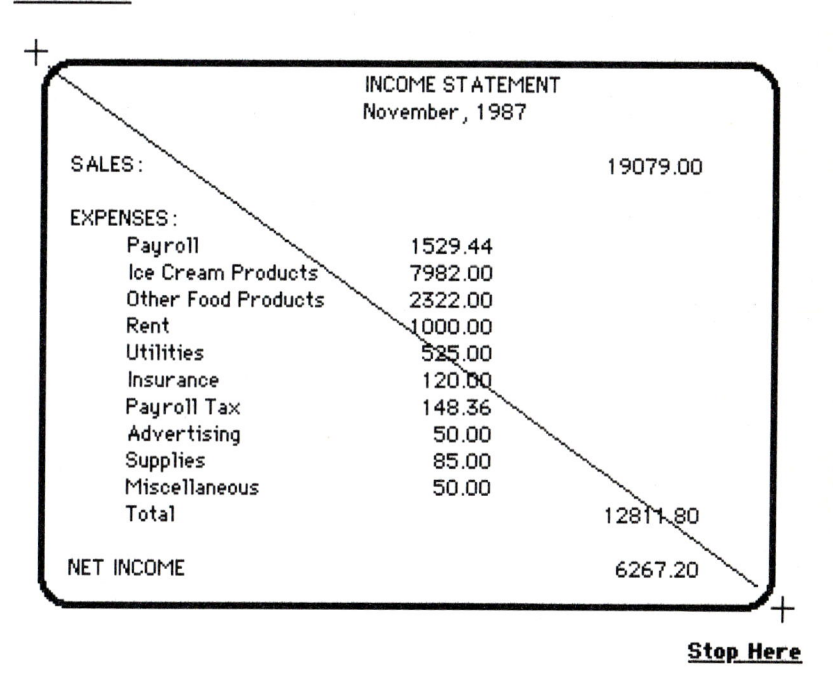

```
+
          INCOME STATEMENT
            November, 1987
  SALES:                         19079.00
  EXPENSES:
       Payroll             1529.44
       Ice Cream Products  7982.00
       Other Food Products 2322.00
       Rent                1000.00
       Utilities            525.00
       Insurance            120.00
       Payroll Tax          148.36
       Advertising           50.00
       Supplies              85.00
       Miscellaneous         50.00
       Total                        12811.80
  NET INCOME                        6267.20
                                          +
```
<u>**Stop Here**</u>

Warning: When you are in the Draw mode, each time you press and then release the mouse button, you will have drawn a picture. If you are not attentive, you may accidentally draw an extremely small object (perhaps just a dot on the screen) and you will overlook it. If you realize your mistake before you press another key, you can easily correct your error by using the Undo command. Practice the Undo command now.

8. **Pull down the Edit Menu and select Undo.** Since the last action you took was to draw the frame, it disappears.

14 Integration **179**

9. **Use Steps 5-7 to draw the frame again.**

10. **Repeat Steps 8 and 9 until you are satisfied with the frame.**

11. **Pull down the Edit Menu and select Draw Off.**

Suppose you decide that you want to delete or change the frame. You simply select and then delete it.

➤ 1. **Place the insertion point anywhere inside the picture (the frame).**

2. **Pull down the Edit Menu and select Select Picture.** The spreadsheet frame is highlighted.

3. **Press: [DEL] or [BACKSPACE].**

The frame disappears. Now redraw the border on your own. Use a different frame if you wish. If you need help, refer to Steps 1-7 and 11 above.

➤ 4. **If you have made other lines or marks that you would like to eliminate, follow these steps.**

a. **Click to the left of the unwanted mark.** The cursor blinks where the left line indent is set for that line.

b. **Pull down the Edit Menu and select Select Picture.** You can use the shortcut [⌘] - [A] instead of the Edit Menu.

c. **Repeat Step b until the mark or line you want to eliminate blinks.** If it does not blink, move the pointer near it, click again, and repeat Step 2. When the unwanted mark blinks,

d. **Press [DELETE].**

Saving a File Under a Different Name

Save the file with a descriptive name: for example, *Income*.

➤ 1. **Pull down the File Menu and select Save As.** When you see the Save As dialog box,

180   *Microsoft Works for the Macintosh*

2. **Type:** **Income** Be certain that your data disk is the active disk. You should see "Works Data" next to the active disk icon. If it is not, click on the Drive button.

3. **Click on the Save button.** Your file is now saved.

Printing a File

1. **Turn on your printer. Check that it is ready to print.**

2. **Pull down the File Menu and select Print.**

You will see a Print dialog box like the one in Figure 14-13. It offers many options. The buttons for the options currently selected are highlighted.

Figure 14-13. The Print dialog box

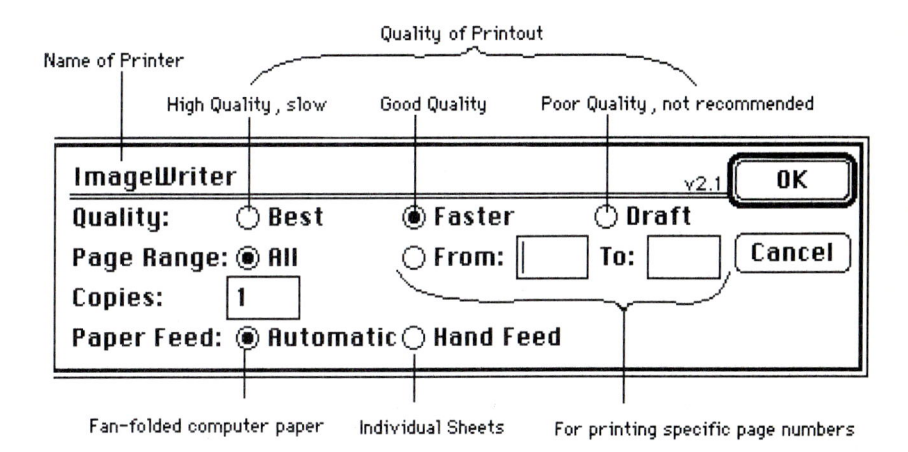

3. **Click the option buttons on your screen to make them conform to Figure 14-13.**

Note: For general use, use Faster printing. Best takes longer to print and quickly wears out ribbons.

4. **Click on the OK button.** The disk drive whirs as the Macintosh reads the Printer file from the system folder and writes a Print file to the disk. You will see the printing message box before printing begins. **If you want to cancel printing, hold down the [⌘] and type a period.** If the paper jams, use the printer on/off button to turn the printer off. Readjust the paper and begin again with Step 1.

14 Integration **181**

Review

If time permits, try some of the activities described in this worksheet without looking at the step-by-step instructions. For example, use the word processor to create amemo to send to all Birthday Club members born in February. Then copy and paste columns of figures from the spreadsheet. Then box the table. Add a drawing from Chris' collection of clip art.

Summary

Congratulations! You have practiced two of the basic integration operations. You have merged addresses from a database document with a form letter in a word processor file, and you have transferred material from a spreadsheet into a word processor document. Also, you have worked with four different files resident in the Macintosh's memory at one time.

If you want to learn more about integration features, check your *Works* manual or select Help from the Window Menu.

Quitting Works

It is always best to formally quit the program before you turn off the Macintosh. If you do not, you may lose information because the Macintosh updates the directories on the disks during the quitting process. Follow the steps to quit *Works*.

➡ 1. **Pull down the File Menu and select Quit.** If you have made any changes to *Income* since saving it, you may see a dialog box as shown in Figure 14-14. If you want to save changes, click on the Yes button. If you do not want to save changes, click on the No button. When the Macintosh has returned you to the desktop, tidy up the desktop for the next person.

Figure 14-14. The Save Changes dialog box

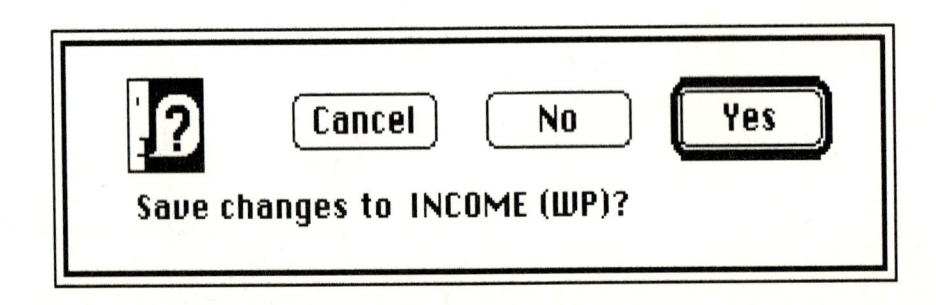

[Dialog box: Cancel | No | Yes — Save changes to INCOME (WP)?]

182   *Microsoft Works for the Macintosh*

2. Close open windows.

3. Pull down the Special Menu and select Shut Down.

4. Remove the disks from the Macintosh and return them to their appropriate places.

5. Turn off the computer.

15 Using the Spelling Checker & Other Finishing Touches

Objectives

In this worksheet, you will learn how to

- Check a document for spelling errors
- Insert manual page breaks
- Add page numbers

Setting the Scene

The editor of your local newspaper has asked you to write a follow up to the *Trivia* article you wrote in Chapter 2. After some research, you have finished the new article and stored it on your data disk under the filename *More Trivia*. Because you know that you sometimes make typographical errors, you plan to use the *Works* spelling checker. But you need to learn how to use it first. The instructions in this worksheet will guide you through the use of the spelling checker.

Using Spellswell™

More Trivia has some misspelled words. It also has some words that are spelled correctly, but are incorrectly used. You will use the Works spelling checker, called **Spellswell**™, to find and correct these words. The Spellswell™ program has a large dictionary and checks every word in a document against its dictionary. It stops and displays a word it does not recognize and offers alternatives to the word.

Your startup procedure will differ slightly from what you have become used to.

1. **Turn on the Macintosh.** When you see the flashing **?** disk,

2. **Insert the *Works* program disk into the upper drive.**

3. **Insert the Spellswell™ disk into the lower drive.** After a few moments, the Spellswell™ disk icon is highlighted.

4. **Pull down File Menu and select Open.** When the desktop appears, click on the Spellswell™ icon to select it.

5. **Pull down the File Menu and select Open**. You see the Spellswell™ copyright information.

6. **Click anywhere on the screen.** The copyright information disappears and you see a screen similar to Figure 15-1a or 15-1b.

Figure 15-1a. The Spellswell Open dialog box to open a dictionary

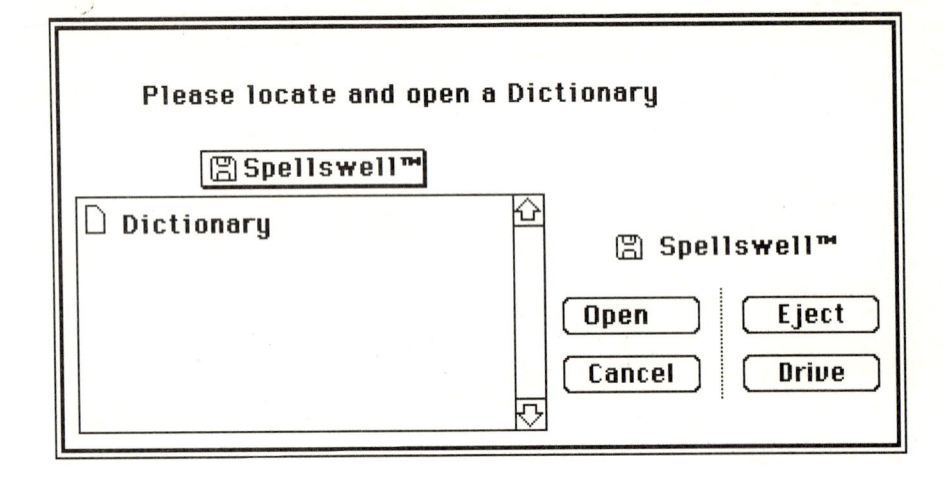

If your screen resembles 15-1a, continue with Step 7. If your screen resembles 15-1b, skip down to the paragraph following Step 7.

Figure 15-1b. The Spellswell Open dialog box to open a document

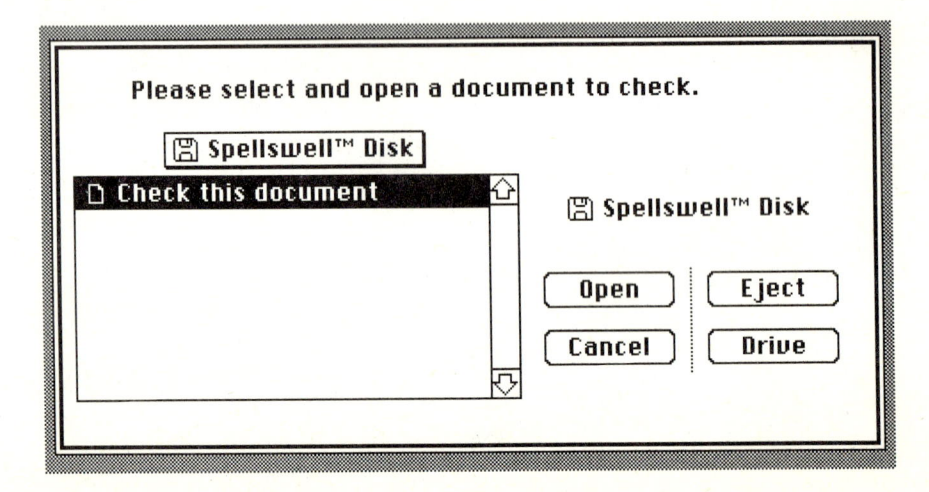

186 *Microsoft Works for the Macintosh*

7. Click on Open to load the Spellswell dictionary into memory. Once the dictionary is installed, you will see a screen resembling figure 15-1b.

Now you want to load a document from your data disk so that you can check it for spelling errors.

1. Click on the Drive button to change the active disk to *Works*.

2. Click on the Eject button.

3. Remove the *Works* **disk and insert your data disk.** When you see the Open dialog box,

4. Select *More Trivia*.

5. Click on the Open button.

The Spellswell™ program starts checking the document.

Be patient, it may take as much as 30 seconds before you see anything on your screen. Also, you may have to do some disk swapping. Just follow the directions from the Macintosh as they appear on the screen.

If a message asks if you want to use the document dictionary, click on the Yes button.

Homonyms

The Spellswell™ program will present you with different screens depending upon the type of problem it finds in the document. For example, the first screen message you will see (shown in Figure 15-2 on page 188) highlights the word "in" in the sentence where it appears.

Although the word is correctly spelled, the program stops at *homonyms* (words that sound the same but have different meanings) because it wants you to be certain you are using the correct word.

You must decide between the following options when the program encounters a homonym for the first time.

15 Using the Spelling Checker **187**

Figure 15-2. The Alternative Spelling dialog box for "in"

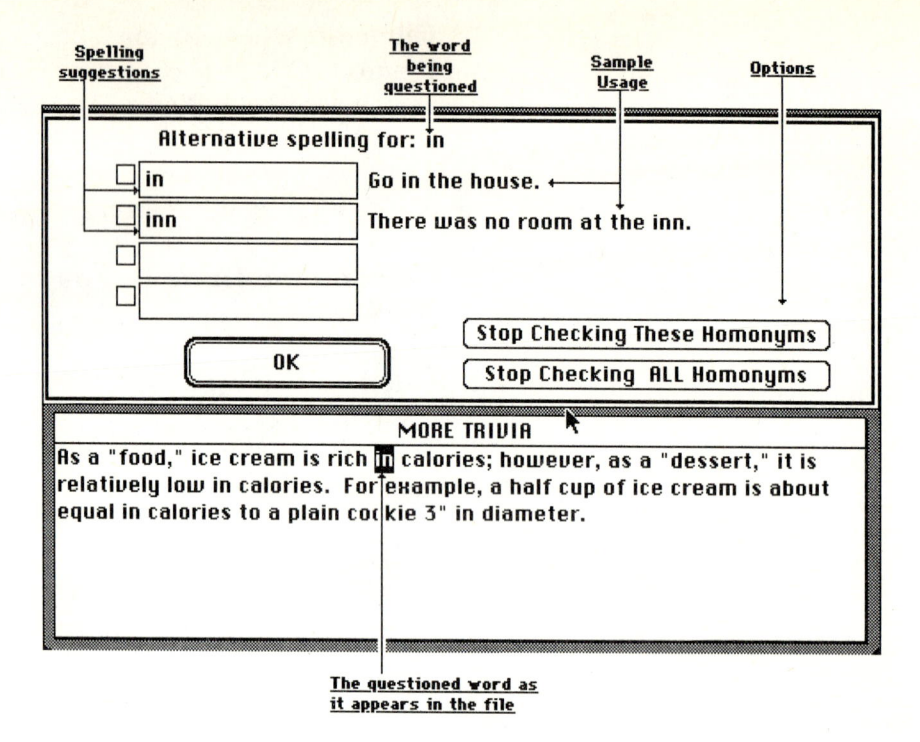

```
Spelling              The word                  Sample
suggestions           being                     Usage          Options
                      questioned

    Alternative spelling for: in
    ☐ in              Go in the house.
    ☐ inn             There was no room at the inn.
    ☐
    ☐
                                          [ Stop Checking These Homonyms ]
           [    OK    ]                   [ Stop Checking ALL Homonyms   ]

═══════════════════ MORE TRIVIA ═══════════════════
As a "food," ice cream is rich in calories; however, as a "dessert," it is
relatively low in calories. For example, a half cup of ice cream is about
equal in calories to a plain cookie 3" in diameter.

                      The questioned word as
                      it appears in the file
```

Option   Action

- **Stop Checking These Homonyms.** The program will no longer stop when it encounters this homonym again (here, the word "in").

- **Stop Checking All Homonyms.** The program will not stop when it encounters any homonym.

- **OK** The program will continue to stop at this word (here, "in") whenever it finds the word.

Since you are certain you have made no errors in using this word,

5. **Click on Stop Checking These Homonyms.** The program will no longer stop when it encounters the homonym "in."

Warning: Even though some words are spelled correctly, they may not be used correctly. For example, the person who typed this document has trouble using "to," "two,"and "too" and types "to" in

188 *Microsoft Works for the Macintosh*

all instances. Whenever the program displays the word "to," select OK if it is correctly used. Select the correct spelling if it is incorrectly used.

Look at Figure 15-3. The program has displayed the word "desert." Here it is incorrectly spelled, although the word you want sounds the same. Replace "desert" with the correctly spelled word, "dessert."

Figure 15-3. The Alternative Spelling dialog box for "desert"

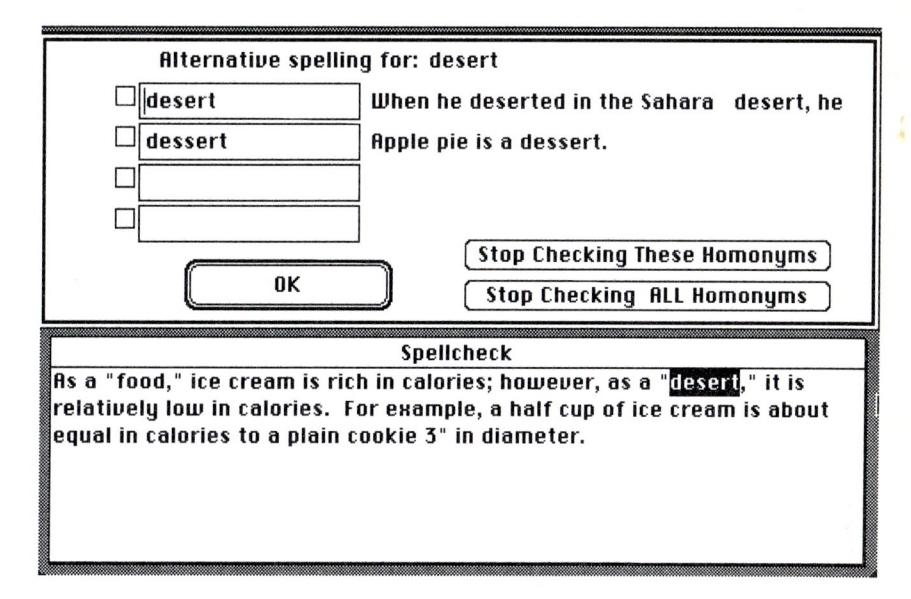

1. **Click in the box next to "dessert."**

2. **Click in the OK box.**

The program makes the correction and continues checking the document for errors. It will stop for several more homonyms, all of which are OK, before it reaches the first incorrect spelling.

Spelling Errors

If a word is spelled incorrectly, the program will suggest a replacement. For example, look at Figure 15-4, page 190. Here the program suggests replacing "ingrediants" with "ingredient." (We will discuss this selection in a moment.)

You are offered several options for a word that the program does not recognize.

15 Using the Spelling Checker **189**

Figure 15-4. The Alternative Spelling dialog box for "ingrediants"

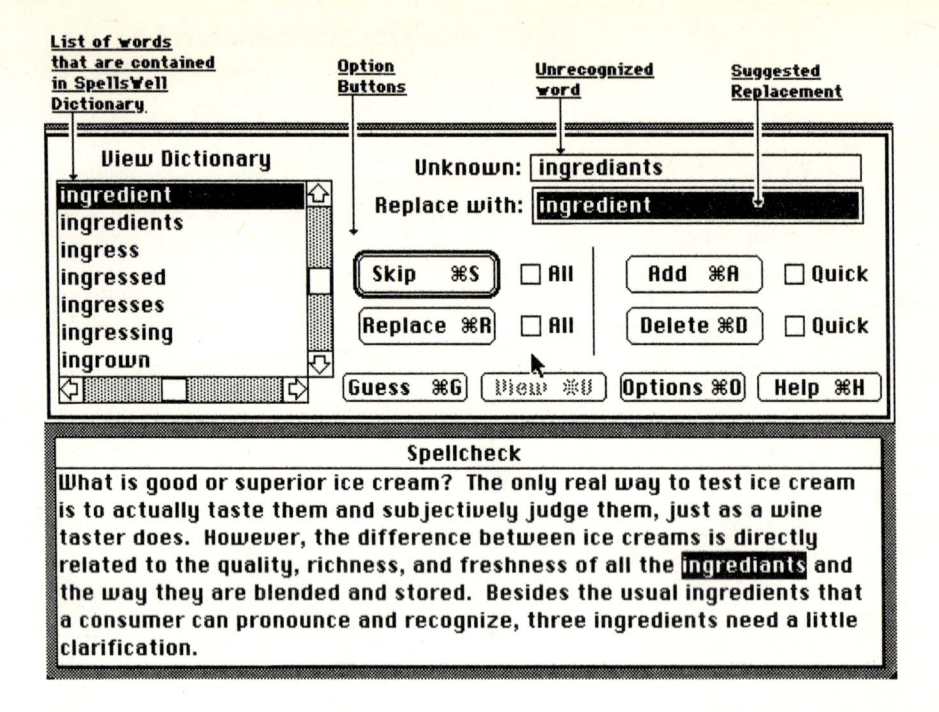

Option	Action
Skip	Skip this word this time. Do not change it.
Replace	Replace this word.
Add	Add this word to the dictionary.
Delete	Delete this word from the dictionary.
Quick	Automatically add word to the dictionary or delete word from the dictionary without prompting for a confirmating response from the user.
Guess	Guess at replacement word(s).
View	Display the dictionary.
Options	Change program options.
Help	Display an explanation of options.

In the View Dictionary box on the left of Figure 15-4, the program has highlighted the word "ingredient" and placed it in the Replace With: box. Because it is singular, this is not the word you want. You must select the plural.

1. **Click on the word "ingredients"** in the View Dictionary box.

This is the correct spelling which you want used all the time,

2. **Click in the All box to the right of the Replace button.** You see an X in the box.

3. **Click on the Replace button.** The program will automatically replace all occurrences of "ingrediants" with "ingredients."

Spellswell™ will continue to check your document and present alternative spellings for each word it cannot find in its dictionary. Before continuing, however, you will need to know more about the dictionary. Read the next three sections before you check the remainder of the document. These explain some general rules about the dictionary and how to respond to the program screens. When you have finished reading these sections, go back to the screen and continue the spelling check.

Viewing the Dictionary

If you are not sure of the spelling of a word and do not see it in the list displayed in the view box, simply use the scroll arrow until you find the word. Click next to it to accept it. When you do, you will see that the Replace With: box now has that spelling. Click the Replace button to continue checking.

Adding Words to the Dictionary

Do not add words to the dictionary even though you would if you were using your own disk. The program will stop at some words (such as "stabilizers" or "additives") because they are not in the dictionary.

If a word is correct, click on the Skip button. The program will ask if you would like to "Skip all occurrences of that word." Answer Yes. If you want to add them to your program, you select the Add button, but *please do not add them* since others who use your

15 Using the Spelling Checker **191**

disk will not then have the opportunity to see what happens when these words are not recognized.

Redundant Words

The program also stops when one word is repeated twice in succession. It assumes that the second appearance is an error. In your document, the word "emulsifiers" does appear twice in succession. (See paragraph 3, line 7.) However, this is no error because the word ends one sentence and begins the next. When you encounter this response, simply click the Skip button. Later in *More Trivia*, you will be questioned about the words "and and." This time the duplication is an error. So you will click the Replace button to accept the Replace With: choice.

Now go back to checking the spelling of *More Trivia*. When you have finished, return here to learn how to quit the spelling program.

Quitting Spellswell™

When the spelling check is completed, you will see a message similar to Figure 15-5.

Figure 15-5

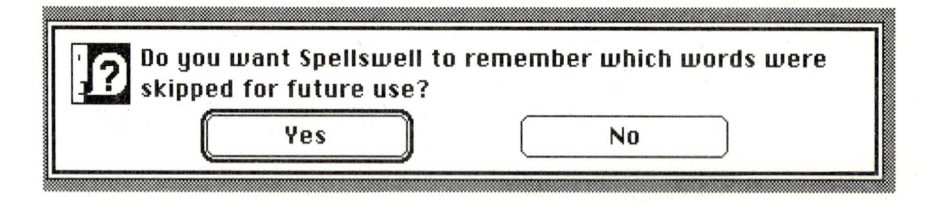

> [?] Do you want Spellswell to remember which words were skipped for future use?
>
> [Yes]   [No]

1. **Click the No button to leave the dictionary unchanged for future users.**

2. **Click the OK button when the program message displays the number of words scanned and number of words questioned.** You may have to do some disk swapping to complete this step. When you see the Open dialog box,

3. **Click on the Cancel button.** When a blank screen appears,

4. **Pull down File Menu and select Quit.** If you see a message regarding Preference settings, select No.

5. **Close the Spellswell™ window.**

6. **Pull down File Menu and select Eject.**

7. **Remove the Spellswell™ disk and insert the *Works* disk if you have not yet done so.**

You have completed the spelling check. Now you will "dress up" the article.

More Scene Setting

Now that you have checked the spelling of *More Trivia,* you can do some formatting to improve its appearance.

1. **Open *Works* to the Open dialog box.** Check to see that your data disk is the active disk.

2. **Select *More Trivia*.**

3. **Pull down the File Menu and select Open.** Your file now appears.

Formatting

As a review, let's make the title bold and change the font size.

1. **Drag the mouse across the title.**

2. **Pull down the Style Menu and select Bold.**

3. **Pull down the Style Menu again and select 14.**

Page Breaks

As you scrolled through *More Trivia*, you may have noticed the number in the box on the right scroll bar. That number indicates the document page presently displayed on the screen.

Works automatically inserts page breaks. These are determined by the Page Setup options in the File Menu. An automatic page break is represented by a series of dots. You can insert your own page breaks. These are represented by a series of hyphens. If you insert your own page break,*Works* will automatically repaginate any subsequent text.

Why would you want to insert your own page breaks? When you scrolled through *More Trivia*, you probably noticed a recipe was split between pages 1 and 2. To prevent this split when you print, place a page break before the recipe so that the entire recipe appears on page 2.

15 Using the Spelling Checker **193**

1. **Place the insertion bar at the beginning of the recipe on the same line as the recipe title.**

2. **Pull down the Format Menu and select Insert Page Break.**

The automatic page break line disappears and the manual page break now appears as a series of hyphens. When you print, the second page will now start with the recipe.

Numbering Pages

Since *More Trivia* is more than one page long, you will instruct the program to print page numbers. You use the Page Setup option.

1. **Pull down the File Menu and select Page Setup.**

2. **Move pointer to the Footer box and click once to place the insertion bar in that box.** To print the page number centered at the bottom of each page,

3. **Type: &CPage &p**   Be sure to put a space after the "e" in "page."

4. **Click on the OK button.**

Saving and Printing Your File

You should save your changed file before you print it.

1. **Pull down the File Menu and select Save As.** You see the Save As dialog box.

2. **Type: Trivia4**

Be certain that you are saving this file to your data disk. You should see "Works Data" next to the active disk icon. If not, click on the Drive button.

3. **Click on the Save button.** Your file is now saved.

4. **Pull down the File Menu and select Print.** You see the Print dialog box.

5. Make any necessary changes in the print options.

6. Click on the OK button to initiate printing of your document.

Quitting Works

It is always best to formally quit the program before you turn off the Macintosh. If you do not, you may lose information because the Macintosh updates the directories on the disks during the quitting process. Follow the steps to quit *Works*.

1. **Pull down the File Menu and select Quit.** If you have made any changes to your file since you last saved it, you may see a dialog box asking if you want to save the changes. If you want to save changes, click the Yes button. If you do not want to save changes, simply click on the No button. When the Macintosh has returned you to the desktop, tidy up the desktop for the next person.

2. **Close open windows.**

3. **Pull down the Special Menu and select Shut Down.**

4. **Remove the disks from the Macintosh and return them to their appropriate place.**

5. **Turn off the Macintosh.**

Review

Type a report for one of your classes. Check the accuracy of your typing by using the spelling checker, add a footer or header to print page numbers, and insert manual page breaks to avoid awkward page endings.

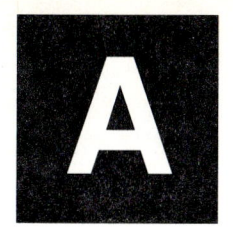

A Meeting the Macintosh

In this worksheet, you willl learn how to

- Get the Macintosh started
- Use the mouse to give commands
- Start Microsoft *Works*

You will need the following:

- A Macintosh computer with mouse
- Microsoft *Works* disk

Getting Started

How you start up *Works* depends on the state of your computer. From Steps 1-3 below, select the numbered step that corresponds to the condition of your computer. Then follow the lettered instructions.

1. If the computer is off

a. Turn the computer on. You see a disk icon with a flashing ? similar to Figure A-1. It reminds you that the computer needs a system disk. An icon is a small picture that represents an object. When the disk icon with the flashing question mark appears, it means that the Macintosh needs a startup disk. (A startup disk is one that has a system folder—more on that later.)

Figure A-1. The question mark disk

b. Insert the Microsoft *Works* program disk into the upper disk drive. At this point, you should see the *Works* program-disk icon in the upper right corner of the screen. Your screen should look like either Figure A-2a Page 198) or Figure A-2b (page 199).

197

Figure A-2a. Desktop with *Works* program-disk icon in the upper right corner

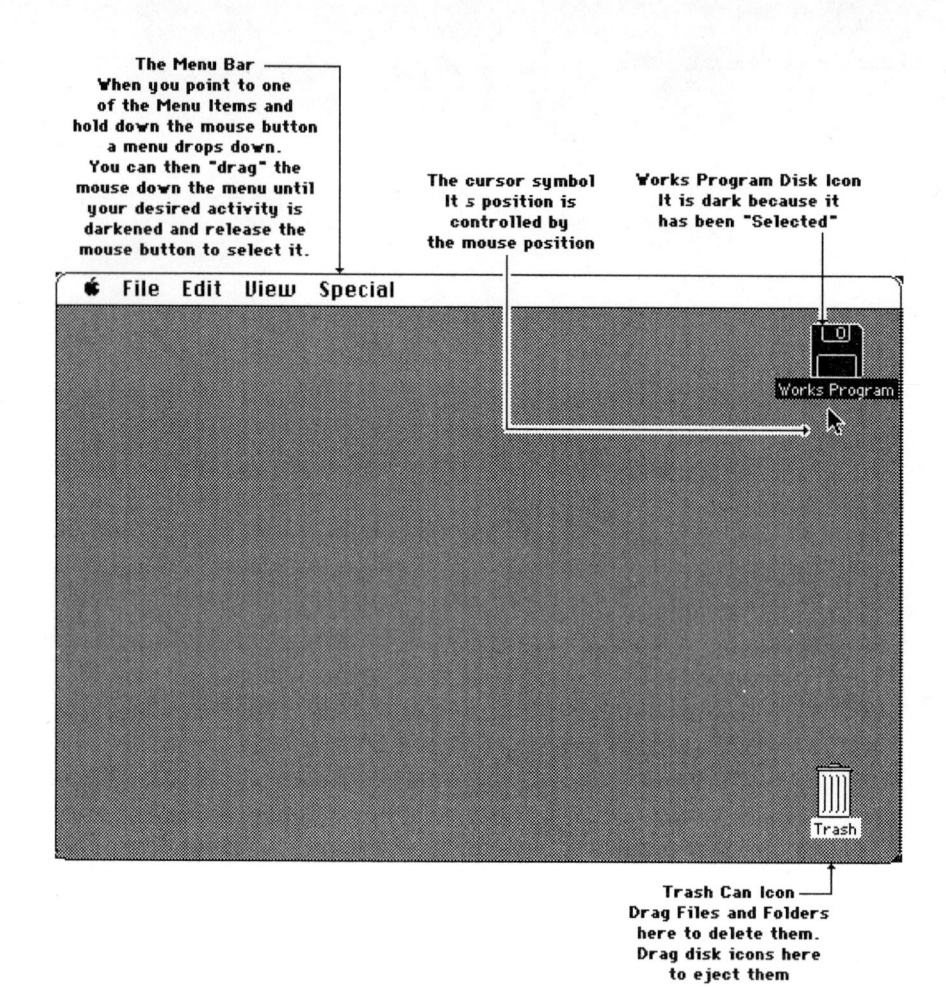

The Menu Bar — When you point to one of the Menu Items and hold down the mouse button a menu drops down. You can then "drag" the mouse down the menu until your desired activity is darkened and release the mouse button to select it.

The cursor symbol It s position is controlled by the mouse position

Works Program Disk Icon It is dark because it has been "Selected"

 File Edit View Special

Works Program

Trash

Trash Can Icon — Drag Files and Folders here to delete them. Drag disk icons here to eject them

c. **If your screen looks like Figure A-2a, continue with Step d. If your screen looks like Figure A-2b, skip down to Step f.**

d. **Click on the *Works* disk icon to select (highlight) it** (if it is not already selected).

e. **Pull down the File Menu and select Open to open the disk onto the desktop.** You see a desktop similar to Figure A-2b.

f. **Click on the *Works* program-disk icon**

198 *Microsoft Works for the Macintosh*

Figure A-2b. Desktop with *Works* program disk open showing file icons

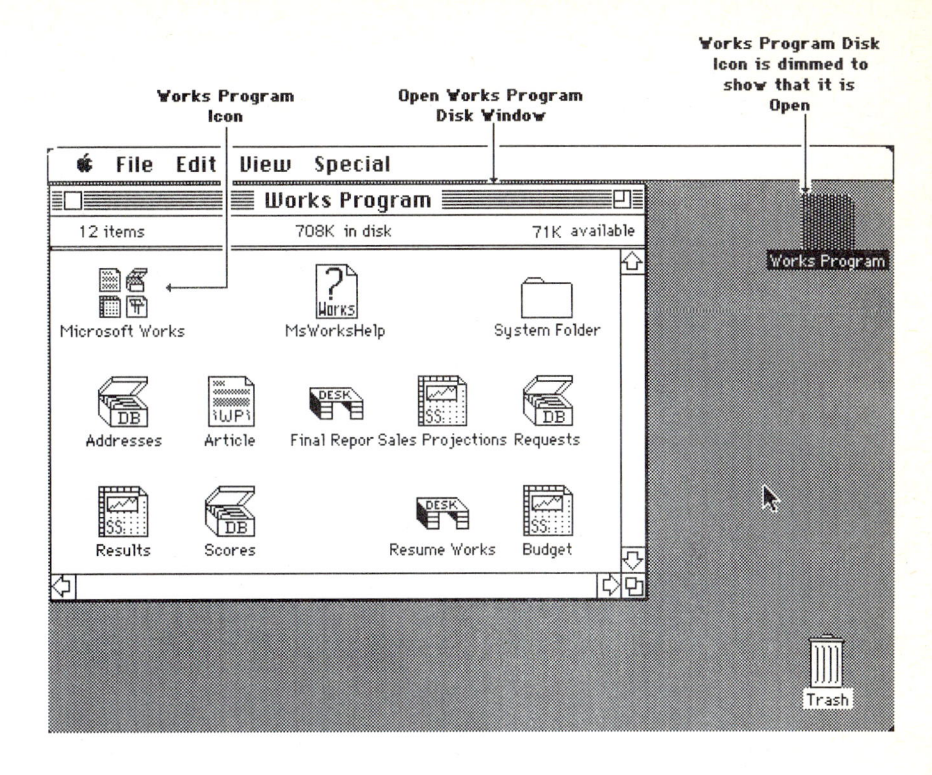

g. **Move the pointer to File. Hold down the mouse button while you drag the pointer down to Open and then release the mouse button.** You see the *Works* open dialog box as shown in Figure A-3 (page 200).

h. **Now read the next section (entitled Scrolling Through a File List Window) that follows the alternative instructions.**

2. **If the computer is on and you see the flashing ? disk from Figure A-1, follow Steps 1b through 1h above.**

3. **If the computer is on and you see anything other than the flashing ? disk, it means that the previous user did not properly shut down the computer.** It is best to close down before beginning your session.

   a. **Pull down the Special Menu and select Shut Down.** The Macintosh will eject any disks in the disk drives and display the flashing ? disk on the screen as shown in Figure A-1.

Appendix A: Meeting the Macintosh **199**

b. Return the ejected disks to their proper storage places.

c. Follow Steps 1b through 1h above.

After a short while, you see the Open dialog box shown in Figure A-3. Study it carefully.

Figure A-3. The *Works* Open dialog box

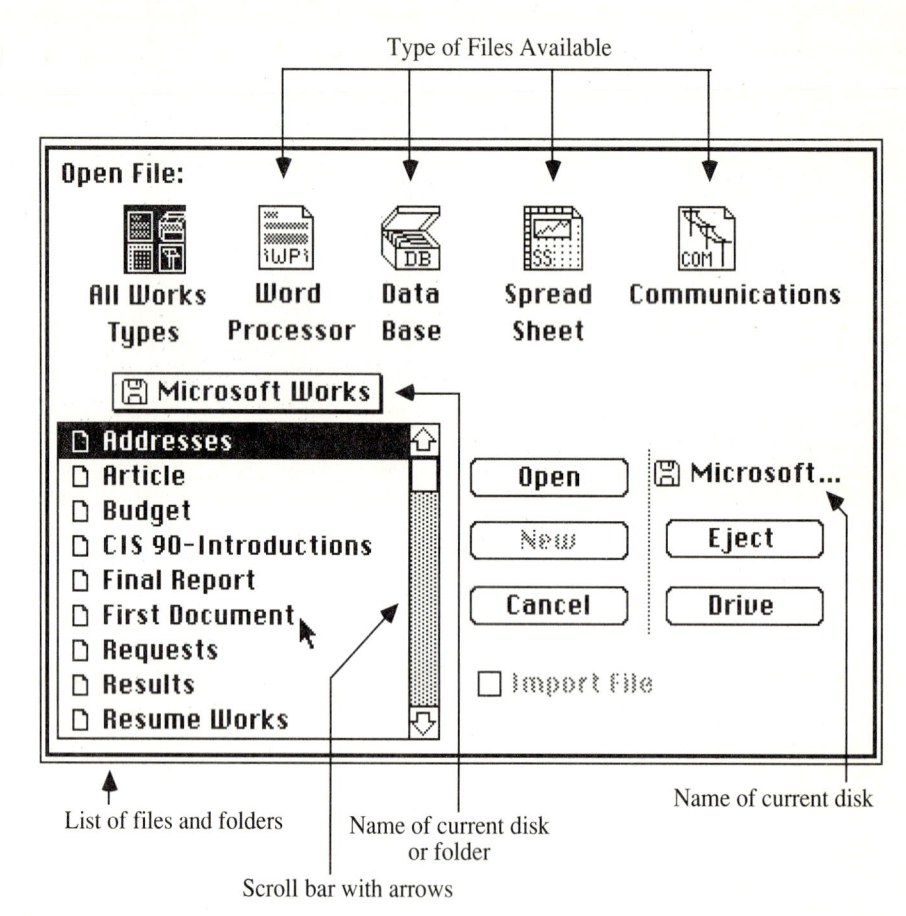

[Figure A-3: The Works Open dialog box, showing icons for "All Works Types," "Word Processor," "Data Base," "Spread Sheet," and "Communications" (labeled as Type of Files Available); a file list containing Addresses, Article, Budget, CIS 90-Introductions, Final Report, First Document, Requests, Results, Resume Works (labeled as List of files and folders); a scroll bar with arrows; buttons for Open, New, Cancel, Eject, Drive; an Import file checkbox; and labels pointing to Name of current disk or folder, and Name of current disk.]

Scrolling Through a File List Window

Notice that the All Works Types icon is highlighted. In the list of files and folders, you will find the names of files produced by all the *Works* applications. You will find word processor, spreadsheet, data base, and communications files. (You will learn more about these when you work with the text.) There may be more files on the disk than will fit in the window. To see others,

1. **Move the pointer to the lower arrow in the scroll bar and click once.** The list of files moves upward and you see a new filename at the bottom of the list.

2. **Continue clicking on the lower arrow until the white box (scroll box) in the scroll bar is at the bottom.** That indicates that you have reached the end of the file.

3. **Return to the beginning of the list by moving the pointer to the upper arrow and clicking several times.**

4. **Practice scrolling back and forward through the list until you feel comfortable with scrolling.** To see only word processing files,

5. **Move the pointer to the Word Processor icon and click once.** Note that the list of files and folders has changed. Now only the files that were produced by the word processor are listed. If you want to, see what happens when you click the icons of the other applications. When you are ready to continue, click the pointer on the Word Processor icon again.

Opening a File

Let's learn more about using *Works* from *First Document:*.

1. **Use the scroll arrows (as in Steps 4 and 5 above) to move up and down the list of files and folders until you see the filename *First Document*.**

2. **Move the pointer to *First Document* and click once.**

3. **Move the pointer to the Open button and click once.**

4. **Read *First Document* and follow the instructions in it.**

5. **When you are finished, come back to this worksheet.**

Opening a Second File

Now that you have finished *First Document,* follow the instructions given below to continue on with *Next Document*.

1. **Position the pointer on the word File in the menu bar.**

Appendix A: Meeting the Macintosh **201**

Figure A-4. The File Menu with Open option selected

2. **Hold down the mouse button while you drag the pointer down the menu to Open.** See Figure A-4. As you drag the pointer down the menu, the various options become highlighted.

3. **When Open is highlighted, release the mouse button.**

Note: The above three steps are called "Pulling down the XXXX menu and selecting XXXX." In the future, we will use this shortened version.

The Open dialog box appears as it did before. Now you will open the file *Next Document*.

4. **Use the scroll arrows to move up and down the list of files until you see the filename *Next Document*.**

5. **Move the pointer to *Next Document* and click once.**

6. **Move the pointer to the Open button and click once.**

7. **Read *Next Document* and follow all the instructions in it.**

8. **When you have completed *Next Document*, come back to this worksheet.**

Welcome Back! You have learned quite a bit about the Macintosh and *Works* while exploring the last two documents. One of the features of *Works* is the ability to work with up to ten documents at the same time. The instructions below will tell you how to move from one document to another when you have more than one open.

Switching Between Documents

1. **Move the pointer to Window in the menu bar and hold the mouse button down while you look at the Window Menu.** It is shown in Figure A-5.

Figure A-5. The Window Menu

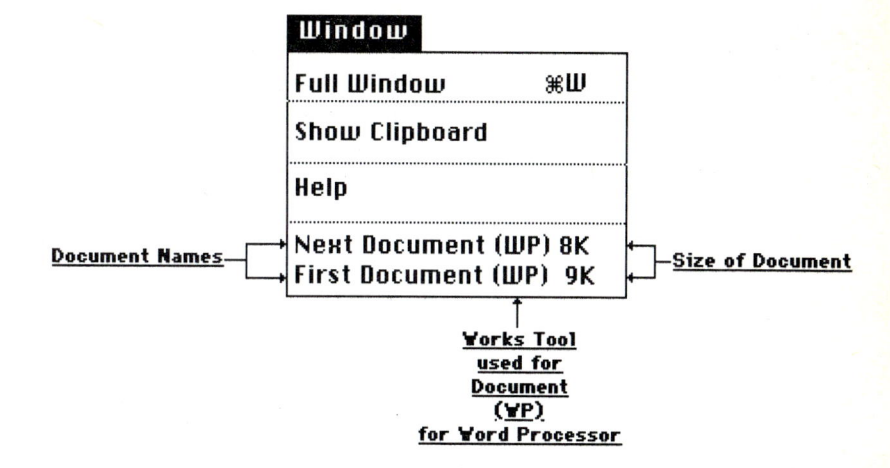

```
Window
Full Window              ⌘W
Show Clipboard
Help
Next Document (WP) 8K
First Document (WP) 9K
```

Document Names → Next Document / First Document
Size of Document ← 8K / 9K
Works Tool used for Document (WP) for Word Processor

2. **Select *First Document* from the Window Menu.** First Document becomes the active window.

3. **Pull down the Window Menu and select *Next Document*.** *Next Document* becomes the active window.

Being able to switch between windows makes it easy to share information between documents.

Quitting Works

- **Pull down the File Menu and select Quit.** You will probably see a dialog box like the one shown in Figure A-6 asking if you want to save the changes you have made in *First Document*.

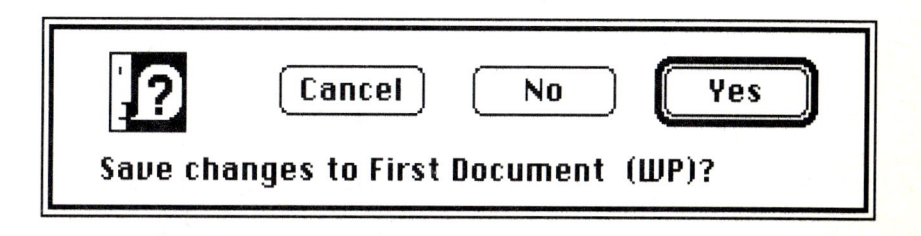

```
[?]   [Cancel]   [No]   [Yes]
Save changes to First Document (WP)?
```

Appendix A: Meeting the Macintosh   **203**

Think About It

- **Cancel** would cancel the Quit command you gave earlier. You could then continue working with the document. Cancel buttons are handy when you have given the wrong command or changed your mind.

- **Yes** would tell the computer that you do want to save the new changed version of *First Document*. Notice that Yes has a dark border around the button. Remember the dark border shows which option you select if you press [RETURN].

To keep *First Document* unchanged for possible use at another time, your response should be **No**.

- **Move the pointer to the No button and click once.**

You should now be back at the Macintosh desktop.

Macintosh Desktop

In order to study the Macintosh desktop closely, close all the open windows on the desktop.

- **Click in the close box of all open windows. See Figure A-7b for the location of the close box.**

Let's get acquainted with the desktop. Look at the top of your screen. You see a menu bar with some familiar titles and some new ones. Follow the instructions below to look at the options listed in each menu.

1. **Move the pointer to File and hold down the mouse button while you look at the options in this menu.** Note that some of the options are dimmed and some are in bold. The bold options are the ones that are available to you at this time. As circumstances change, the available options also change.

2. **Now move the pointer to each of the other menu titles and hold down the mouse button while you examine the options available in each of them.**

3. **Finally, move the pointer to the Apple icon in the upper left corner and hold down the mouse button while you examine those options.** Certain options in each menu will be explained as we use them. If you are curious, you may look up others in the Macintosh manual.

Figure A-7a. Desktop showing *Works* disk window open with icon view

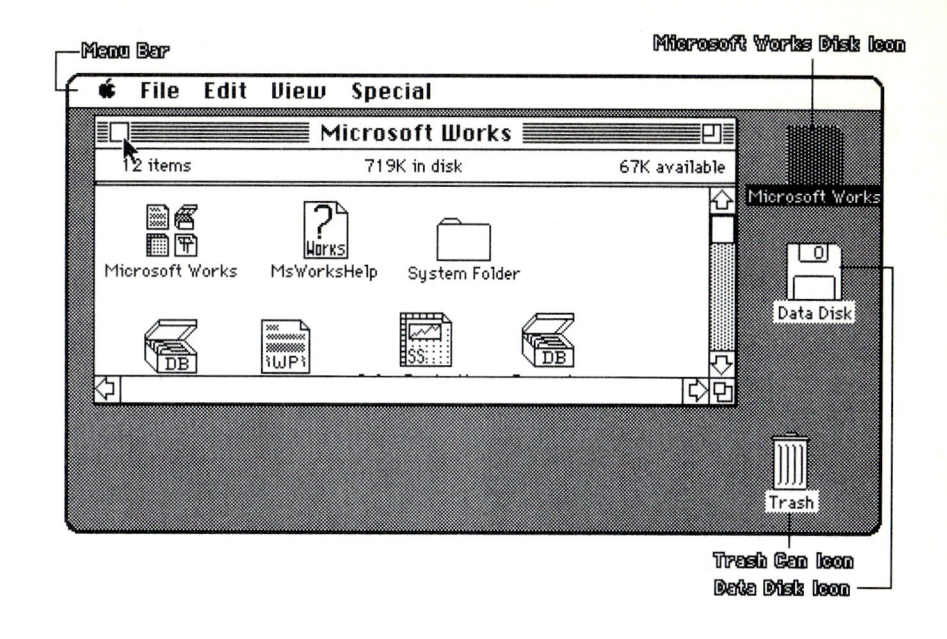

Figure A-7b. *Works* disk window with name view

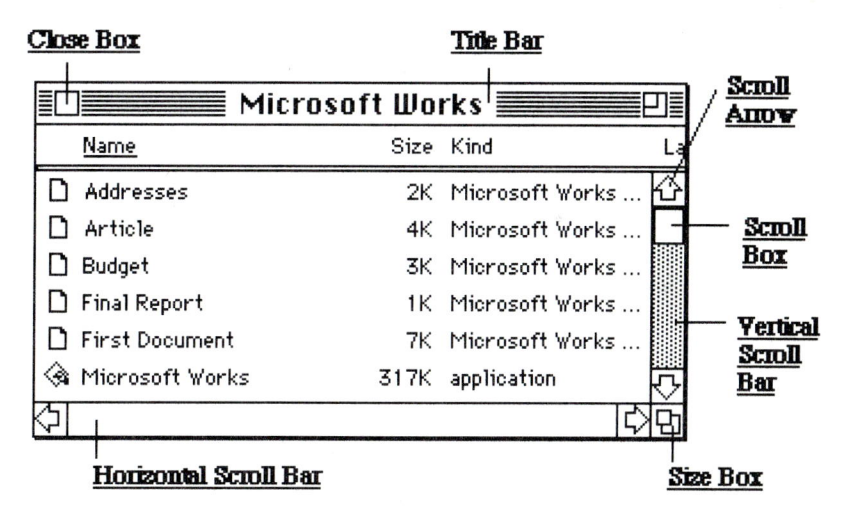

Opening a Disk Window

On the desktop are three icons. The trash can icon allows you to delete files from your disk by throwing them away into the trash can. The disk icons represent disks in the Macintosh's disk drives. To see what information is saved on a disk (the *Works* program disk for example), you must open it.

➡ 1. **Move the pointer to the *Works* disk icon and click once. The disk icon becomes highlighted (if it wasn't already).**

Appendix A: Meeting the Macintosh **205**

2. **Pull down the File Menu and select Open.**

A window similar to one of those in Figure A-7 opens on the desktop.

Viewing the Disk Contents

Your window may not look exactly like either one in Figure A-7. That's because the desktop offers many views through a disk window. Follow the instructions to see these different views.

➡ 1. **Pull down the View Menu and keep it down while you examine the options.** One of the options will have a check mark beside it. That is the current view.

2. **Select a different view from the View Menu.**

3. **Experiment with different views.**

4. **Pay particular attention to how the information in the window changes with different views.**

5. **Look at the vertical scroll bar and the horizontal scroll bar.** If either or both of them are gray, it means that there is information available that does not fit in the window. **Use the scroll arrows on the gray scroll bar to scroll the window so that the rest of the information becomes visible.**

6. **Finally, pull down the View Menu and select By Name.** We prefer the By Name view because it lists files in alphabetical order, making them easier to find.

This window is very similar to the word processor window.

Closing a Window

When you click the close box, the window goes away. Try it now. Here are the instructions.

➡ 1. **Move the pointer to the close box (Figure A-7b) and click once.** The window disappears! Don't worry, we can get it back. Just continue with the instructions.

2. **Pull down the File Menu and select Open.** The window reappears.

Changing Window Size

The size box allows you to change the size of a window. Follow these instructions to find out how to do it.

➡ 1. **Move the pointer to the size box (Figure A-7b) and hold down the mouse button while you drag the mouse down and to the right.** Note that a shadow outline of the window follows the mouse as you drag it.

2. **Release the mouse button when the window shadow reaches the lower right corner of the screen.** The window will fill in.

3. **Make the window small again.** Move the pointer to the size box and hold down the mouse button while you drag the mouse up and to the left. Release the mouse button when the shadow outline of the window is the size you want it.

Moving a Window

You can also move the window to other parts of the desktop.

➡ 1. **Move the pointer to the title bar (Figure A-7b) and hold down the mouse button while you drag the mouse in the direction you want the window to move.** Note that a shadow outline of the window follows the mouse as you drag it.

2. **Release the mouse button when the window shadow reaches the position where you want it.** The window will fill in.

Note that the icons in the disk window associated with *First Document* and *Works* are different. That is because *Works* is an applications program (a computer program which turns the computer into a specialized tool) while *First Document* is a document prepared using an application program.

The System Folder

You should become familiar with the system folder. The instructions below will help you.

➡ 1. **Look through the list of files until you find the system folder.**

Appendix A: Meeting the Macintosh **207**

2. **Move the pointer to the system folder and click once.**

3. **Pull down the File Menu and select Open.**

4. **Pull down the View Menu and select By Icon.**

You should see a window similar to the one in Figure A-8. A system folder that contains at least the Finder and system files must be present on any startup disk. Disks without system folders are either program disks (storage for a computer program) or data disks (storage for documents created by computer programs). For example, to complete the worksheets in this book, you use the Works program disk (which is also a startup disk) and you store the documents you create on your own data disk.

Figure A-8. The system folder window

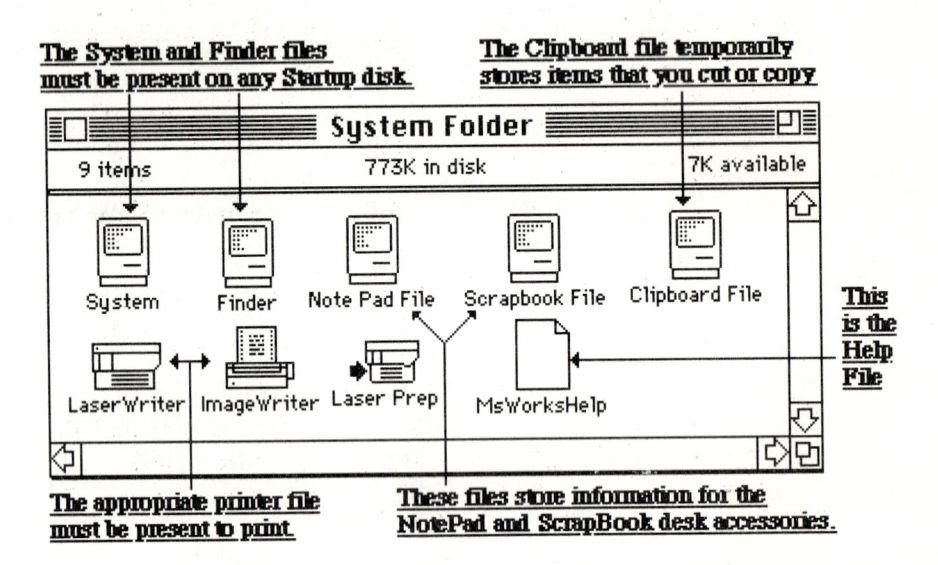

Desk Accessories

Now look at the Apple on the left side of the menu bar. Under the Apple are many desk accessories. These are small special purpose programs that you can use any time you are working on the computer. A limited number of desk accessories may be installed on the system file of the startup disk. In this section, you will view the desk accessories that are stored under your Apple.

The Scrapbook

1. **Move the pointer to the Apple in the menu bar. Hold down the mouse button.**

208 *Microsoft Works for the Macintosh*

2. **Move the mouse down the Apple Menu until the Scrapbook is highlighted.**

3. **Release the mouse button.** A screen similar to Figure A-9 should appear. If you see a picture instead of the message screen, don't worry — it simply means that someone else has been playing with the Scrapbook. **Just continue to Step 4.**

Figure A-9. Scrapbook message

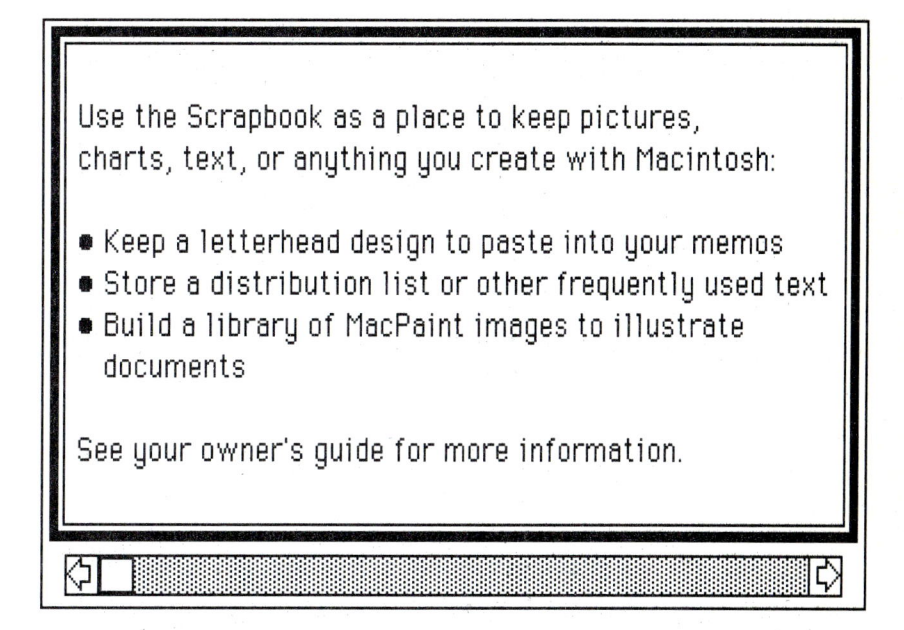

```
Use the Scrapbook as a place to keep pictures,
charts, text, or anything you create with Macintosh:

• Keep a letterhead design to paste into your memos
• Store a distribution list or other frequently used text
• Build a library of MacPaint images to illustrate
  documents

See your owner's guide for more information.
```

4. **Look at the scroll bar along the bottom of the screen.** Clicking on the left or right arrow will move you through the pages of the Scrapbook. Pictures and documents can be posted into and copied from the Scrapbook at any time. Scroll through the pages in the Scrapbook to see what has been stored in it.

5. **Click the close box at the top left corner of the Scrapbook screen to close the screen when you are finished looking through it.**

The Chooser

Let's look at another desk accessory called the *Chooser*. Before any document can be printed, a printer must be correctly selected. You select printers in the Chooser.

Appendix A: Meeting the Macintosh **209**

➡ 1. **Move the pointer to the Apple.**

2. **Hold down the mouse button.**

3. **Move down to select Chooser.** You should see a screen similar to Figure A-10.

Figure A-10. The Chooser window

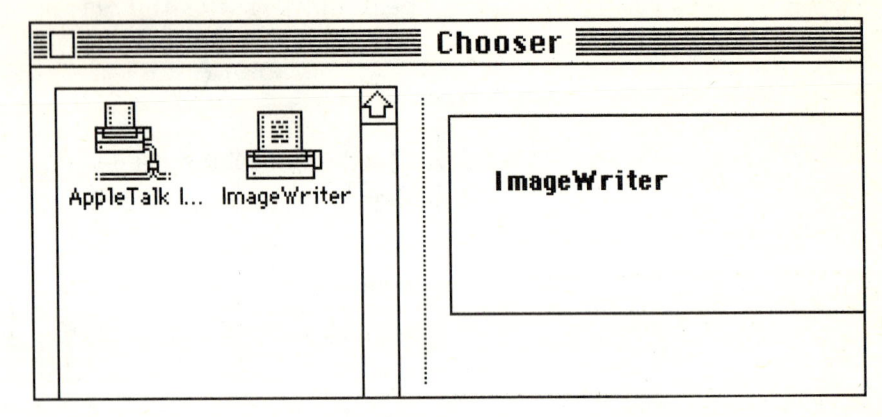

4. **Click on the ImageWriter icon.** The printer is selected.

5. **Click on the close box of the Chooser window.**

If you wish, you can try some of the other desk accessories that are listed under the Apple Menu. When you finish with a desk accessory, just click on the close box and it will disappear.

Quitting This Session

Before you leave, tidy up the desktop for the next person.

➡ 1. **Close each Open window by moving the pointer to the close box and clicking once.**

2. **Pull down the Special Menu and select Shut Down.**

3. **Remove any ejected disk from the Macintosh.**

4. **Turn off the Macintosh.**

5. **Return the *Works* disk to your instructor or to the lab assistant.**

B Laboratory Procedures

The following rules are designed to protect the Macintosh in the laboratory and to help prevent the loss of your valuable time and data. By protecting the equipment, more computers will be available for you to use more of the time.

Do's

- The Mac is on a very restricted diet. Keep food, gum, or drinks out of the lab.

- Leave the Mac on unless directed otherwise by your instructor or the lab assistant.

- Turn the Mac off before moving it or electrical connections. You could accidentally unplug the computer and lose work in progress.

- Treat the computers with the care you would give any expensive electronic device.

- Feel free to ask questions of your neighbors, the lab assistant, and your instructor.

Disk Handling

Some authors use the word *diskette* instead of the more common term, *disk*. We prefer "disk" and use that term. In some cases, you may see the alternate form "diskette" on your computer screen. (It depends on the program you are using.) In any case, the two words mean exactly the same thing—a device used for the electronic storage of information used by the computer. Disks for the Macintosh look likeFigure B-1.

When the write protect notch is open, the Mac cannot write or erase any information on the disk. However, it can still read information from the disk.

211

Figure B-1. The Macintosh Floppy disk

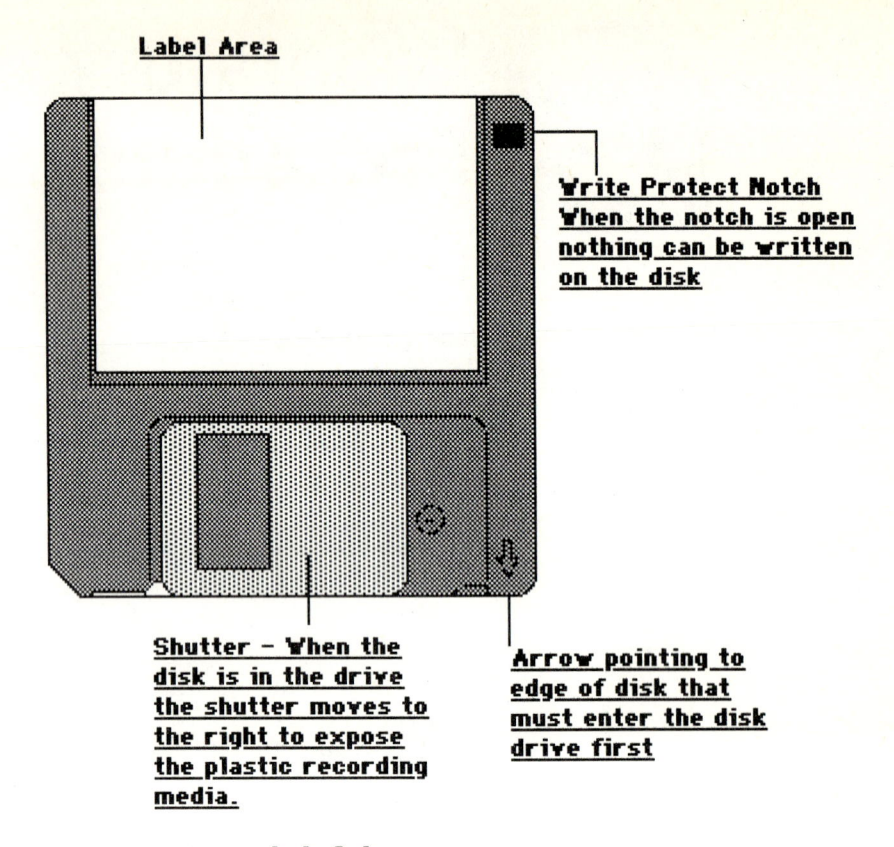

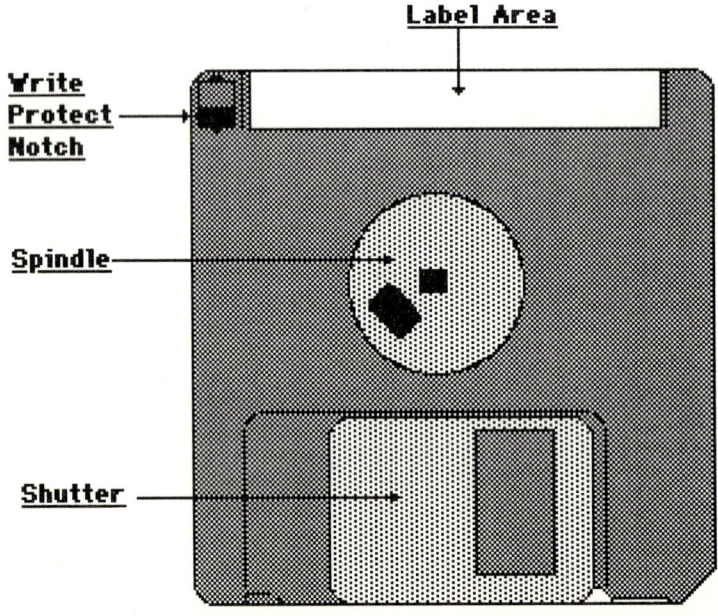

Top of Disk

Label Area

Write Protect Notch When the notch is open nothing can be written on the disk

Shutter — When the disk is in the drive the shutter moves to the right to expose the plastic recording media.

Arrow pointing to edge of disk that must enter the disk drive first

Label Area

Write Protect Notch

Spindle

Shutter

Bottom of Disk

212 *Microsoft Works for the Macintosh*

Certain precautions must be taken to protect the disks and the programs and data contained on the disks.

- Keep disks away from magnets, magnetized objects, telephones, electric motors, excessive heat or sunlight, dust, dirt, and moisture.

- Avoid placing heavy objects on the disk.

- Use a soft tip pen when writing on the disk label.

C Printing With a LaserWriter

In order to use the LaserWriter, you must connect the printer to the Macintosh with a special AppleTalk cable, and you must have a LaserWriter printer driver document in your system folder. You should have received this software with your LaserWriter. If you have problems, consult the manual accompanying your LaserWriter.

Once the proper software is included in your system folder, you still must select the LaserWriter with the Chooser, as directed below. After making the Chooser selection, you will notice some differences in the Page Setup dialog box and the Print dialog box. Those dialog boxes are displayed in Figures C-2 and C-3.

Selecting the LaserWriter With the Chooser

The Chooser is a small program installed in all Apple systems and accessible through the Apple Menu. You use the Chooser to switch between the ImageWriter and the LaserWriter printers. Once your LaserWriter printer driver is installed,

1. **Pull down the Apple Menu and select Chooser.**

2. **Check to see if you have the correct settings as shown in Figure C-1.** When you are satisfied that all settings are correct,

3. **Click once on the close box in the upper left corner of the Chooser window.**

The Page Setup Dialog Box

Figure C-2 shows the LaserWriter Page Setup dialog box. Note that a few paper options are not available with the LaserWriter. For example, there is no Custom Paper Size option.

Note the Help button in this dialog box. When you click that button, you are presented with a screen that gives information

214

Figure C-1. The Chooser window

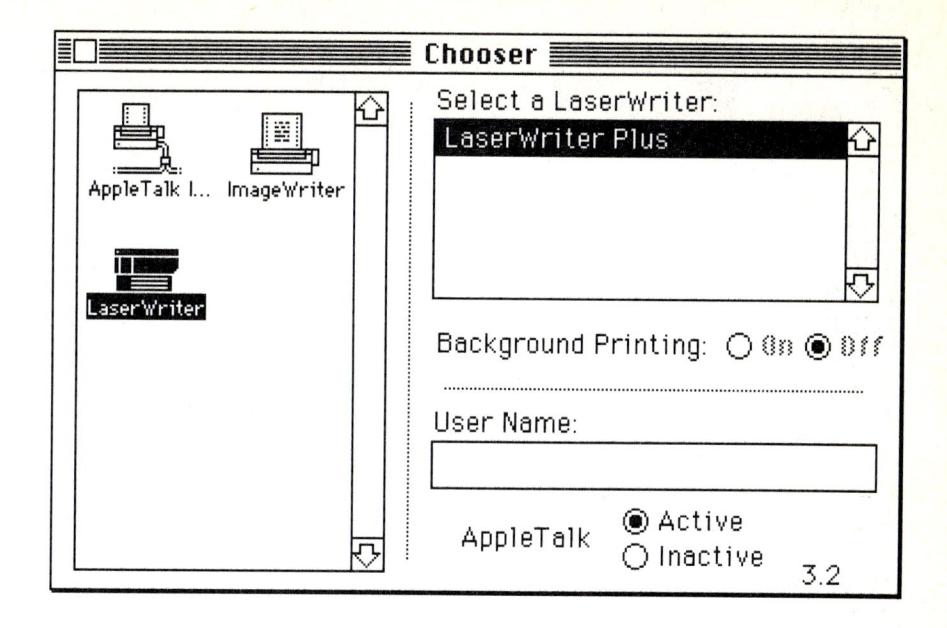

Figure C-2. Page Setup dialog box

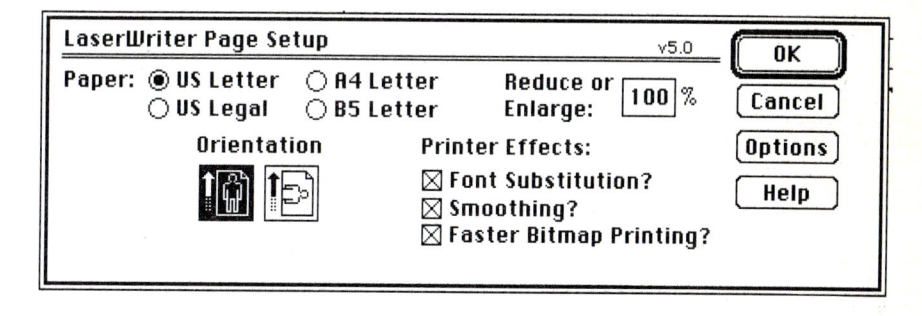

about some of the other options available in the Page Setup dialog box. Try that now.

➡ 1. **Pull down the File Menu and select Page Setup.**

2. **Move the pointer to the Help button and click once.**
   When you have finished reading the Help screen,

3. **Move the pointer to the OK button on the Help screen and click once.**

4. **Leave the Page Setup dialog box showing while you read the rest of this section.**

Appendix C: Printing With a LaserWriter **215**

When printing with the ImageWriter, you have a choice of printing full size or at a 50% reduction. With the LaserWriter, you can reduce or enlarge the size of the material being printed. However, use this option with care. For example, if you specify a reduction option of 80%, it increases the amount of information you can print on a page. If you specify 110%, it is an enlargement option. Whenever you specify anything other than 100%, Works makes whatever changes are necessary in the document being printed. For a Database document, *Works* adjusts the right-edge marker in the Report window. For the Word Processor and the Spreadsheet, *Works* also adjusts the page break indicators.

5. When you have examined all the buttons in the Page Setup dialog box, **move the pointer to the Cancel button and click once.**

The Print Dialog Box

The Print dialog box for the LaserWriter, as shown in Figure C-3, is not too different from the one for the ImageWriter. Note the Help button in this dialog box. When you click Help, you are presented with a screen that gives instructions for printing envelopes and using the manual feed ability of your LaserWriter.

Figure C-3. The Print dialog box

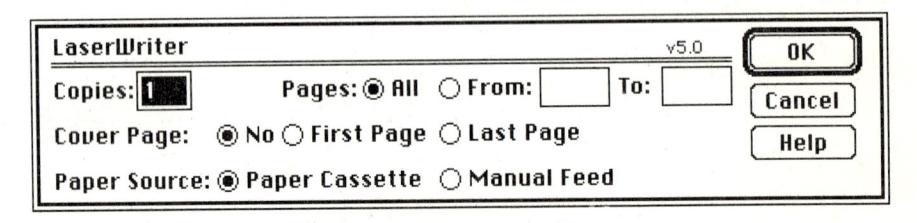

216 *Microsoft Works for the Macintosh*

D Installing Works on a Hard Disk

Your *Works* manual describes the installation procedure on a hard disk. However, here is a brief summary of the procedure.

1. **Turn on your Macintosh.** After the drive lights go off and your desktop appears with the hard disk icon in the upper right corner,

2. **Open the hard disk icon.** A window displaying the contents of the hard disk appears.

3. **Pull down the File Menu and select New Folder.** A highlighted folder will appear on the hard disk window labeled "Empty Folder." To rename the folder for Microsoft Works,

4. **Type:**   **MSWorks** That name will appear as the new name of the folder.

5. **Insert the *Works* program disk into the floppy drive.**

Remember that your hard disk should contain only one system file and one Finder. Since your hard disk already contains those files, you need to be certain that you do not copy the entire Works program disk onto your hard disk.

6. **Open the *Works* program disk.**

7. **Drag all the icons on the Works program disk except the system folder to the newly created file on the hard disk.** In order to complete this step, you may have to reduce the size of the windows by using the size boxes and to reposition the windows by dragging on the title bars. The Spellswell disk also contains some files you will need.

8. **Pull down the File Menu and select Eject.**

Figure D-1. Desktop with hard disk and Works program disks opened

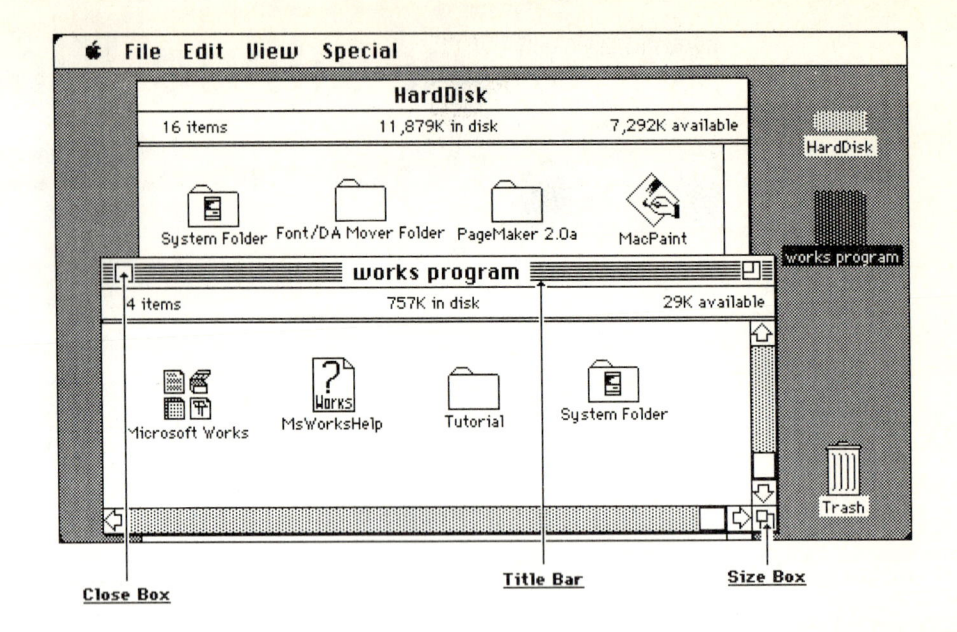

9. Remove the *Works* program disk and insert the Spellswell disk.

10. Open the Spellswell disk.

11. Drag Spellswell, Dictionary, Homonym, and Homonym Table files and icons to the new MSWorks folder.

12. **Shut down the computer.** The installation process is complete.

Launching Works From the Hard Disk

When you want to open (*launch*) *Works* from your hard disk,

1. **Turn the computer on.** When the hard disk icon appears,

2. **Open the hard disk.**

3. **Open the MSWorks folder.**

4. **Open** *Works*.

E Communications

Computers can "talk" to each other! You can use a properly equipped computer to exchange messages with a friend or to access the data and services of large computers anywhere in the world. Communications capabilities enable you to

- Use electronic mail to send messages and files
- Search on-line databases for information
- Obtain business, finance, and investment information
- Conduct electronic conferences
- Shop electronically

What's Needed?

To send a message with a personal computer, you will need the following items:

- Computer
- Modem and its related phone number
- Communications software
- Telephone line
- Cables

Modem is short for *modulation/demodulation*. A physical device called a *modem* is needed on the sending computer to change the electronic signals of the computer to sounds that travel over telephone lines. This is called *modulation*.

Another modem is needed at the receiving end to convert the sound waves back to electronic signals that the computer can understand. This is called *demodulation*.

There are two types of modems: *internal* and *external*. Internal modems fit into slots inside the computer's system unit. Most modern external modems are small boxes with direct cable connections to the computer and the telephone lines. Some external modems are called *acoustic couplers*. These are connected to the computer just like any other modem, but the connection to the telephone lines is made by placing a standard telephone handset into a special cradle.

To better understand how computers communicate, you may want to know how a modem transmits computer data. Personal computers use a combination of eight binary numbers, or *bits*, to represent one letter. For example the letter "A" is represented by the numbers 01000001. When this combination of bits is translated into sound signals, a 1 is transmitted as a "high" signal and a 0 is transmitted as a "low" signal. To send the letter "A" over telephone lines, 8 signals must be sent. The modem sends each signal sequentially (serially) through a device known as an RS-232-C interface. (RS-232-C stands for "Recommended standard number 232, version C.")

One of the identifying features of a modem is the rate at which it transmits and receives data (baud rate). The baud rates most commonly used are 300, 1200, 2400, and 9600. The baud rate of the sending computer must match that of the receiving computer.

Before you can begin communications, you must find out the baud rate of the receiving computer. You will use your communication software to set the baud rate, as well as several other important settings, sometimes called *parameters*. Information services usually publish their modem speed, which you match with your software. Other parameters have to do with checking for errors in transmission.

You don't have to understand what it all means for now—just type in the proper settings, or parameters, of the modem you are calling. The exercises in this chapter will lead you through the process of using two modem-equipped computers for direct communications. You will be able to participate in a "conversation" with a colleague at another computer. You will also be able to send a file from one computer to the other one.

The exercises assume that you have available two Macintosh computers equipped with Hayes compatible modems. The computers will communicate through the phone lines. One computer will be referred to as the *Sending Mac* or *MAC A* and the other will be the *Receiving Mac* or *MAC B*.

Setting up the Receiving Mac: MAC B

1. Double click on Microsoft *Works*.

2. Double click on the Communications icon.

You see a **screen** similar to Figure E-1.

Figure E-1

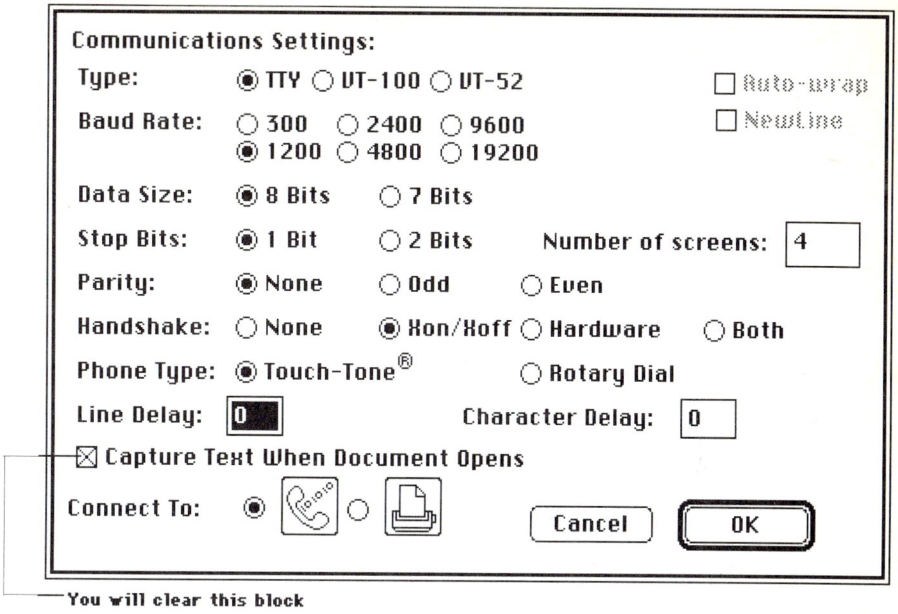

```
Communications Settings:
Type:           ● TTY  ○ VT-100  ○ VT-52          □ Auto-wrap
Baud Rate:      ○ 300    ○ 2400   ○ 9600          □ NewLine
                ● 1200   ○ 4800   ○ 19200
Data Size:      ● 8 Bits    ○ 7 Bits
Stop Bits:      ● 1 Bit     ○ 2 Bits     Number of screens: [4]
Parity:         ● None      ○ Odd        ○ Even
Handshake:      ○ None      ● Xon/Xoff   ○ Hardware    ○ Both
Phone Type:     ● Touch-Tone®            ○ Rotary Dial
Line Delay:     [0]                      Character Delay: [0]
                ⊠ Capture Text When Document Opens
Connect To:     ●  📞   ○  🖨       [ Cancel ]   [  OK  ]
```
—You will clear this block

This is your opportunity to select the proper settings for communication with another computer. The most common selections (the default settings) are already highlighted. So your work in this dialog box will be minimal. One setting should be changed: "Capture Text..." It directs the computer to create a file and save everything that appears on the screen during the communication. This is extremely valuable when searching data bases for important data, but it is not necessary during exercises such as this.

3. **Click on the box "Capture Text When Document Opens" so that the box does *not* have an X.** If your screen does not contain the "Capture Text" option, this step is unnecessary.

4. **Click on OK.**

5. **Pull down the Communications Menu and select Answer Phone.** You see a screen similar to Figure E-2.

Appendix E: Communications

Figure E-2

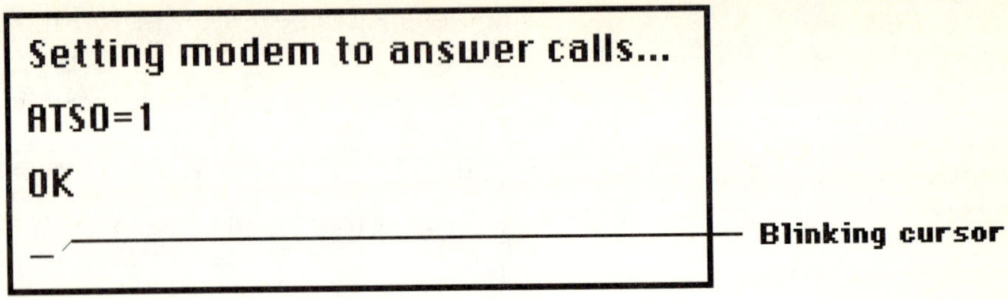

```
Setting modem to answer calls...
ATS0=1
OK
_/                                    ———— Blinking cursor
```

Setting Up Sending Mac: MAC A

From the keyboard of MAC A,

1. **Click on Microsoft *Works*.**

2. **Double click on the Communications icon.**

You see a screen similar to that in Figure E-1. Since the settings must be the same on the sending and receiving computer, leave all settings as is except the "Capture Text" option.

3. **Click on the box "Capture Text When Document Opens" so that the box does *not* have an X.**

4. **Click on OK.**

Dialing Using MAC A

From the keyboard of MAC A,

1. **Pull down the Communications Menu and select Dial.**
   You see a screen similar to that in Figure E-3.

You will use this screen to record the phone number(s) you wish to call and the name(s) that will identify those numbers. With the cursor in the first Name field,

2. **Type: MAC B**

3. **Press: [TAB].**

4. **Type the phone number of the modem attached to MAC A.**

To initiate the call,

222 *Microsoft Works for the Macintosh*

Figure E-3

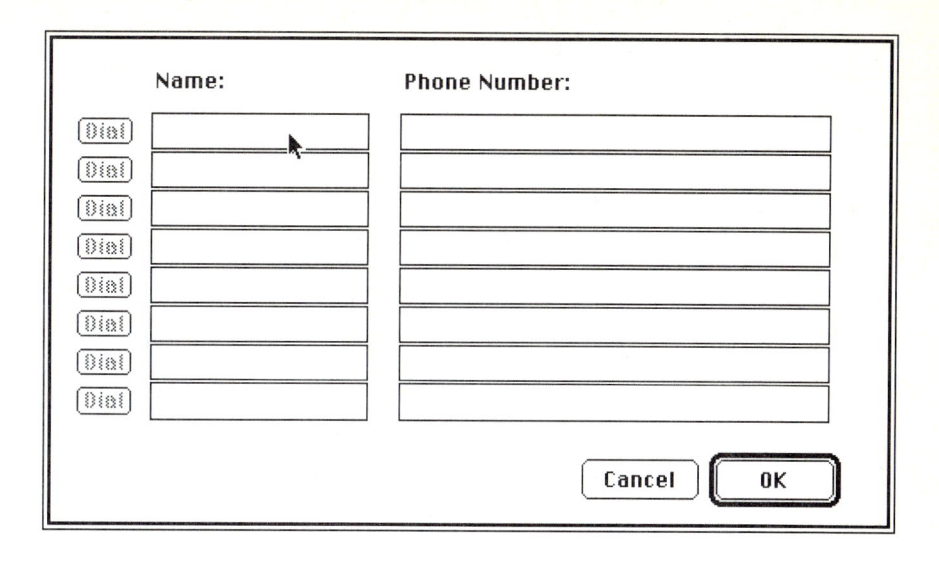

[Dialog box showing Name and Phone Number fields with Dial buttons, Cancel and OK buttons]

5. **Click the Dial button preceding the MAC A phone number.**

6. **Listen for the dial tones and a high pitched tone signaling that the other modem has answered.** You should see "Ring" on the receiving computer and then the word "Connect" on both screens. Try dialing again if you do not connect.

Typing Messages on MAC A

1. **Type:** Hello, MAC B.

2. **Press:** **[ENTER] or [RETURN]** to move the cursor to the next line. The message "Hello, MAC B" should appear on both screens.

3. **Carry on a conversation between the two computers by typing messages alternately on one keyboard and then the next.**

Messages can be sent quickly over telephone lines from your computer to another thousands of miles away. You could have communicated the previous message by using a regular telephone, but a computer with modem enables you to quickly send entire files. In the next section, you will send a document to the other computer.

Appendix E: Communications **223**

Sending a File From MAC A to MAC B

Figure E-4

1. **Insert your data disk into MAC A.**

2. **Pull down the Communications Menu and select Send Text.** You see a screen similar to Figure E-4.

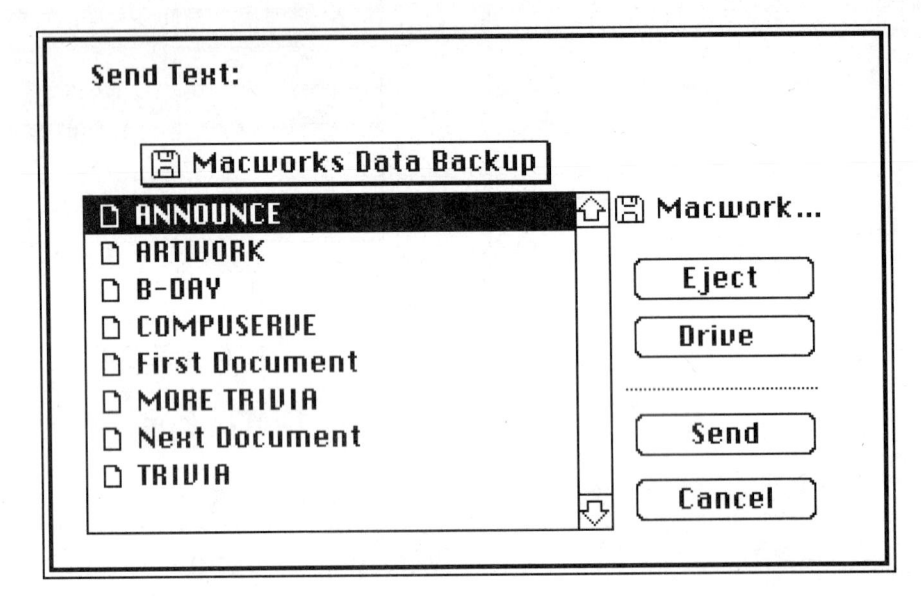

```
Send Text:

         [💾 Macworks Data Backup]
   📄 ANNOUNCE              ⬆  💾 Macwork...
   📄 ARTWORK
   📄 B-DAY                    [ Eject  ]
   📄 COMPUSERVE               [ Drive  ]
   📄 First Document
   📄 MORE TRIVIA
   📄 Next Document            [ Send   ]
   📄 TRIVIA
                            ⬇  [ Cancel ]
```

If your data disk is not in the active drive, click on the Drive button. To select the *Announce* file for transmission,

3. **Click on the filename *Announce* in the list box.**

4. **Click on Send.**

The announcement will immediately display on both screens. MAC B has received the file into the memory of the computer, but it did not save it onto disk since it was not instructed to do so. In the next section, you will save a transmitted file onto a disk instead of displaying it on the screen.

Saving a File on Disk As It Is Received by MAC B

Since communication costs are calculated by the minute, the most cost-effective method of communicating is for the sender using Mac A to prepare the file off line (without using a telephone line) before sending it. Once completed, the file can be sent directly to the disk of the receiving computer. After disconnecting, the recipient using MAC B can read the file. In this way, both users will be

Microsoft Works for the Macintosh

charged only for the time spent on line (using a telephone line) and not for the time it takes for the recipient to read the file.

The receiving MAC must first be prepared to receive the type of file being transmitted:

➡ **1. Insert a second data disk into MAC B.**

2. Pull down the Communications Menu and select Receive File.

If your data disk is not in the active drive, click on the Drive button. You see a screen similar to Figure E-5.

Figure E-5

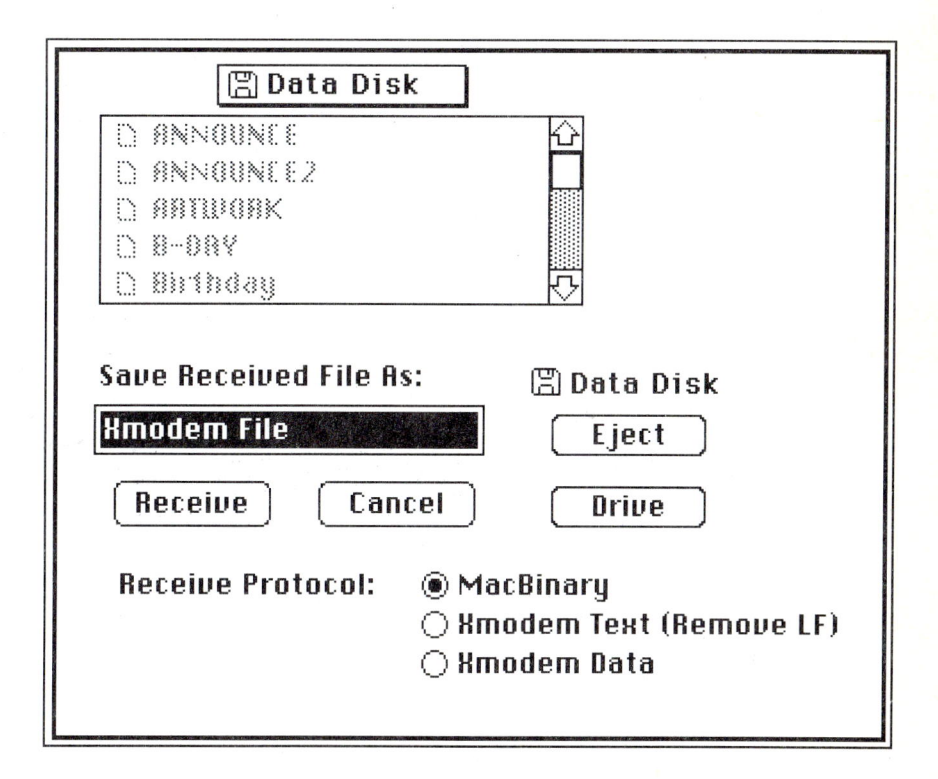

```
┌─────────────────────────────────────────────┐
│              💾 Data Disk                    │
│  ┌───────────────────────────────────┐ ▲   │
│  │ 🗋 ANNOUNCE                        │ ┃   │
│  │ 🗋 ANNOUNCE 2                      │ ┃   │
│  │ 🗋 ARTWORK                         │ ┃   │
│  │ 🗋 B-DAY                           │ ┃   │
│  │ 🗋 Birthday                        │ ▼   │
│  └───────────────────────────────────┘     │
│                                             │
│  Save Received File As:     💾 Data Disk   │
│  ┌─────────────────────┐   ┌──────────┐    │
│  │ Xmodem File         │   │  Eject   │    │
│  └─────────────────────┘   └──────────┘    │
│  ┌──────────┐  ┌──────────┐ ┌──────────┐   │
│  │ Receive  │  │  Cancel  │ │  Drive   │   │
│  └──────────┘  └──────────┘ └──────────┘   │
│                                             │
│      Receive Protocol:  ⦿ MacBinary        │
│                         ○ Xmodem Text (Remove LF) │
│                         ○ Xmodem Data      │
└─────────────────────────────────────────────┘
```

This screen enables you to change the type of the file from the default MacBinary to another format. To prepare to receive a MacBinary file,

➡ • **Click on Receive.** You see a screen similar to Figure E-6.

Appendix E: Communications **225**

Figure E-6

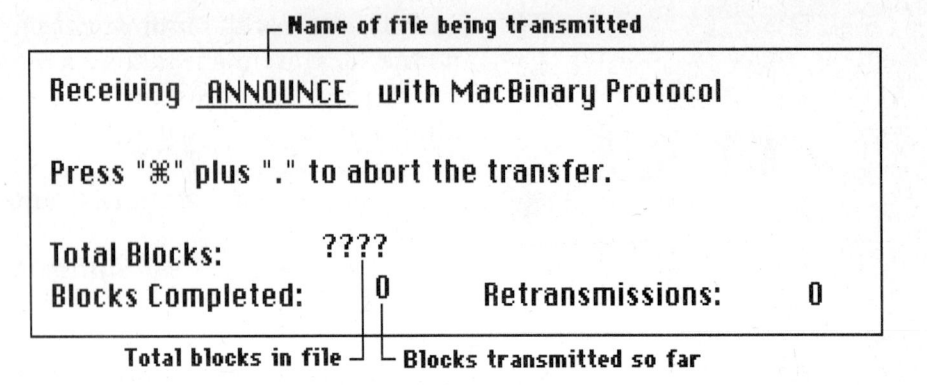

```
                          ┌─ Name of file being transmitted
                          │
┌─────────────────────────┼──────────────────────────────┐
│  Receiving  ANNOUNCE  with MacBinary Protocol          │
│                                                         │
│  Press "⌘" plus "." to abort the transfer.             │
│                                                         │
│  Total Blocks:        ????                              │
│  Blocks Completed:     0      Retransmissions:    0    │
└─────────────────────────┬──┬───────────────────────────┘
         Total blocks in file ┘  └ Blocks transmitted so far
```

The screen will change as the file is transmitted so that you can view the name of the file being transmitted and the progress of the transfer as blocks of data are received.

Sending a File for Disk Storage: MAC A

From the keyboard of MAC A,

1. **Pull down the Communications Menu and select Send Text.**

2. **Click on the file *Trivia*.**

3. **Click on Send.** You see a screen similar to Figure E-7.

Figure E-7

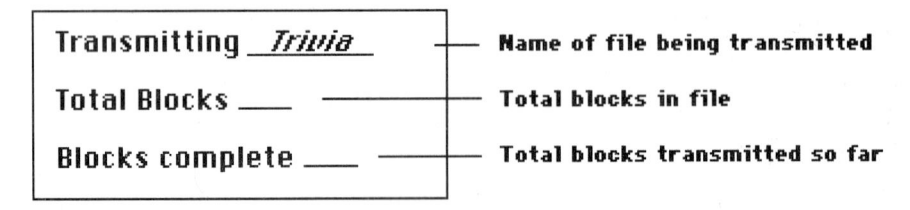

```
┌──────────────────────────────┐
│ Transmitting  Trivia   ├──── Name of file being transmitted
│                              │
│ Total Blocks ___       ├──── Total blocks in file
│                              │
│ Blocks complete ___    ├──── Total blocks transmitted so far
└──────────────────────────────┘
```

The blanks will be updated as the file is transmitted. Note that the file will not appear on the screen of the receiving computer when the file is sent to disk, but the dialog box (Figure E-7) is being updated to disclose the progress of the transmission. A "beep" will signal that the transmission is complete, at which time "Blocks Completed" will equal "Total Blocks" in the dialog box.

Disconnecting: MAC A

It is very important that you hang up when through with transmission because you are being charged by the minute for the use of the phone lines.

➡ • **Pull down the Communications Menu and select Hang Up.** "OK" appears on the screen of MAC A to indicate that the computer did disconnect from the phone lines, and "+++..." appears on the receiving screen to indicate that the transmission has been aborted.

Disconnecting: MAC B

Even though MAC A has disconnected from the phone line, MAC B has not. From the MAC B keyboard,

➡ • **Pull down the Communications Menu and select Hand Up.** "OK" appears on the screen of MAC B to indicate that the computer is now disconnected from the phone lines. Note that "+++" does not appear on the screen of MAC A because it has already been disconnected and no longer knows what MAC B is doing.

Viewing the Disk File: MAC B

From the keyboard of MAC B,

➡ 1. **Pull down the File Menu and select Open.**

2. **Select the file *Trivia*.**

3. **Select Open.** The *Trivia* file displays on the screen.

Summary

The Microsoft *Works* communications module contains basic features that enable you to call another computer or bulletin board, connect to a remote mainframe computer, or access information services. Modems can help you communicate with large computers across the country. Companies such as Compuserve, Dialog, and Dow Jones provide many data bases of information, electronic mail services, electronic shopping and electronic conferences for a fee. Many free, local electronic bulletin boards may be available in your area. You can also connect to large computers using the steps presented in this worksheet.

F Version 2.0 Changes

Introduction

If you are fortunate enough to have a hard disk with Microsoft *Works* Version 2.0 installed (see Appendix D for installation procedure), you will have more capabilities available to you. Listed below are some corrections to apply when using this manual.

Please note that where the differences in Version 2.0 and Version 1.1 are slight and would not affect the use of this text (such as changes in symbol design or the addition or deletion of a limited number of items in menus or dialog boxes), the changes are not addressed. These and other differences can be explored by using the Help feature of the program.

Word Processing

Chapter 1, pages 2-4. Getting Started. Replace Steps 1 through 3 with:

1. **If the computer is off**

   a. **Turn the computer on.** A screen similar to Figure 1-2a will appear except the disk icon will say "Hard Disk."

   b. **Pull down the File Menu and select Open.** A desktop similar to Figure 1-2b will appear. The *Works* program is in the folder labeled MSWORKS.

   c. **Click on the MSWORKS folder to select it.**

   d. **Pull down the File Menu and select Open**. The window showing the Works icon (along with a few other folders or files) is now visible.

   e. **Click on the Microsoft *Works* icon, pull down the File Menu, and select Open.**

f. Continue with Dialog Boxes on page 4.

2. **If the computer is on and the screen resembles Figure 1-2a with the exception that the disk icon reads Hard Disk, follow Steps 1b through 1f above.**

3. **If the computer is on and the screen resembles Figure 1-2b with the exception that the disk icon reads Hard Disk, follow Steps 1c through 1f above.**

4. **If the computer is on and your screen does not resemble either Figure 1-2a or 1-2b, it means that the previous user did not properly shut down.**

   a. **Close any open windows by clicking the close box in the upper left corner of each open window.** (See Figure 1-2b.) If option boxes appear asking if you would like to save changes, click on No.

   b. **When your desktop is empty and all windows have been closed, pull down the Special Menu and select Restart.** The result will be the same as turning the computer on in Step 1a.

   c. **Follow Steps 1b through 1f above.**

Chapter 1, page 5. Figure 1-3. The filenames in the files box may be different.

Chapter 1, page 6. Opening a File. The first sentence in Step 1 should read: "Insert the data disk into the internal disk drive."

Chapter 1, page 8. Centering Text. Font and Style are not separate menu items in Version 2.0. Both of these are options with submenus under the Format Menu. The Format Menu also contains the option Justification which has a submenu. See the explanation in Figure 1-5V2 below.

Chapter 1, page 8. Figure 1-5. Replace with Figure 1-5V2 below. As you can see, the Font and Style Menu items are replaced by Spell and Macro respectively.

Appendix F: Version 2.0 Changes **229**

Figure 1-5V2. Format Menu with the submenu for justification displayed

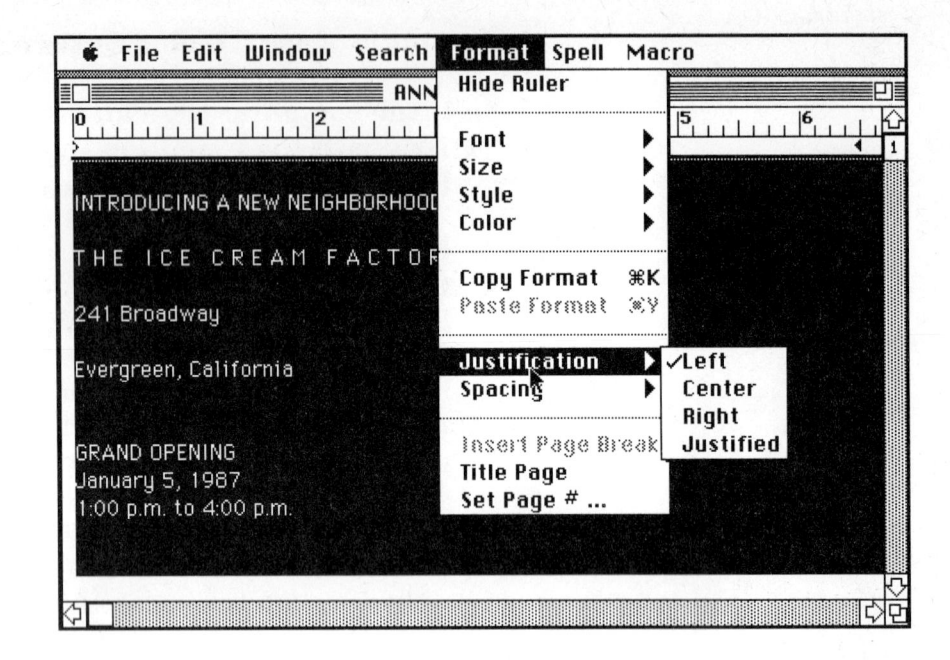

Chapter 1, page 8. Step 3. Replace the second sentence with: "Hold down the mouse button and drag the pointer down to Justification. Note the arrow pointing to the submenu at the right with Left justification selected (checked). All menu items with such right arrows have pop-out submenus. Drag to the right and down to select Center. Then release the mouse button."

Chapter 1, page 10. Changing Text Size and Style. The first sentence in Step 2 should read: "Pull down the Format Menu, drag to highlight Font, and then drag to the right and down to select a font other than Geneva. Release the mouse button."

The first sentence in Step 3 should read: "Pull down the Format Menu, highlight Size, then drag to the right and down to select 18."

Step 4 should read: "Pull down the Format Menu, highlight Style, then drag to the right and down to select Outline."

The first sentence in Step 5 should read: "Pull down the Format Menu, highlight Style, and then drag to the right and down to select Shadow."

230   *Microsoft Works for the Macintosh*

Chapter 1, pages 11-14. Figures 1-8, 1-9, 1-10, and 1-11 have slight differences in menus or dialog boxes.

Chapter 2, page 18. Getting Started. Use procedures outlined in Chapter 1 of this Appendix.

Chapter 2, page 21. Typing a Centered Bold Heading. First sentence in Step 2 should read: "Pull down Format Menu, highlight Justification, and drag to the right and down to select Center."

Replace Step 4 with: "Pull down Format Menu, highlight Style, then drag to the right and down to select Bold."

Chapter 2, page 23. Underlining Text. All references to Style Menu in this paragraph as well as in the remainder of the text should be changed to the Format Menu. When using the Format Menu, drag down to highlight Style, then drag to the right to select the appropriate option. For example, Step 2 should read:

2. **Pull down the Format Menu, highlight Style, and then drag to the right and down to select Underline.**

Chapter 2, pages 26-31. Figures 2-11, 2-13, 2-14, and 2-15 dialog boxes have minor differences.

Chapter 3, page 36. Typing a Byline. Replace Step 3 with:

3. **Pull down the Format Menu, highlight Style, and then drag to the right and down to select Normal.**

Chapter 3, page 38. Remember that the menu bar in Version 2.0 is slightly different.

Chapter 3, page 40. Double Spacing Paragraphs. Replace Steps 3-5 with

3. **Pull down the Format Menu, highlight Spacing, and then select Double.**

4. **Continue with Step 6.**

Appendix F: Version 2.0 Changes

Chapter 4. No significant changes in Chapter 4.

Chapter 5, page 56. Figure 5-1. The File Menu is slightly longer.

Chapter 5, page 56. Table at the bottom of the page. Replace "Style" in the menu column with "Format."

Chapter 5, page 59. Formatting Hints. To see the four options listed, pull down the Format Menu and select the Style option.

Spreadsheets

Chapter 6, page 65. Getting Started. Use procedures outlined in Chapter 1 of this Appendix.

Chapter 6, page 65. Figure 6-2. The menu bar has a new option, Macro, added on the right.

Chapter 6, page 66. Opening a File. The first sentence in Step 1 should read: "Insert the data disk into the internal disk drive."

Chapter 6, page 70 on. Selecting Parts of a Spreadsheet. Whenever only one cell is selected, that cell will not be highlighted (darkened). Instead, only the cell's border will be darkened. If more that one cell is selected, the active cell's border will be darkened and the remaining selected cells will be highlighted. See Figure 6-7V2.

Chapter 6, page 71. Figure 6-7. Replace with Figure 6-7V2 below.

Chapter 6, page 72. Using the Go To Method. Replace this section with the following:

- Pull down the Select Menu and select Find Cell. A dialog box will appear with the cursor blinking in the Enter Cell to Select or Text to Find box. Type either the cell location or the specific value you wish to find.

Use the "Go to Cell" option in the Select Menu only if you wish to view a distant cell. This option will make the chosen cell visible on the screen, but does not select it, whereas the "Find Cell" option both makes the chosen cell visible and selects it.

Figure 6-7V2. Note that A5, the active cell, has a dark border but the remainder of the selected cells in Row 5 are highlighted.

```
 File   Edit   Window   Select   Format   Options   Chart   Macro
 A5              Sunday
════════════════════════════ RECEIPTS (SS) ═══════════════════════════
        A           B        C        D       E      F       G       H        I
  1  DAILY RECEIPTS
  2  Week of    December 21, 1987
  3                                                     Total   Taxes     Total
  4  Day        Cone/Cup Fountain Party Pre-pk Hand-pk  Sales Collect  Receipts
  5  Sunday         251     123    186     24     51     635    0.21    635.21
  6  Monday         125      67    125     13     32     362    0.24    362.24
  7  Tuesday        164      68     95     18     42     387    0.21    387.21
  8  Wednesday      159      73    152     38     39     461    0.18    461.18
  9  Thursday       186      86    152     21     35     480    0.12    480.12
 10  Friday         248     106    168     17     57     596    0.36    596.36
 11  Saturday       287     157    211     32     65     752    0.45    752.45
 12  TOTALS       1,420     680  1,089    163    321   3,673    1.77   3,674.8
 13              ======== ======= ====== ====== ======= ======= ======= ========
 14
 15
 16
 17
```

Chapter 6, page 73. Figure 6-8. Remember that the selected cell is merely outlined by a bold border.

Chapter 6, page 82. Figure 6-13. Your Page Setup has one added option box—Print Cell Notes. **Note**: The files on your data disk were created using Version 1.1. If you open a file created using 1.1 and then make corrections using 2.0, you may not be able to "Save" it with the same filename. You may have to rename that file using Save As.

Chapter 7, page 93. Formatting Numeric Values. Replace Step 2 at the top of the page with the following:

2. **Pull down the Format Menu and select Set Cell Attributes. . .** The three dots following that option indicates that another dialog box will be displayed.

Figure 7-5. Replace with Figures 7-5aV2 and 7-5bV2 below.

3. **Click on the Fixed option in the Set Cell Attributes dialog box.**

4. **Click OK.**

Appendix F: Version 2.0 Changes **233**

Figure 7-5aV2. Format Menu

Figure 7-5bV2. Set Cell Attributes dialog box

To experiment with some of the other options in the Set Cell Attributes dialog box, follow the same procedure as above.

Chapter 7, page 94. Formatting Labels. Replace Step 2 with the following:

2. **Pull down the Format Menu and select Set Cell Attributes.** A dialog box appears.

3. **Select the Center option in the Align: column.**

4. **Click OK. The labels are now centered.**

Chapter 8, page 102. Aligning Columns of Data and Their Headings. Replace Step 2 with the following:

234   *Microsoft Works for the Macintosh*

2. **Pull down the Format Menu and select Set Cell Attributes.** A dialog box appears.

3. **Select the Center option from the Align column in the dialog box.**

4. **Click OK**. Both labels and amounts are now centered.

Chapter 8, page 102. Aligning Columns of Data and Their Headings. Aligning cells at the right is done using the same technique as above. Change old Step 3 to Step 4. Replace old Step 4 with the following:

5. **Pull down the Format Menu, select Set Cell Attributes, select the Right option, and click OK.**

Change old Step 5 to Step 6.

Chapter 9. No significant changes in Chapter 9.

Database

Chapter 10. Reminder As in the spreadsheet application, the active field will have a dark border, it will not be highlighted. However, if a range is selected, the other selected fields will be highlighted.

Chapter 11. No significant changes in Chapter 11.

Chapter 12, page 147. Creating a New Report. Replace the end of the last paragraph starting with the words "The upside-down triangle..." with the following: "The darkened left and right-edge markers, which resemble the left indent and right-indent markers in word processing, mark the boundaries of the print area. Any field that is even partially within those markers will be printed. You may have to scroll to the right to see the right-edge marker." See Figure 12-3V2.

Chapter 12, page 148. Figure 12-3. Replace with Figure 12-3V2 below.

Chapter 12, page 153. Widening Columns. Replace the paragraph following Step 3 at the top of the page with the following:

Appendix F: Version 2.0 Changes **235**

Figure 12-3V2

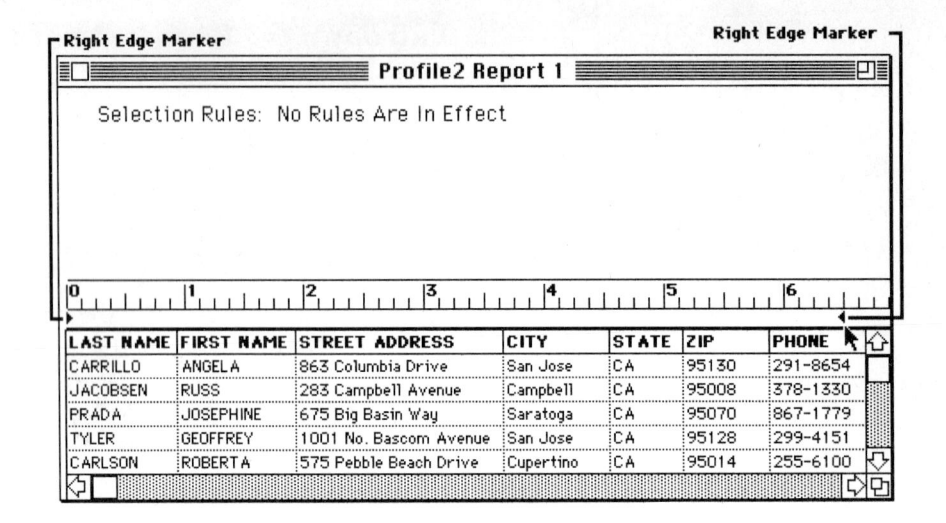

"After widening the columns, your right-edge marker should be on the right side of the "Time Available" field. If it is not, simply drag the marker to that position."

Chapter 12, page 154. Printing Without Lines. The instructional step should read:

- Pull down the Format Menu. Notice that the Show Grid option is selected (a check mark precedes it). This is a toggle option. To disable it, select Show Grid. The check mark disappears and the grid will not print.

Figure 14-8V2. Tools palette box

Chapter 13. No significant changes.

Integration

Chapter 14, page 174. Adding a Picture. Replace Steps 4-8 with the following:

To select one of the pictures from the Artwork file,

4. **Pull down the Edit Menu and select Draw On.** A "Tools" palette box appears on the left side of your screen. (See Figure 14-8V2 on the right.) Since the selection tool (arrow) is already highlighted,

5. **Click on the picture you want to paste into your form letter.** "Handles" will appear around the

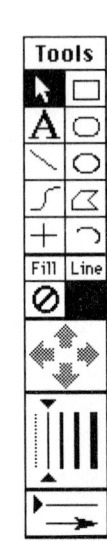

236 *Microsoft Works for the Macintosh*

chosen picture. (See Figure 14-9V2.) If you change your mind and want to use another drawing, simply click on the desired picture and the handles will move to the new selection.

Continue with Step 9 on page 175.

Figure 14-9V2

Look at Figure 14-9V2. The square "handles" around the selected picture can be used to change the size and shape of the picture. The handles at the corners of the picture can be dragged up, down, left, right, or diagonally. The other handles can move left and right or up and down.

Chapter 14, page 175. Adding a Picture. Replace Steps 14-17 with the following:

14. **Move the arrow anywhere over the picture, hold down the mouse button, and drag the picture to the desired location.** When you start to drag the picture, the picture itself will not move. However, a rectangle representing the picture will move to show the position of the picture if dragging were concluded at that time.

15. **Release the mouse button.** The picture will appear in its new location.

Appendix F: Version 2.0 Changes **237**

16. **If you would like to increase or decrease the size of the picture, click on any one of the handles and drag following the directions accompanying Figure 14-9V2.** When you are satisfied with the picture and its location,

17. **Pull down the Edit Menu and select Draw Off.** The tools box will disappear and the pointer will again become the insertion bar.

Chapter 14, page 178. Drawing a Frame. Before drawing a rectangular border around the statement portion of your memo, use the right vertical scroll arrow so that only the statement shows on your screen.

Replace Steps 1-4 with the following:

1. **Pull down the Edit Menu and select Draw On.** The "Tools" palette appears on the left side of your screen. Because the Tools box is covering part of the statement, you will need to move it out of the way. To do this,

2. **Click on the word "Tools" and drag the box to the right side of the screen.** Your screen should resemble Figure 14-11V2.

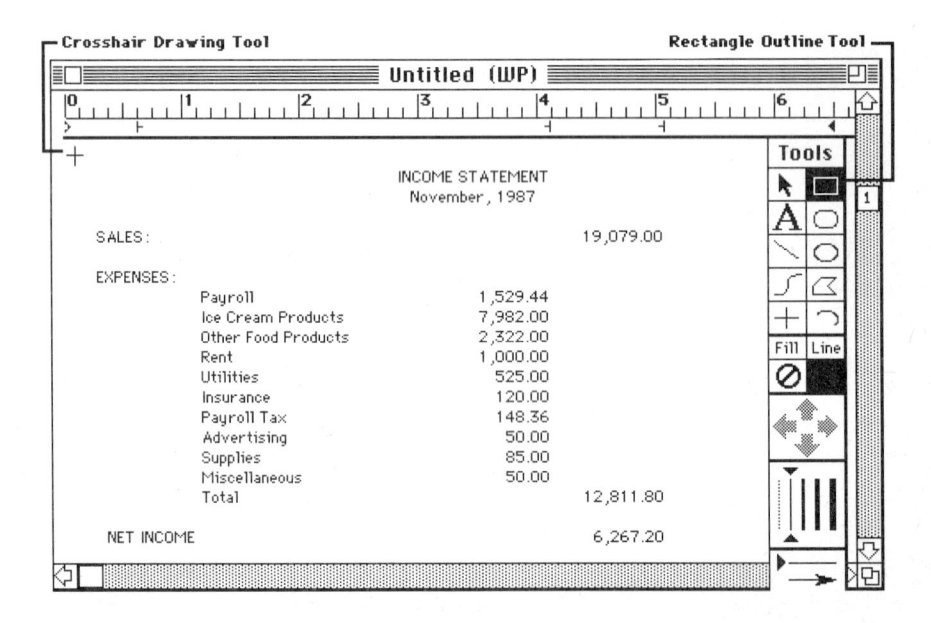

Figure 14-11V2

238   *Microsoft Works for the Macintosh*

To draw a box around the statement,

3. Click on the rectangle outline tool to select it. (See Figure 14-11V2.) The arrow now becomes a crosshair.

4. Continue with Step 5 on page 179. Remember: To eliminate the "handles" or deselect a drawing, click anywhere outside the lines.

Chapter 14, page 180. Drawing a Frame. The large section in the middle of the page which includes Steps 1-3 and Steps1-4 contains instructions for deleting or changing borders. Replace that entire section with the following:

1. Pull down the Edit Menu and select Draw On. With the selection tool (arrow) highlighted,

2. Click on any of the lines in the unwanted frame. The handles will appear.

3. Press: [Del] or [Backspace]

You can now redraw the frame on your own using a different style border if you desire. If you need help, refer to Steps 4-5 of the previous exercise.

If you made any other lines or marks you would like to eliminate, follow Steps 2-3 above. When you are through,

4. Pull down the Edit Menu and select Draw Off . You are now ready for the section entitled Saving the File Under a Different Name which begins at the bottom of page 180.

Chapter 15, page 185. Using Spellswell™. Read the first paragraph, but replace the remainder of this section with the following. You will be using Works' built-in spelling checker rather than a separate program named Spellswell™. As a result, getting started and quitting will be much easier. To begin,

1. Open the Works program as usual.

2. Insert your Data Disk in the internal disk drive.

Appendix F: Version 2.0 Changes   **239**

3. Open the file named *MORE TRIVIA*.

4. **Pull down the Spell Menu and select Options**. A screen similar to Figure 15-1V2 will appear.

Figure 15-1V2

Compare your screen with Figure 15-1V2. The options selected (checked) in that figure may be more or less than you would want. However, these selections will give you an opportunity to see how the program works.

```
Options:
☒ Must capitalize after period
☒ Proper noun capitalization
☐ Mix numbers and letters
☒ Double word errors
☒ Two spaces after period
☒ Homonyms
☐ Treat hyphens as spaces
[ Cancel ]    [  OK  ]
```

5. Click in any box that needs to be selected or deselected.

6. Click on OK when your options box matches Figure 15-1V2.

7. **Pull down the Spell Menu and select Correct Spelling.**

The spelling program will now start checking and will stop at the first word to be checked—the word "in." (See Figure 15-2.)

8. Read the information given on pages 187-191.

9. If you see a word highlighted and it is obviously correct, simply click on the OK button even if the alternative spelling box shows other possibilities.

As mentioned before, except for such common and troublesome homonyms as to, too, and two, you may want to click on the "Stop Checking These Homonyms" box to speed up the corrections.

When spell checking is complete, the last word checked will be highlighted.

10. Click anywhere on the screen to deselect the last word checked. Continue with the section titled Formatting.

Reminder: Whenever the directions ask you to pull down the Style Menu, pull down the Format Menu and highlight the Style option. The Style submenu will then pop out to the right where you can make your selection.

Appendixes

Figure D-1V2

Appendix D, page 218. Figure D-1. Replace with Figure D-1V2.

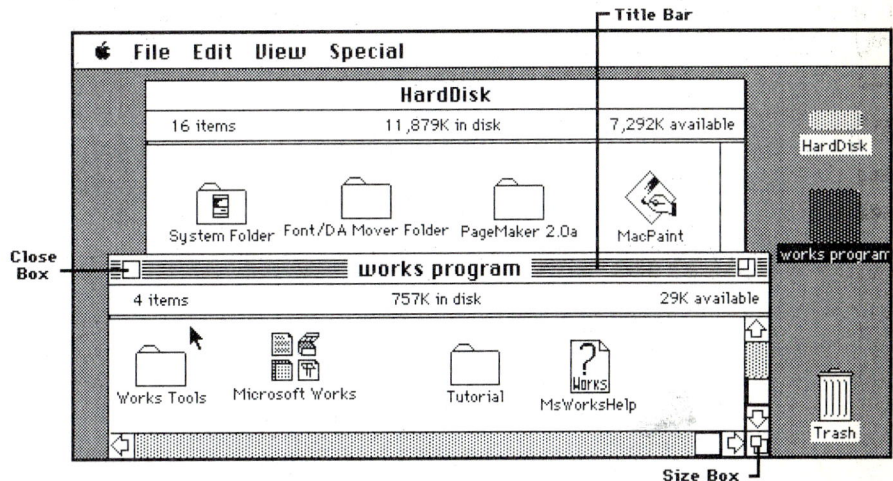

Appendix D, page 217. Replace Steps 7 on with the following:

7. **Drag all the icons on the Works program disk to the newly created file on the hard disk.** To complete this step, you may have to reduce the windows using the size boxes and reposition the windows by dragging on the title bars.

The Startup disk contains a Dictionary folder which *Works* will need when using the spelling checker.

8. **Pull down the File Menu and select Eject.**

9. **Remove the *Works* Program disk and insert the *Works* Startup disk.**

10. **Open the *Works* Startup disk.**

11. **Drag the *Works* Dictionary folder to the new MSWorks folder on the hard disk.**

12. **Shut down the computer.** Installation process is complete.

Appendix F: Version 2.0 Changes **241**

Glossary Of Computer Terms

Absolute cell reference. In the spreadsheet application, a reference to a cell location that remains unchanged if a formula that contains the reference is copied or moved to a new location. See *Relative reference.*

Active window. The window where the present action is taking place. On the Macintosh, the title bar of the active window is visible.

Apple Menu. Menu option on the far left of the Macintosh. It has as its title the apple symbol.

Analog signals. Electrical signals (such as the human voice) that change continuously in wave form. The telephone is an analog device since it turns voice vibrations into analogous electrical vibrations. See *Digital signals.*

Application software. Computer programs that apply the resources and capabilities of the computer and its peripheral devices. Programs include word processing, database management, graphics, or communications. Compare *System software* definition.

ASCII code. Acronym for American Standard Code for Information Interchange. Used by almost all personal computers for data communications and character representation.

Auxiliary memory. The component of a computer used to permanently store programs and data. Disks and tapes are used for auxiliary memory.

Backup. As a verb, to make a duplicate of a file or program on a disk in case the original is lost or destroyed. As a noun, the duplicate copy itself.

BASIC. Beginner's All-purpose Symbolic Instruction Code. A computer language developed at Dartmouth College during late 60's and early 70's. BASIC is available in most personal computers and is relatively easy for programming novices to learn.

Baud rate. A unit for measuring the speed of data transmission.

Bit. Binary Digit. The smallest unit of data stored in a computer. The value of an individual bit is represented by the number 1 (on) or the number 0 (off).

Buffer. A group of storage locations within which data are stored while waiting to be transferred between the computer and a peripheral device.

Bulletin board. A program stored on a host computer. It allows messages to be posted and read via a modem.

Button. Circular or rectangular areas in dialog boxes where you click with the mouse button to confirm an action

Byte. A set of 8 bits grouped together to form a storage location in the computer's main memory. A computer's memory is usually described in terms of bytes. One byte can store one typed character. In some computers, each byte is individually addressable. In other computers sets of bytes are grouped together to form an addressable computer word.

Cell. Intersection of a row and column in a spreadsheet.

Chips. Integrated circuits made by photographically etching electronic circuits onto a tiny wafer of silicon no larger than a fraction of an inch on each side.

Chooser. Desk accessory found under the Apple Menu. It enables the user to select a printer.

Click. Positioning the pointer on something and then quickly pressing and releasing the mouse button.

Clipboard. Area in memory that stores the last item cut or copied from a file.

Close. To remove a window from the desktop. When a window is closed, the document it represents is no longer available. Closing can be achieved by selecting Close from the File Menu or by clicking in the window's close box.

Close box. Small box in the upper left corner of active window. When clicked, it closes window.

Command. An order for the computer to execute some specific task. On the Macintosh, all commands are selectable from the menus and some commands can be transmitted to the computer by using the Command key together with another key or keys.

Command key. On a Macintosh, the key [⌘]. When held down while another key is pressed, the command key causes a command to take effect.

Communications. The capability of a computer to send information to and receive information from another computer.

Computer. An electronic device that performs predefined and internally stored (programmed) computations at high speed and with great accuracy.

Computer language. A code for writing a computer program. Some common computer languages are BASIC, Pascal, FORTRAN, and COBOL. A set of instructions written in a computer language is called a *program*. Computer languages are also called *programming* languages.

Control key. A special key on the computer's keyboard. Used in conjunction with other keys to change their normal meaning. The Control key usually must be held down while another key is depressed.

Control panel. The desk accessory through which you can change aspects of the Macintosh user interface (such as the background pattern of the desktop, response speed of the keyboard and mouse, and speaker volume).

CPU. The Central Processing Unit. Also called the *microprocessor*. The part of the computer that directs the flow of information within the computer, performs all calculations, and controls all other components of the computer.

CRT. Cathode Ray Tube in a video display terminal (VDT). Computer jargon for the display screen connected to a computer.

Cursor. A marker displayed on the computer monitor. It usually designates where the next typed character will be displayed.

Cut. To remove something from a document in memory. The material cut is placed temporarily on the Clipboard and can be recalled until something else is cut or copied.

Database. A collection of data or information concerning one major topic maintained in one central storage place or file (for example, the telephone book or card catalog at a library).

Data disk. A disk used for storing documents created or used by the user. Includes letters, memos, graphs. Compare with *Program disk* definition.

Decimal tab stop. Automatically lines up the decimal points in a column of numbers.

Default. The standard setting or action performed by the software when no specific direction is given to the computer by the user.

Desk accessories. Small Macintosh programs that are available under the Apple Menu regardless of what application you are using.

Desktop. The menu bar and shaded screen with the trash can in the lower right corner. The desktop greets you when the Macintosh is first turned on with a startup disk. Also, the area of the Macintosh screen where you do your work.

Device. A unit of computer hardware, such as a disk drive or printer. Sometimes called a *peripheral* or peripheral *device*.

Dialog box. Windows that request information. The user must respond to a dialog box before the activity can continue.

Digital signals. Unlike analog signals, digital signals can have only two (binary) levels and nothing in between. All standard microcomputers use digital logic. Additional components must be added to intercept signals for transmission and reception of analog signals.

Directory. An index file containing the names of all the files contained in a folder or disk.

Disk. A flat, circular piece of plastic (flexible) or metal (rigid) onto which information is recorded magnetically. A flexible disk is also called a *"floppy."* The 3.50-inch floppy disk encased in a rigid container is sometimes called a *"microfloppy."*

Disk drive. A device that can read information from and write information onto a disk in much the same way that a tape recorder plays from or records onto a magnetic tape. Inside the drive, a motor spins the disk and a read/write head performs the reading or writing operation.

Disk operating system (DOS). An operating system that allows a computer to use disks for data storage. Many computer manufacturers incorporate the acronym DOS into the name of the operating system for a particular computer (for example, IBM PC/DOS or MS/DOS for IBM personal computers). On many personal computers, the operating system is loaded into RAM when the computer is booted with a system master disk. Some personal computers may have an operating system resident in ROM. On the Macintosh, DOS operations are carried out by the programs stored in the system folder. See *Operating system*.

Display. As a noun, the screen connected to the computer. See *CRT* or *Monitor*. As a verb, to cause material to appear on the computer screen.

Documentation. Written instructions describing how to use computer hardware or software.

Download. To save a program or file sent to your computer by another computer, as opposed to letting it disappear as it scrolls off the screen.

Drag. To position the pointer at the beginning point, hold down the mouse button, move the mouse to the ending point, and then release the button.

Duplex. "Full Duplex" is data transmission in both

directions at the same time. "Half duplex" is transmission in one direction only.

Field. Smallest unit of a database record.

File. A unit of information that is stored on disk and given a filename. The contents of a file may be anything—a letter, a financial model, a graph, or a program.

Finder. A Macintosh program that allows a user to manage documents and applications and to get information to and from disks no matter what application is being used.

Firmware. A computer program or set of programs stored in the computer's ROM memory. Firmware is not lost when the computer is turned off.

Floppy disk. See *Disk*.

Folder. A holder of documents, applications, or other folders. Used to organize the contents of Macintosh disks. Analogous to subdirectories in IBM terminology.

Font. In *Works* terminology, the typeface or design used to print characters (for example, Courier or Helvetica). In typesetting terminology, describes the combination of typeface and typestyle used to print characters (for example, Courier/bold).

Form feed. The manual control that causes the printer to advance the paper to the top of the next page for continuous feed paper. If single sheets are being used, the current sheet will be ejected.

Format. As a verb, to prepare the surface of a floppy disk so that you can use it for storing data. As a noun, the pattern which must be written on the disk before you can use it for storing data. Different computers require different disk formats. Also used to describe the manner in which text is set up on a page.

Formula. A rule expressed as an equation.

Function keys. Special keys that, when depressed, will begin an activity as prescribed by the software.

Hard copy. The printed material generated by a computer. Also called *printout*.

Hard disk. Fast auxiliary storage mounted in its own case or permanently encased inside a computer. Capable of storing millions of characters.

Hardware. The physical components of a computer system.

Hayes modem. The standard communication device used by the majority of communication programs. "Hayes compatible" means that a communication device will operate like the Hayes modem.

Hierarchical file system. Use of folders to orgranize information on disk on the Macintosh. Folders can be nested in other folders to develop as many levels of hierarchy as is needed.

High-level language. A computer programming language that employs English-like words and statements rather than numeric codes.

Icon. A graphic representation of an object, concept, or message. Prominently used in the Macintosh environment.

Initialize. See *Format*, definition 1.

Instruction. One statement in a computer program.

Integrated program. Software that combines two or more applications. *Works* is an integrated program that combines word processing, database, spreadsheet, and communication applications. Data is easily exchanged between them.

Interactive program. A program that allows the computer and the user to respond to each other.

Interface. A hardware device or a computer program that allows one component of the computer to communicate with another. Interfaces are commonly used between the computer and a printer or between the computer and a modem.

Justification. Pertaining to alignment of text at the left margin, right margin, or both.

Keyboard. A device used to enter information into the computer's RAM memory.

Kilobyte. A measure of memory size, often abbreviated as K. One kilobyte (1K) is 1,024 characters or bytes. See *Megabyte*.

Label. Non-numeric entries in a spreadsheet. Calculations cannot be performed on cells containing labels.

Launch. A term used in Macintosh documentation that means to start a program.

Layout. The physical placement of text or data on the printed page.

Line feed. The manual control that advances the paper one line at a time.

Load. A common command that tells a computer to transfer a program or data file from a disk or tape into its main memory.

Log off. Also *Logoff*. To break an established connection with a computer that serves more than one user. The log off procedure varies from system to system. Some typical log off commands are "Exit," "Logoff," "LO," and "Bye."

Log on. Also *Logon*. To gain access to a computer that serves more than one user. The log on procedure varies from system to system, but it usually requires that the computer be supplied with a predetermined account name and unique password for each user.

Mainframe. In terms of physical size, size of memory, and speed of calculations, a large computer — in contrast to a minicomputer or a microcomputer (personal computer).

Main memory. The component of a computer used to temporarily store programs and data for quick access by the CPU. Personal computers use RAM chips for main memory.

Megabyte. One million bytes (or one million characters). Commonly abbreviated as M. See *Kilobyte*.

Menu or **Menu bar**. A visual display on the computer's monitor. It lists the activities that the computer can perform.

Microprocessor. The most important chip in the computer. It executes instructions from programs and controls all the components of the system. See *CPU*.

Modem. A peripheral device that enables one computer to communicate directly with another computer by using telephone communications channels. MODEM is an acronym for MOdulator/DEModulator. A modem changes the digital electronic signals used by a computer into analog-wave forms that can be transmitted by telephone and vice versa.

Monitor. A video display connected to the computer and used as an output device. See *CRT*.

Monochrome. Single color display.

Motherboard. Main circuit board of a microcomputer.

Mouse. Device used to control the pointer on the

Macintosh. The pointer moves in correspondence to the movement of the mouse.

Mouse button. Button on the top of the mouse. When you press it, the action indicated under the on-screen pointer is initiated. When you release it, action is taken.

Offline. In the communications application, this means that the computers are not electronically connected.

Online. In the communications application, this means that the computer is electronically connected to another computer.

On-line light. The indicator that shows that the printer is ready to print and receive commands from the computer. When the light is off, the printer will respond to manual controls only.

Operating system. A collection of system software that controls the internal operations of the computer and provides utility functions to the user. Different operating systems are designed for different computers. In the Macintosh environment, the operating system is found in the system folder.

Option key. A key used in conjunction with other keys to produce special symbols and foreign characters.

Parallel ports. The input/output outlet in which some fixed number of bits are transmitted simultaneously instead of one at a time (serially). See *Serial ports*.

Parameters. As used in the communications application, software settings that enable computers to send and receive data via modem.

Parity. In communications, a form of error checking used to increase the chances that each character has been received correctly.

Paste. To place a copy of the contents of the Clipboard at the insertion point.

Peripherals. Devices connected to a computer system but not essential to its operation. Modems and printers are peripherals.

Personal computer. A microcomputer. See *Mainframe*.

Placeholders. In *Works,* special characters used in word processing documents to set off fields that are to be replaced by database data during printing.

Point. The unit of measurement for type size.

Printer. The hardware that is used to obtain printed copies of data produced by the computer.

Program. Causes the computer to do something. Programs are also called *software*. See *Application software* and *System software*.

Program disk. A disk containing a program. Compare with *Data disk*.

Prompt. A character or message provided by the computer to indicate that it is ready to accept keyboard input.

Query. Question process that allows you to search a database for records that meet selected criteria.

RAM. Random Access Memory. Temporary memory on chips. The main memory of a computer. All programs are loaded into RAM memory before they can be run. RAM memory is called "volatile" or "temporary" because the programs or data stored there are lost when the computer is turned off.

RAM cache. A section of RAM that may be designated for special use through the control panel of the Macintosh. It may cause problems when used with memory intensive applications.

Relative reference. In the spreadsheet application, a reference to a cell that changes if the formula is copied or moved to a new location. See *Absolute reference*.

Read. To take data from a disk, tape, or keyboard, and place it into the computer's memory. Reading is an input operation.

Record. A collection of related items of information treated as a unit. Description of an item in a database.

ROM. Read Only Memory. Permanent memory stored on chips and providing fast access. Anything stored in ROM remains there even when the computer is turned off. ROM chips are programmed at the time of manufacture.

RS-232-C. A standard developed by the Electronics Industry Association specifying what signals and voltages will be used to transmit data from a computer to a modem.

Save. A common command that tells a computer to transfer a program or a file from main memory to a disk or tape.

Scrapbook. A desk accessory used to save frequently needed pictures or text.

Screen. The surface portion of a video terminal on which information is displayed.

Scroll. Process of viewing a program or file by having it continuously display on the screen from beginning to end.

Scroll box. The small box on the scroll bars of the Macintosh indicate the position of the window content relative to the entire document.

SCSI. Small Computer System Interface, pronounced "scuzzy." Provides high-speed access to peripheral devices on the Macintosh.

Select. Clicking or dragging across the screen to designate where the next action will take place.

Serial port. Data is transferred one bit at a time through a serial port. Used for modem and printer connections. See *Parallel port*.

Silicon. A basic semiconductor material obtained from sand and used for the development of computer chips.

Size box. The box in the bottom-right corner of active windows. It lets you resize the window.

Software. Another name for programs. Software may be written by the computer user, it may be purchased for a special purpose, or it may be delivered with the computer.

Split screen. Command that divides the computer screen into two or more windows (work areas). Each window can show a different part of the same file.

Spreadsheet. A type of program that arranges data and formulas in a matrix of cells.

Startup disk. A disk that has the system software that the computer needs to get itself started. Macintosh startup disks must have at least a Finder and a system file. An IBM startup disk must have at least DOS.

Style. In Macintosh terminology, the variation of typeface used, such as bold, italic, underline.

System software. The set of computer programs that make up the operating system. They are usually supplied with the computer and are always computer specific.

Template. A frequently-used form stored as a file

that can be used whenever the information varies but not the format.

Terminal. Input/Output devices (keyboard/display or keyboard/printer).

Toggle key. A key that alternately turns an activity on and off when you press it more than one time.

Typeface. The design of the printed characters (for example, Courier, Helvetica, Times). See *Font*.

Typestyle. The variation of typeface used, such as bold, italic, underline. Called *style* in the Macintosh world.

Undo. A command that will reverse the most recent user action.

Utility program. Program that performs common tasks or tasks essential to file maintenance.

Value. In spreadsheet terminology, numeric entries or formulas. Contrast with *Label*.

Window. A viewing area of a portion of computer memory as displayed on the video screen. Some programs and computers allow multiple windows to be displayed at the same time so that the viewer can see different files or different parts of the same file at the same time.

Word processing. Technique of electronically storing, editing, and manipulating text by using a computer.

Wordwrap. In word processing, when a word exceeds the right margin, the program will automatically move the word to the next line.

Write. To transfer data or programs from the computer's memory to disks, tapes, monitors, or printer. An output operation.

Write-protect. A procedure to prevent accidental writing to a disk or tape.

X-axis. In charting, the horizontal line usually showing the way data is classified, such as days, months, years, products, etc.

Y-axis. In charting, the vertical line that represents the unit of measurement or amount, such as dollars, number of products sold, etc.

Zoom box. The small box in the upper right corner on the title bar. It acts as a toggle: click on it once and the window will expand to maximum size. Click on it again and it returns window to the original size.

Index

absolute reference, 91
absolute value, 90-91
acoustic coupler, 219-20
active cell, 66
Add New Field, 130
address, 66
Align Center, 102
aligning columns, 101-2
Align Right, 102
All Cells, 71, 177
Alternative Spelling dialog box, 188-90
Answer Phone, 221
arithmetical operators, 78
Artwork, 174

bar chart, creating, 113-16
baud rate, 220
bits, 220
byline, typing, 35-36

calculated field, using, 161-62
cancel box, 73
capitalizing titles, 35
cells, 63
   changing contents, 76-77
   contents, 67-68
   identifying, 66
   protecting, 103
   selecting, 70
centering headings, 21-23
centering text, 8-9
Change Field Name, 161
Change Report Title, 155
changing cell contents, 76-77
changing column size, 141
changing column width, 88
changing fields, 137-38
changing formulas, 91-92
changing margins, 57
changing tabs, 42-43, 57
changing text, 172-73
changing window size, 207
Chart dialog box, 116
charting, 107

Chart Menu, 108, 113, 118
charts
   printing, 116-17
   saving, 117-18
Chooser, 209-10
   selecting LaserWriter, 214
Clear, 160
Close, 14, 117
closing files, 6
closing windows, 206
columns, 63
   aligning, 101-2
   changing size, 141
   changing width, 88
   deleting, 75-76
   identifying, 66
   inserting, 86-87
   selecting, 71
   widening for reports, 151-53
communications, 219-27
Communications Menu, 221-27
Copy, 158, 175, 178
copying database records, 158-61
copying formulas, 92, 101
creating bar charts, 113-16
creating database files, 135-36
creating forms, 136-37
creating formulas, 101
creating new reports, 147-48
creating pie charts, 107-9
creating top margins, 34-35
cursor, 18
Cut, 45, 76

data
   database, entering, 127-28, 138-40
   spreadsheet, entering, 72-74
database
   changing column size, 141
   changing size and location of fields, 137-38
   copying information, 158-61
   creating files, 135-36
   creating forms, 136-37
   creating new reports, 147-48

   dividing list window into panes, 162-64
   entering new data, 127-28, 138-40
   modifying forms, 129-31
   opening files, 122-23, 145-46
   opening two files at one time, 167-68
   printing reports, 154-55
   printing reports without lines, 154
   renaming reports, 155
   saving files, 132-33, 143
   saving reports, 155
   searching, 131-32
   selecting data, 173
   selecting fields for reports, 148-50
   selecting records, 125-27
   shortcuts, 157-58
   sorting, 129
   sorting fields in report, 146-47
   sorting files, 141-43
   using calculated fields, 161-62
   using report headers, 153-54
   viewing as form, 125
   viewing as list, 123-24
   viewing open documents, 169-72
   widening columns for reports, 151-53
   widening margins for reports, 150-51
default filenames, 50
Delete Field, 161
deleting columns, 75-76
deleting lines, 9
demodulation, 219
desk accessories, 206-10
Dial, 222
dialog boxes, 4-6
   Alternative Spelling, 188-90
   Chart, 116
   Draw Pattern, 178
   Match Records, 173
   Open, 4-5, 18-19, 28-29, 57, 65, 122, 193, 200, 202
   Page Setup, 50, 52, 57, 59, 214-16
   Pie Chart Definition, 108

Prepare to Merge, 170
Print, 13, 29, 95, 155, 181, 194, 216
Replace, 25
Save, 82
Save As, 12, 28
Save Changes, 14, 31, 182
Sort, 129
Spellswell Open, 186
dictionary
  adding words, 191-92
  viewing, 191
disk contents, viewing, 206
disk handling, 211-13
disk windows, opening, 205-6
dividing list windows, 162-64
documents
  merged
    adding art, 173-75
      changing text, 172-73
      drawing a frame, 178-80
      printing, 176, 181
      saving, 180-81
      selecting data, 173
      typing memo, 176-77
    numbering pages, 194
    spreadsheet, opening, 177-78
    switching, 203
    viewing open, 169-72
    word processor, opening new, 176
Done, 137
Double, 41
double spacing, 40-41
dragging, 69
Draw, 178
Draw Off, 180
Draw Pattern dialog box, 178
Drive, 12, 123, 135, 168, 187

Edit, 8
Edit Menu, 11, 45, 57, 76, 87, 89, 92, 98-99, 100-1, 106, 130, 155, 158, 160-61, 170-71, 173, 175, 178-80
Eject, 193
entering database data, 127-28, 138-40
entering functions, 106
entering spreadsheet data, 72-74

entry bar, 66, 123
entry box, 73

fields, 121, 123
  calculated, 161-62
  changing size and location, 137-38
  selecting for reports, 148-50
  sorting in report, 146-47
File, 3
file list window, scrolling, 200-1
File Menu, 3, 12-14, 28-30, 46-47, 50, 52-53, 55-56, 81-83, 95-96, 113, 117-18, 120, 132-33, 143-44, 150, 153-56, 161, 168, 174, 176-77, 180-82, 186, 192-95, 198, 202-3, 206, 208, 215, 217, 227
filenames, default, 50
files
  closing, 6
  database
    creating, 135-36
    opening, 122-23, 145-46
    saving, 132-33, 143
    sorting, 141-43
    viewing as form, 125
    viewing as list, 123-24
  opening, 6-7, 201-2
  opening two at one time, 167-68
  printing, 13-14, 194-95
  saving, 6, 11-12, 194-95
  spreadsheet
    opening, 66, 86, 97-98, 107
    printing, 81-82, 95, 104
    saving, 82-83, 95, 104
  viewing open, 28-29
  word processing
    opening, 18-21, 34, 57
    printing, 29-30, 46, 53
    saving, 26-28, 46, 52-53
Fill Down, 88-90, 92, 101
Fill Right, 89-90, 101
Find Cell, 72
Find Field, 131
Find Next, 72, 132
Find What box, 25-26
Fixed, 93-94
Font Menu, 10
fonts, 10
Format, 8

Format Menu, 21, 38, 41, 59-61, 93-94, 102, 125, 128-30, 141, 154, 194
formatting, 193
formatting labels, 94
formatting numeric values, 92-94
forms
  creating, 136-37
  modifying, 129-31
formulas
  changing, 91-92
  copying, 92, 101
  creating, 101
  predefined, 78
  showing, 118
  user-defined, 77-78
  viewing, 77-78
form window, 159
functions, 78
  entering, 106
  using, 78-80

Go To method, 72
grids, 154

hanging paragraphs, 36-37, 60
Hang Up, 227
hard disk, installing Microsoft Works, 217-18
headings, centering, 21-23
Hide Ruler, 38
homonyms, 187-89

I-beam, 8
If Statement, 119-20
indents, setting, 36-40
Insert, 87, 99-100
inserting blank lines, 43-44
inserting columns, 86-87
inserting paragraphs, 36
inserting text, 8, 23-24
insertion bar, 8, 24
Insert Page Break, 60, 194
installing Microsoft Works on hard disk, 217-18
Install Rule, 127

justification, 59

labels, 68
  formatting, 94
LaserWriter, 214-16
  selecting with Chooser, 214
letters, replacing, 24
lines
  deleting, 9
  inserting blank, 43-44
list window, 159-60
  dividing into panes, 162-64
  scrolling, 200-1
logical operators, 78

Macintosh
  communications, 219-27
  opening files, 201-2
  scrolling file list window, 200-1
  starting, 197-200
Macintosh desktop, 204-5
  opening disk windows, 205-6
  viewing disk contents, 206
margins
  changing, 57
  creating, 34-35
  widening for reports, 150-51
Match Records, 173
Match Records dialog box, 173
menu bar, 8
Merge, 171, 173
merged documents
  adding art, 173-75
  changing text, 172-73
  drawing a frame, 178-80
  printing, 176, 181
  saving, 180-81
  selecting data, 173
  typing memo, 176-77
Microsoft Works
  installing on hard disk, 217-18
  loading, 2-4
  quitting, 14-15, 30-31, 47, 53, 83, 96, 104, 120, 133, 144, 156, 164, 182-83, 195, 203, 210
modems, 219-20
modifying forms, 129-31
modulation, 219
Move, 98
moving paragraphs, 44-45
moving windows, 207

New, 136, 176
New Folder, 217
New Pie Chart, 108
New Report, 147
New Series Chart, 113
No Grid, 154
Normal Text, 36
numbering pages, 194
numeric values, formatting, 92-94

Open, 3, 7, 20, 28, 66, 98, 123, 146, 168, 174, 177, 186, 187, 193, 198-99, 206, 208, 227
Open dialog box, 4-5, 18-19, 28-29, 57, 65, 122, 193, 200, 202
opening database files, 122-23, 145-46
opening disk windows, 205-6
opening files, 6-7, 201-2
opening programs, 57
opening spreadsheet documents, 177-78
opening spreadsheet files, 66, 86, 97-98, 107
opening two files at one time, 167-68
opening word processor documents, 18-21, 34, 57, 176
Option Menu, 118
Options Menu, 103
Organize Menu, 126-27, 129, 131, 142, 147, 173
outdents, 36-37, 60
Outline, 10

page breaks, 60-61, 193-94
pages, numbering, 194
Page Setup, 50, 81, 150, 153, 176, 193, 194, 215
Page Setup dialog box, 50, 52, 57, 59, 214-16
paragraphs
  double spacing, 40-41
  hanging, 36-37, 60
  inserting, 36
  moving, 44-45
parameters, 220
Paste, 45, 106, 160, 175, 178
Pie Chart Definition dialog box, 108
pie charts

creating, 107-9
printing, 112-13
placeholders, 169
predefined formulas, 78
Prepare to Merge, 170-71, 173
Prepare to Merge dialog box, 170
Print, 13, 29, 46, 53, 55, 82, 95, 118, 154, 181, 194
Print dialog box, 13, 29, 95, 155, 181, 194, 216
printing, LaserWriter, 214-16
printing charts, 116-17
printing files, 13-14, 194-95
printing merged documents, 176, 181
printing pie charts, 112-13
printing reports, 154-55
printing spreadsheet files, 81-82, 95, 104
printing word processor files, 29-30, 46, 53
Print Merge, 176
Print/Page Setup Menu, 60
Print Window, 113, 117
programs, opening, 57
Protected, 103
protecting cells, 103

Quit, 14, 30, 47, 53, 83, 96, 120, 133, 144, 156, 182, 192, 195, 203
quitting Microsoft Works, 14-15, 30-31, 47, 53, 83, 96, 104, 120, 133, 144, 156, 164, 182-83, 195, 203, 210
quitting Spellswell, 192-93

Receive File, 225
Record Comparison Information box, 126
records, 121, 123
  selecting, 125-27
Record Selection, 126
Record Selection Criteria box, 126
Record Selector box, 158
relative values, 90-91
Remove Page Break, 61
renaming reports, 155
Replace, 25, 191
Replace dialog box, 25

Index **253**

Replace With box, 25-26
replacing letters, 24
replacing text, 25-26
replacing words, 24-25
Report Menu, 147
reports
   creating new, 147-48
   printing, 154-55
   renaming, 155
   saving, 155
   selecting fields, 148-50
   sorting fields, 146-47
   using headers, 153-54
   widening columns, 151-53
   widening margins, 150-51
report window, 147-48
repositioning spreadsheet titles, 98-99
rows, 63
   identifying, 66
   inserting at end of range, 99-101
   inserting blank, 99
   selecting, 70
RS-232-C interface, 220

Save, 12, 28, 46, 53, 133, 143, 155, 181, 194
Save As, 12, 28, 46, 52, 82, 95, 118, 132, 143, 161, 180, 194
Save As dialog box, 12, 28
Save Changes dialog box, 14, 31, 182
Save dialog box, 82
saving charts, 117-18
saving database files, 132-33, 143
saving files, 6, 11-12, 194-95
saving merged documents, 180-81
saving reports, 155
saving specifications, 117-18
saving spreadsheet files, 82-83, 95, 104
saving word processor files, 26-28, 46
Scrapbook, 208-9
scroll bar, 69-70
scroll box, 20-21, 69-70
scrolling a file list window, 200-1
scrolling spreadsheets, 68-70
searching databases, 131-32
searching text, 25-26
Search Menu, 25

Search Text Fields Only box, 131
Select, 127
Select All, 8, 57, 160
Select Definition, 118
selecting fields for reports, 148-50
selecting records, 125-27
selecting text, 57
Select Menu, 71-72, 177
Select Picture, 180
Send Text, 224, 226
setting indents, 36-40
Shadow, 10
Show All Records, 127
Show Form, 125, 128, 130
Show formulas, 118
showing formulas, 118
Show List, 125, 129, 141
Show Ruler, 38
Shut Down, 4, 15, 31, 47, 53, 83, 96, 104, 120, 133, 156, 183, 195, 199, 210
sizing windows, 109-12
Skip, 191-92
Sort, 129, 142, 147
Sort dialog box, 129
sorting database files, 129, 141-43
sorting fields in report, 146-47
Spacing..., 41
Special Menu, 4, 15, 31, 47, 53, 83, 96, 104, 120, 133, 144, 156, 183, 195, 199, 210
specifications, saving, 117-18
spelling checker. See Spellswell
spelling errors, 189-91
Spellswell
   dictionary, 191-92
   homonyms, 187-89
   quitting, 192-93
   redundant words, 192
   spelling errors, 189-91
   using, 185-87
Spellswell Open dialog box, 186
spreadsheet
   aligning columns and headings, 101-2
   cell contents, 67-68
   changing cell contents, 76-77
   changing column width, 88
   changing formulas, 91-92

charting, 107
copying formulas, 92, 101
correcting errors, 74
creating bar charts, 113-16
creating formulas, 101
creating pie charts, 107-9
deleting columns, 75-76
entering data, 72-74
entering functions, 106
formatting labels, 94
formatting numeric values, 92-94
Go To method, 72
identifying rows, columns, and cells, 66
identifying your work, 94-95, 103
inserting blank rows, 99
inserting columns, 86-87
inserting rows at end of range, 99-101
labels, 68
opening documents, 177-78
opening files, 66, 86, 97-98, 107
printing charts, 116-17
printing files, 81-82, 95, 104
printing options, 118
printing pie charts, 112-13
protecting cells, 103
relative and absolute values, 90-91
repositioning titles, 98-99
saving charts, 117-18
saving files, 82-83, 95, 104
scrolling, 68-70
selecting rows, cells, and columns, 70-71
shortcuts, 105-6
showing formulas, 118
sizing windows, 109-12
If Statement, 119-20
using Fill Down, 88-90
using functions, 78-80
values and alignments, 75
viewing formulas, 77-78
"What If" analysis, 80-81
Style Menu, 10, 21, 23, 36, 193
switching between documents, 203
system folder, 207-8

tabs, changing, 42-43, 57

254 *Microsoft Works for the Macintosh*

templates, 80, 90
text
    centering, 8-9
    changing, 172-73
    changing size and style, 10-11
    inserting, 8, 23-24
    searching and replacing, 25-26
    selecting, 57
    underlining, 23
titles
    capitalizing, 35
    spreadsheet, repositioning, 98-99
typefaces, 10
typestyle, 10
typing bylines, 35-36

Underline, 23
underlining text, 23
Undo, 11, 23, 179
user-defined formulas, 77-78
using calculated fields, 161-62
using Fill Down, 88-90
using functions, 78-80
using Spellswell, 185-87

values, 75
    formatting numeric, 92-94
    relative and absolute, 90-91

vertical scroll bar, 20-21
View Dictionary box, 191
viewing database file as list, 123-24
viewing dictionary, 191
viewing disk contents, 206
viewing formulas, 77-78
viewing open documents, 169-72
viewing open files, 28-29
View Menu, 206, 208

"What If" analysis, 80-81
widening columns for reports, 151-53
widening margins for reports, 150-51
Window Menu, 28-29, 169, 173, 175, 178, 203
windows
    changing size, 207
    closing, 206
    moving, 207
    sizing, 109-12
word processing
    capitalizing titles, 35
    centering bold headings, 21-23
    changing margins and tabs, 57
    changing page setup, 50-52
    changing tab stops, 42-43
    creating top margins, 34-35
    double spacing paragraphs, 40-41

formatting hints, 59-60
inserting blank lines, 43-44
inserting paragraphs, 36
inserting text, 23-24
moving paragraphs, 44-45
opening files, 18-21, 34
opening new documents, 176
opening programs and files, 57
opening two files at one time, 167-68
page breaks, 60-61
printing files, 29-30, 46, 53
replacing letters, 24
replacing words, 24-25
saving files, 26-28, 46, 52-53
searching and replacing text, 25-26
selecting text, 57
setting first-line indents, 36-40
shortcuts, 55-56
typing bylines, 35-36
typing letters, 50
underlining text, 23
viewing open documents, 169-72
viewing two open files, 28-29
words, replacing, 24-25
wordwrap, 18